ANETTA PIZAG

35 SMART CHOICES

Bring out the best
in yourself and your team
through powerful decisions about
when, where and how you work

'*35 Smart Choices* is a highly engaging and incredibly timely guide to being our best selves at work – wherever and whenever that may be. However timely, the book is not a superficial attempt to ride the post-pandemic "hybrid work" media wave. Anetta's meticulous research started well before 2020, and as a result presents a well-rounded and grounded approach to building impactful work practices.

With her second book Anetta has found her author's voice and even though most of the content was familiar to me as an expert reviewer, her style is highly engaging and pulls together a lot of threads in one easy-to-digest handbook. I enjoyed the analogous stories and found many takeaways as both a business leader and team member. *35 Smart Choices* will definitely be on the bookshelf of all my team!'

Caroline Burns, Founder & Managing Director, Workplace Revolution

'Rarely do we consciously stop and think about how we work. We roll from deadline to deadline, email to email, without stopping to think, "How can we do this better?" Anetta Pizag's book is timely. At a point in time where work is being turned on its head, more than ever we need to stop, reflect and change.

35 Smart Choices is your perfect guidebook through this journey. Anetta has assembled a helpful list of little things that you can do to make a big difference in your work and in your life. I enjoyed the writing style; it's easy to access and well-illustrated with entertaining life examples. Read it, act on it, and share it with your colleagues.'

Peter Andrew, Head of CBRE Workplace Centre of Excellence, Asia Pacific

'*35 Smart Choices* couldn't be more timely. As we face into the confusion and complexity of a hybrid working future, Anetta clearly lays out a plan to improve personal and team performance and deliver on purpose. The evidence-based tips and tricks are so easy to digest and will have you wanting to employ them straight away.'

Caroline Boyce, Workplace Strategy, Place Futures, Lendlease

'In our world of infinite distractions and competing commitments, this is a fresh and practical approach towards mastering work "flow". Whether working together or remotely, Anetta Pizag offers choices that we can all make towards a more inspired and fulfilling work experience.'

Su Lim, Global Managing Director, FreeState

'Powerful, practical, heartfelt advice to find your flow. Anetta beautifully blends science and practical advice in very human ways. The topics are timely given the disruption to our pre-pandemic routines and are a perfect guide to help navigate a new path to more authentic ways of working.

Read through it from cover to cover for some thought-provoking advice or dip into it when you feel stuck or need some inspiration. The style is both refreshingly engaging and conversational. You'll feel like you are talking to a friend rather than reading a book.'

Gerry Marcus, Associate Director, Learning & Capability, Colliers

'Every once in a while, a publication crosses your desk that actually hits the mark like a bullseye, resonates greatly and offers something actionable and meaningful. *35 Smart Choices* is one such book, and I just can't put it down, as each page-turn is enlightening or reminding me of a useful and pertinent piece of clear and considered information that today's rapidly changing and ultra-conscious world needs to consider.

You've only got to read the contents pages to grasp just how relevant this book is right now, with topics that cover all aspects of the remote working challenge, to mental health, productivity, connectivity, adequate breaks, virtual meetings, motivation, energy and creative inspiration.

It's riveting reading. There's been plenty of commentary and insights around many of these topics over the past two years, but until now, I haven't seen them addressed in such a concise and approachable manner. It's akin to a "workplace bible" for all to gain from. Engaging, meaningful and with real-life actionable ideas that can and will make a difference.'

Richard Duerden, Client Development Director | Associate, Diadem

'Reading *35 Smart Choices* felt as if I was sitting in a comfortable armchair next to the author. Anetta writes with astonishing honesty and clarity. At times it was as if she was holding up a mirror saying, "Your emotions and experiences are valid. How can I help? Here are some choices, now what is the next best step?"

Dipping in and out of this book with anticipation, I rediscovered aspects of myself and my work style that I knew but had forgotten, and what I wanted to change. I found myself making small adjustments as I read – in my posture, my walking gait, my music, my schedule of daily and weekly activities. Anetta lit a spark. I'm now excited by the possibility of further enhancing my work patterns.

An overwhelming amount of science and psychology-based data has been distilled into useful and clever tips. *35 Smart Choices* is also riddled with humorous and sometimes painful anecdotes. Not only captivating and mobilising, this book is a treasure chest of informative and inspiring resources. Work it!'

Katherine McPherson, Workplace Strategy Lead, Developing Property Solutions

'There are few authors who put as much thought and attention into their books as Anetta Pizag, and *35 Smart Choices* is no different. A powerful book for the times we find ourselves living in, now that we are rethinking so much, especially around how we work. *35 Smart Choices* is thought-provoking and practical, and the ideal read for anyone who knows they could do what they do so much easier and with much less stress, if they were simply shown a better path. That's exactly what Anetta does.'

Andrew Griffiths, International Bestselling Author and Global Speaker

'A practical and easy-to-read go-to guide on the trials and tribulations of being part of a work team. Anetta's dive into the conundrum of being your full self in a work situation is refreshing and honest in a world that requires us to fit into an unseen mould of what is and is not acceptable.'

Eminè Mehmet, CEO, Sacred Feminine Empowerment

'If you ever wondered what the term "work smarter and not harder" really means and how to master this mantra, *35 Smart Choices* is for you. I thoroughly enjoyed Anetta's engaging narration, which at times felt like being in conversation with an older sister. The book encouraged me to reflect on my own work habits, and reminded me to be more strategic and disciplined about when, where, and how I work.

As a full-time working mother, it is very easy to step into the trap of always delivering and being available. *35 Smart Choices* makes it very clear though, that focused rest is just as important as focused work. I look forward to saying "no" more often from now on, which really means saying "yes" to things that matter to me. As a team leader, I also enjoyed the suggested team activities, enabling me to share *35 Smart Choices* with my colleagues – allowing us as a team to strive for greater performance and happiness.'

Johanna Trickett, Associate | Sustainability, Arup

'*35 Smart Choices* is observant, provocative and compelling. Anetta Pizag offers an in-depth framework for moving individuals and teams from a detached criteria of productivity to the creation of value. The text is incredibly useful for overcoming blockages in performance and developing greater strength and resilience.

The book lays out its thesis with a mix of applied research and storytelling, and Anetta's self-deprecating, humorous and intelligent style lends itself well to building rapport between reader and writer.

Anetta recognises the critical contribution of emotional states, health and energy flow towards personal performance and interpersonal relationships, and without descending to the language of "self-help" books, offers realistic strategies to redirect them to advantage.'

Maurice Kiely, Director, chow:hill architects

'In an increasingly dynamic and hybrid world, Anetta Pizag's book is filled with timely and practical ideas on how leaders, employees and businesses can continue to adapt in a human-centred way. It's a great read for anyone curious about what might happen in tomorrow's workplace.'

Scott Ko, Director, ColourSpace Gallery

'With any book that promises lots of rich food for thought, I like to start with the 'menu' (aka table of contents). I found a couple of Choices – chapters – that had been playing at the fringes of my thinking, like #25 about music and #6 on taking breaks. Anetta provided great information, not token advice, and now I feel smarter because I'm making informed choices that work for my unique work style. Thanks Anetta for helping me become the master of my precious resources of time, attention and energy!'

Helen Palmer, Creator, Self unLimited

'The ability to consciously design our work lives is a new concept for many of us, thanks to the silver lining of the greatest social experiment we are all living through. This is a guidebook to navigating the opportunities and pitfalls that come with a more flexible approach to work, covering the three critical areas of collaboration, connection and communication.

Anetta paints contrasting pictures of our environments and the opportunities at our fingertips to shake things up for the better, and the influence that our space and the simple things, such as our furniture, can have on how we show up and contribute.

We spend a lot of time at work and it should be fun! This book is full of practical ways to make it so!'

Melissa Marsden, Founder & Director, COMUNiTI

'Anetta's voice is both pragmatic and human, taking the reader on a personal journey through their own workday, guiding them on the little choices that can make a big difference. *35 Smart Choices* is an easy to read – and share – guide with actionable tips, tools and exercises for optimising the dozens of choices we make during our workday that we might otherwise take for granted. It will become an essential resource for high-performance professionals and their teams. The world of work is always changing but these tips are as relevant today as they will be years from now, and with the easy, accessible structure of the book, it is sure to be referenced again and again.'

Monica Parker, Founder, HATCH Analytics

CONTENTS

PART VI: HOW CAN I TURN CHALLENGES INTO OPPORTUNITIES? AND WHAT ARE MY LIMITS? **326**

LET'S GET STARTED

GOOD DAYS, BAD DAYS

It might have been yesterday – or ages ago – the last time it happened, but I'm sure you're blessed with days when work doesn't really feel like work. Everything flows, you're focused and effective, and ideas come to you effortlessly. You're in sync with your teammates and clients, and you know that you're contributing to something meaningful. You tick off one task after the next, solve problems like there's no tomorrow, and surprise yourself with how much you can achieve in a single day.

And perhaps you also know *those* days when work is just hard going, and despite being busy all day you can't make any headway. You seem to be taking one step forward and three steps back. Everything is distracting, you feel scattered and overwhelmed, and you struggle to think straight. By the time you clock off, you're so exhausted that you can't even enjoy your well-deserved break.

Now, let me ask ... When you recall some of your best and worst days at work, what do you think makes the difference? How can you be on top of your game one day, and see things spiral out of control the next?

I often put these questions to my colleagues, clients and friends. And as it turns out, very few of them believe that their good and bad experiences at work are simply a matter of luck, written in the stars, or the result of getting up on the right or the wrong side of the bed.

Instead, they usually talk about the *choices* they make. On bad days, they tend to jump from task to task, react impulsively to interruptions and setbacks, and fail to look after their bodies and minds. And on good days, they plan their work more thoughtfully, manage their attention and energy better, collaborate more skillfully, and work in environments that help them find their flow. They make many of these choices routinely, without giving them much thought – but these are choices nonetheless.

ARE YOU MAKING THE RIGHT CHOICES?

Scientific research and my own observations lead to the same conclusion: it's in our power to swing the pendulum from struggling to thriving at work.

Especially in recent years, with flexible and remote work practices becoming more common, we have plenty of freedom to choose when, where and how we work. But even if you're based in a traditional office, you probably have more control than you realise.

You can start your day with an easy task, or a difficult one. You can jot down that idea on a piece of paper, or a laptop. You can answer that email straight away, or later in the day. You can sit or stand. You can put on headphones and listen to your choice of music, or tune into the sounds of your office. You can have a quick break to refresh your mind at any given moment, or press on a bit longer. When you actually take a break, you can go for a walk, or just mess around on the internet. You can meet your team in a conference room, or in an informal space. You can see your clients in person, or catch up with them over a video call ... You're making choices like these dozens of times each day.

The issue is we tend to underestimate the impact of such simple decisions, and do things out of routine. But in truth, making smart, considered choices – even in the most mundane situations – can make a huge difference to how we feel, think and behave, and what we achieve.

Unfortunately, we don't learn much in school or in professional training about these seemingly mundane aspects of work. And probably not many people have ever discussed with you how you can discover your own unique work style and become your natural best.

When it comes to professional development, what could be more important? So many brilliant people struggle to reach their potential and to see the results they deserve. Being left to their own devices, they battle with endless setbacks, while putting their health and happiness on the line. This is a huge problem – but I hope that with this book, I can contribute to the solution.

WHAT YOU WILL LEARN

Before we get into the juicy stuff, let me clarify what this book is not. It's not about time management, task management, gaining control over your inbox or getting stuff done. You won't be assigned a label defining your 'productivity style', 'creativity style' or 'collaboration style'. And you won't see recommendations for 'exciting new' productivity apps.

Instead, I'd like to help you find answers to some bigger questions:

- Who do you need to be to make the most of your talent?

- How can you tap into your best thinking to solve big problems?

- How can you find your groove and share your magic?

- How can you improve the quality of your work – and your life?

- How can you make work an amazing experience?

- What can you do to make every day a good day?

- And how can you help others achieve the same?

Thriving at work is not about putting in more hours. It's about working smarter, so that you create more value with your time, energy and knowledge while staying happy and healthy.

35 Smart Choices will take you on a journey where you'll discover how you can bring your best self to any situation. You'll find out when, where and how to approach different tasks and challenges to give yourself the best chance to succeed. You'll learn to overcome unproductive habits, develop effective routines, and create or choose supportive physical spaces that help you live up to your potential. Once you get the 'externals' right, your internal world will shift, and your genius will be free to surface.

HOW YOU WORK BEST IS UNIQUE

Science offers plenty of insights about what makes the average person more effective, and you'll learn about many fascinating studies in this book.

However, science doesn't know who you are and what you need in order to become your best self. (Do you know anyone who has ever used a dating app with a 'science-based' algorithm to find their match? I'm sure they have some stories to tell.)

Your natural work style is unique, just like your personality, skills, experiences, goals and passions. What inspires you, what sparks your creativity and what helps you find your groove are different from the person next to you.

In recent years, researchers have developed an automated system to evaluate employee performance. It collects data about your behaviour and your physical and emotional states (via a smartphone and a wearable fitness tracker), and after analysing the data, decides whether you're a high or a low performer. I'm not sure about you, but I find this invention rather disturbing. Can you imagine that a piece of software can meaningfully evaluate whether you collaborate effectively, find original solutions to problems, make quality decisions or build empathic relationships? You probably find that even your closest colleagues can't always tell when and how you do your best work.

You're not an interchangeable part of a system. And there is no such thing as the 'right work style'. To rise above the crowd and create exceptional value, you need to know what makes you tick and be able to decide which strategies are right for you.

WHO WILL GET THE MOST FROM THIS BOOK

35 Smart Choices is for everyone who uses knowledge and creativity to solve non-routine problems for work. So if you spend a lot of time researching, analysing, strategising, planning, designing, writing, innovating, engineering, coding, consulting, advising or negotiating, the ideas in this book are for you.

Whether you're based in a traditional office, in a flexible workplace, in a coworking space or at home – and even if you spend a lot of time working in cafes, hotel rooms or on the road – I'm confident that you'll find many useful insights.

You may be an employee, a contractor, a team leader or a manager – working in a small business or a large corporation. Or perhaps you're a business owner, entrepreneur or freelancer. Whichever position you're in, game on!

However, this book is not for everyone. To get the most out of it, you need to be ready to play your part. So I trust that you recognise these qualities in yourself:

- You care more about your work than just collecting a 'pay cheque'. You genuinely want to do your best and make a difference. And you believe that work is an important part of life, which is meant to be meaningful and enjoyable.

- You're driven to think for yourself, act proactively and look for solutions to your problems. (Organisational psychologists tell me that many employees choose to act like sheep; they want to be told what to do all the time. If you'd like to up your game and remain a valuable contributor in the current economy, avoiding effort and responsibility won't cut it.)

- You're willing to experiment, try new ways of working and let go of old habits. You're happy to challenge assumptions and shake up the status quo. And you love asking great questions as much as you love finding the answers. You know that you don't know it all, and never will.

- You have a deep desire to understand yourself better and to live with self-awareness. You certainly want to know more about yourself than giant tech and media companies know about you, and to make conscious choices rather than drifting with the tide.

If you are in a leadership position

You may see yourself as a leader, manager, coach or guide. Whichever role you're in, my intention is to help you bring out the best in your people. I'm not here to offer leadership advice; however, for you to benefit most from this book, we need to agree on a few fundamental principles:

- The vast majority of people want to perform well, contribute and grow.

- People need to feel valued, trusted and safe to bring their best selves to work.

- Humans are complex and sensitive creatures, easily influenced by their environments.

- People are more likely to excel when they are treated as equal partners in the workplace.

- The number of hours people spend at their desks is a terrible measure of performance.

YOUR TICKET TO **THRIVE**

By exploring and honing your work style, you'll develop an array of skills and personal qualities that will help you succeed at work, now and in the future. Let me spell out six of these, which I believe are your ticket to a THRIVE-ing work life …

Team player

You'll learn to understand many different work styles, which will help you become a more flexible and empathic communicator. As such, you'll find it much easier to collaborate with people who think and work differently from you – not only with your closest colleagues, but also with members of other disciplines, organisations and industries.

Honest and humane

By getting to know yourself better, you'll be more comfortable expressing your true personality, sharing your honest thoughts and feelings, and diving into deep conversations. Others will feel safer and more relaxed around you, which will certainly help you develop trusting, connected relationships. You'll also find it easier to tap into your emotions, run with your imagination and find innovative solutions.

Responsive

Through this process of learning and discovery, you'll become more agile and better equipped to deal with uncertainty and change. As a result, you'll have what it takes to innovate quickly and meet new challenges as they arise. And with the right skills and a fresh mindset, riding new waves will be an exciting experience rather than an ordeal.

Intelligent

Once you understand all your options, you'll approach different tasks and problems more effectively. Even in complex and difficult situations, you'll be ready to make quality decisions that bring you closer to the team's goals. You'll be more self-aware and switched on, and you'll know how to bring out the best in yourself and others.

Venturous

During this journey, you'll gain courage and confidence in what you and your team can achieve. You'll think bigger, aim higher, and get more thrills from pursuing ambitious goals while proving the skeptics wrong. Your curiosity and adventurous spirit will likely take you to uncharted territory where risks are abundant and outcomes are uncertain. You may have some failures along the way, but you'll also experience more breakthroughs and epiphanies.

Eternal learner

You'll learn a lot about learning, about people and performance, and about yourself – and hopefully, you'll be left with a deep love for knowledge. As an avid learner, you'll find it easier to keep your skills up to date, unlearn old ways of doing things and stay ahead of the game. You'll be able to think more creatively and to capitalise on new opportunities.

WHAT ELSE IS IN IT FOR YOU

I'm sure you agree – being able to perform to your potential and to make a difference with your talent is incredibly rewarding. But once you embrace your unique work style, you'll notice that all aspects of your work life will improve. You'll more often experience a state of flow where progress is effortless and insights come to you naturally. You will feel more motivated and fulfilled, and become healthier both physically and mentally. And as a result, you'll also get more out of life outside of work.

If you are a leader

As a starting point, you'll reap an array of personal performance and well-being benefits. But when you also take your people on the same journey, things will reach a whole new level. Ultimately, you'll have the privilege of leading a star team: skilled, flexible and engaged collaborators who are ready for change and are eager to evolve.

Your people will better understand not only their own work styles, but also how their teammates are wired. Consequently, they will have a better sense of their place in the team, and a greater respect for the diverse range of qualities others bring into the mix. They will more likely see their differences as an opportunity to create something extraordinary, rather than an obstacle to collaboration.

Your team members will also learn how to organise themselves more effectively, and to support and elevate each other. They will be better prepared to address issues proactively and share their knowledge freely. With greater collaboration, agility and awareness, your team will have what it takes to successfully navigate competing priorities and to turn challenges into opportunities.

Naturally, you'll also learn a lot about your people through this process, and gain new insights into how you can offer every single individual the best possible support.

WHY I HAD TO WRITE THIS BOOK

It's been a winding journey that has led me to this point, which is very personal to me. I was brought up in Hungary, in a cerebral world. The wall dividing East and West was standing strong until I reached my teens. My father was a military officer, my mother worked in the financial departments of technology companies, and my sister specialised in chemistry. As a family, we loved solving logic puzzles over lunch, and I excelled in maths and physics competitions for many years … Yep, I was the textbook nerd. School teachers loved me. (Some of my classmates didn't. Such is life.)

I learned early on that 'knowledge', 'logic' and 'honesty' were some of the most powerful forces in life. And in my naivety, living a successful life was a bit like playing chess: when you take the right steps, you win. It was all black and white.

Eventually, this illusion started to crumble. I studied and practised architecture, worked as an environmental consultant and workplace specialist, and also immersed myself in the fascinating worlds of coaching and psychology. Over the years, I encountered plenty of 'Santa Claus moments' where I learned that some of the ideas I'd picked up in my childhood were not exactly true … Just to be clear, I'm not talking about finding out that Santa doesn't exist. What I experienced was rather the opposite: I realised that there's much more magic in life than I used to believe.

Nature, and especially human nature, never ceases to amaze me. (Did you know, for example, that if your sport drink is coloured pink, you'll likely run faster and with less effort compared to having the same drink without the food dye?) We are emotion-driven and often illogical creatures with many quirks and flaws – which is awesome. This is why we're able to create art, innovate beyond our wildest dreams, and build rich, meaningful relationships.

I still value knowledge, logic and honesty, but they mean different things to me now. Knowledge is not just about information and facts – it's also about knowing yourself. Logic is not just about rational reasoning – it's also about making smart decisions in conflict-ridden and emotionally charged situations. Honesty is not just about telling what you know is true, but also about allowing others to see into your soul.

And if life is like playing chess, you can spice it up with your own rules, and the board has no limits.

I've always felt the calling to create great experiences and to help people succeed at work, but one question has been nagging me lately: how can I help you find your own unique way to shine? To become your best self, you need more than just good advice. You need a one-of-a-kind plan to play your best game.

This is why I had to write *35 Smart Choices*. With this book, my aim is to offer you a guiding hand along your journey of discovery.

HOW TO USE THIS BOOK

As the title suggests, this book explores 35 Choices – one per chapter. Of course, there are many more smart choices you can make about the way you work, but I selected those which I believe will make the greatest difference.

You'll probably find it easier to digest it all if you read the Choices in sequence, but you can also go through them in any order you wish. However, before diving into the Choices, I recommend you first read the next section, 'What does high performance mean to me?' It will help you create a clear picture of what you want to achieve, allowing you to get the most out of this book. Too many people have a very narrow definition of performance, and are caught up spinning the hamster wheel at an incredible speed – you don't want to be one of them!

I'm going to share lots of scientifically supported tips and tricks, along with insights from interesting research studies. (I won't bombard you with too many scientific details, but you'll find references to relevant literature in the 'Sources' section at the end of the book.) Please keep in mind that none of this information is a prescription for success. Instead, I'd like you to see the ideas presented as food for thought – and action.

You can't discover your work style just by thinking about it, so keep experimenting and putting what you've learned into practice. Wherever you work, pay attention to your choices, your thoughts and feelings, and your results – and when there's room for improvement, try something different. You'll also find a set of individual and team exercises at the end of each Choice to assist you with this.

I'm confident that you'll enjoy discovering your work style – but if you can join forces with your team and jump into this together, you'll have an even richer experience. I suggest you compare notes, and support and motivate each other as you go. And why not start a fun competition to see who has the most interesting light-bulb moments and breakthroughs?

IF YOU'RE A TEAM LEADER

I recommend that you first read this book with a focus on your own work style and performance. If you then give it to your team, you'll have a better sense of what they will experience and how you can support them.

When it comes to exploring new work practices, I suggest you discuss with your people what's acceptable and encouraged, and let them experiment freely within these agreed boundaries.

The activities in this book are intended to promote engagement and learning without disrupting the flow of work. Some of these activities will require planning and facilitation, but I'm confident your efforts will pay off in spades.

Apart from these exercises, it's a good idea to regularly discuss with your people how they could work more effectively, both as individuals and as a team. Understanding your team members' work styles should also make it easier for you to communicate with them, lead them and help them reach their potential.

If you're planning a workplace change project – such as an office relocation or upgrade, a cultural transformation, a technology upgrade, or a shift in the organisation's work style – this book will give you a clear idea of what kind of information is worth collecting from employees in the lead up to the changes. In addition, people who have read this book will be able to give you more insightful and well-considered input compared to those who have never really been encouraged to rethink how they work.

Think beyond staff surveys and focus groups. Encourage each individual to question how work is done, and to make smarter choices. When it comes to innovation and change, they will be equal partners in the conversation. They will organise themselves more efficiently and work more proactively. And instead of approaching you with problems, they will more often come to you with solutions and stories of success.

WHAT DOES HIGH PERFORMANCE MEAN TO ME?

How do I know when I'm performing at my best?
What does it look and feel like when I'm doing my best work?

What does high performance mean to you? For some people, it means getting things done as efficiently as possible. At work, they are in a never-ending race to tick things off their to-do lists faster than the rate at which new tasks appear. This is an exhausting place to be where progress is often just an illusion.

If you're reading this book, I'm sure you realise that high performance has a deeper meaning. It's not just about getting things done, but also about doing the *right* things, in pursuit of your individual and team goals as well as the purpose of your organisation. You need to carefully balance efficiency and effectiveness. On one hand, you need to find solutions to unique and complex problems, which can be a slow and risky process, and on the other, you have to produce deliverables efficiently, streamlining and automating as much as possible.

The path that navigates between these two aspects of work is littered with pitfalls. Focus too much on superficial measures like the number of emails and reports you write, phone calls you make or clients you meet in a week, and you may get caught up in a hamster wheel, losing sight of the bigger picture. Get lost in innovation, and you may find yourself in real trouble, missing deadlines, blowing budgets, and facing angry colleagues and clients.

YOUR EXPERIENCE IS PART OF THE PICTURE

Strictly speaking, 'productivity' means the ratio between input and output. If you can achieve more without working harder, by definition you're working more productively. Many people still believe that working longer hours equates to higher productivity, which is a distorted view. But I understand where this confusion might come from; productivity is a narrow metric.

'Performance' is a more holistic measure. It doesn't only take into account how effectively you work, but also the quality of your results. It looks at how much value you create for your organisation, your clients and the greater good, using your skills and talent. And in my view, part of your performance is how you create a better life for yourself and your loved ones.

Yes, the quality of your life is part of the picture. Regardless of what you achieve, if you hate your job and dread Monday mornings, I can't say you're performing wonderfully. And if after a day of transformative work you're left completely spent, unable to spend your personal time in a meaningful way, again, you're not doing great. You're investing a large part of your life – your time, attention, energy and emotions – into your work, and you should be able to enjoy the returns.

SHOULD YOU MEASURE YOUR PERFORMANCE?

There are a lot of ways to measure performance. Organisations often focus on tasks and deliverables completed in a given time, on billable hours, and on financial and business results. Many of them also regularly assess different aspects of employees' wellbeing and engagement. You'll probably find that certain measures are more relevant to you than others.

Evaluating creative work is also possible – for example, by assessing the quantity and quality of ideas and the number of innovations produced by a team. But getting it right can be challenging. Some authors are committed to writing a specific number of words in an hour, and as an author myself, this makes me cringe. What does the number of words have to do with sharing knowledge?

I know organisations that are obsessed with setting the right targets, and still they don't measure everything – because certain aspects of work simply shouldn't be analysed or planned. When you measure something, you're inclined to compare it to past results, or to other people's or teams' performances. And this is not helpful when you're creating something unique or disruptive. Being hooked on targets also makes it difficult to tune into your intuition, find your flow and enjoy what you do.

I encourage you to do your best to identify the performance measures and targets that will allow you to shine, perhaps in discussion with your team. These metrics will form a map to your goals. And with this book, what I offer you is a compass, assisting you to move in the right direction wherever you are on your journey.

FOCUS ON THE RIGHT QUESTIONS

How do you do your best work?

You naturally want to know the answer; otherwise you wouldn't be here. But this is a big question and there's no short answer. How you do your best work depends on many factors, including your task, your circumstances, and even the way you feel in the moment.

I'm confident that after reading this book, you'll have a clear idea of how you can perform to your best in different situations. But for now, let's ask an easier yet equally important question:

What do you need to be really good at?

In other words, how can you bring your best to your team and put your unique skills and knowledge to great use?

Here is my own answer, as an example. To succeed in my mission, I need to engage in open and trusting conversations with my teams and clients, ask thought-provoking questions, listen intently and read between the lines. I also need to be able to discover meaningful patterns in large volumes of data, develop customised design solutions that resolve conflicting priorities, and write articles and reports that are easy to read and act upon.

Your answer will be different from mine (unless we miraculously share the same talents and do similar jobs). So it's worth spending a moment thinking about the skills and abilities that allow you to make the greatest difference.

Which leads me to one of my favourite questions …

How do you recognise when you're doing your best work?

Every time I pose this to my clients, colleagues and friends, the answer bubbles to the surface straight away. People go to that special place where they feel deeply connected with the purpose of their work. Their eyes brighten and their passion shines through as they relive some of the most meaningful and transformative moments in their work lives.

When describing powerful moments at work, no-one raves about empty mailboxes or shrinking to-do lists. Technical reports, spreadsheets or routine meetings are nowhere on the radar. Put simply, the kinds of activities we dedicate most of our time and attention to hardly get a mention in these conversations.

In fact, people say very little about what they actually do, and talk mostly about their *emotions* and *experiences*. For example, they describe the pride they feel about collaborating with amazing people. They speak of the excitement of stumbling upon a game-changing idea during a spontaneous catch-up. And they share what an incredible feeling it is to see their clients' faces light up as the solution to their problems suddenly becomes tangible.

I also like to ask people in different roles to describe what it's like when they are in their element, and again, the answers are not miles apart. It seems that we all have similar experiences. We are focused, courageous and optimistic. We're in touch with our intuition, and open to new ideas and change. We're clear on our priorities, and about what's right and wrong. And we care deeply about the people we serve.

When doing impactful work, we tend to experience intense emotions. We breathe deeply, and on occasion we may become a bit teary. Sometimes we have a lot of fun, and at other times we're fuelled by frustration or the burning desire to defy the odds. Either way, we're ready to tackle obstacles, because we know that if we succeed we'll create something extraordinary.

Can you relate? And what can you add from your own experiences?

RECOGNISE YOUR HIGH-PERFORMING MOMENTS

Measuring your progress can be tricky, especially when you're immersed in the day-to-day demands of your work. But noticing when you're performing at your best is easy – you just need to pay attention to your experience in the moment. When you feel you're on top of your game, check what you're doing and learn from it. If you can refine your own formula for high performance, you'll be able to get to that place more often.

In reality, your workdays are probably filled with time-consuming tasks, some of which are not that exciting. But keep in mind that you can create immense value in just a few minutes, by stumbling upon a brilliant idea, making a connection with someone or coming to a critical decision. And these moments can occur anywhere and at any time – while having a quick catch-up with your mates, walking your dog or riding your bike.

So, to improve your performance, I suggest you focus more on creating transformative moments, and don't get caught up in how many hours you spend on different tasks or in different places. You want your talent to shine, and you need to open the door for it.

35 SMART CHOICES PART I

PART I

HOW CAN I BUILD MOMENTUM AND MAKE THE MOST OF MY DAY?

Transformative work requires a lot of energy and focus – if it were child's play, everyone would be a star. Your success therefore greatly depends on how wisely you use your mental resources. The way you organise your tasks and respond to challenges can skyrocket your productivity, or put you into a downward spiral.

Sometimes it seems crazy how much distraction and negative influence we all need to overcome at work. You might feel like Super Mario at times, having to jump obstacles and navigate your way around threats at every step while trying to make progress. Emails, phone calls, notifications, distracting noises, and interruptions from colleagues are only the start. You also need to deal with temptations to drop what you're doing, as well as your own distracting thoughts and emotions.

To reach your goals on time and with the least amount of effort, you need to choose your path wisely and treat your mental energy as your most precious resource.

In this Part we'll look into planning your day strategically, ensuring that each task acts as a springboard to the next, rather than slowing you down. We'll also explore how you can achieve flow by scheduling your work around your body clock.

You'll find out what it takes to build up your mental energy, protect it from energy-draining situations and habits, and use it most efficiently. You'll learn about getting on a roll and maintaining momentum with little effort. And you'll find out how you can recharge your batteries by taking breaks at the right times and in the right ways.

Hitting milestones and kicking goals are deeply satisfying. By mastering your energy and attention, you could get hooked on making fast progress, and surprise yourself with what you can achieve.

CHOICE 1

HOW SHOULD I PLAN MY DAY TO MAKE THE MOST OF IT?

How should I organise my tasks?

How can I build and maintain great momentum?

How can I make sure I achieve what I've planned for the day?

Do you know people who always manage to get on a roll and make impressive progress every day, rain, hail or shine? Seasoned hikers are great examples. By learning some of their secrets, you too could plan your days and manage your energy and time with the skills of a serious hiker – without even leaving the comfort of your workplace. Let's unpack what they are doing so right.

It's been years since I last climbed a decent mountain and I miss the experience. I love wandering across ridges and valleys, even if it's exhausting at times. My mind always becomes clearer while exploring beautiful natural environments and things just fall into perspective. Reaching a summit is an exhilarating moment when I feel I'm exactly where I'm supposed to be. Some people call this 'the moment of truth'.

For many years I regularly ventured out with much more experienced hikers whose stories and achievements were truly impressive. They were able to cover more ground in a day than I could comprehend and reach their destinations on time through any conditions, rain or shine. What inspired me most is that while walking through rugged terrain and jumping over hurdles, they were having a wonderful time.

Not all hikers I've come to know are particularly athletic. Some of them may give you the first impression that they won't even make it around the block, yet they're able to conquer massive peaks. What's the key to their success? I've learned that the best hikers plan each adventure carefully, ensuring that they can get the best out of the experience and reach their destination with the least amount of effort.

PLANNING YOUR PATH PAYS OFF

As the saying goes, preparation is half the battle, and I find this lesson highly relevant not only in the wild but also when it comes to tackling mountainous goals at work. After spending a few moments in the morning thinking about my day ahead, as seasoned hikers do, things tend to flow more easily. I quickly gain momentum as I check off one task after another with sharp focus and abundant energy. I usually feel more optimistic and in control, confident that I'll be able to complete my projects in time.

However, my days look very different when I neglect this lesson and impulsively dive into work. Without a well-thought-out approach, I often find myself losing direction and going down rabbit holes. Failing to make any meaningful progress, my motivation and focus eventually start to fade. Are you able to relate?

I've actually noticed that when I'm messing around, whether out in the wild or in the office, the consequences are surprisingly similar. When I'm progressing too slowly or being sidetracked in the mountains, I risk falling behind and facing an unpleasant situation; I might need to spend the night in the cold and damp, in the companion of crawly creatures. Similarly, after an unproductive day at work, I often find myself tossing and turning in a cold sweat most of the night. I'm kept up by disturbing head chatter, mulling over how I'm going to catch up, and how I'll face my unhappy team and clients. If I could choose, I'd much prefer the crawlies.

So how can you plan your day wisely, and ensure you make the most of every ounce of effort you put in while enjoying the journey? Let me share six tips that are proven to work both in the wilderness and in the workplace.

1. SET ACHIEVABLE TARGETS

From experience, I know I'm able to handle around 1400 metres change in elevation when climbing, and around 1000 metres descending, in one day. In undulating terrain, I'm able to walk a distance of 28 kilometres. If I try to exceed these limits, there's a good chance I will short of my destination or injure myself. I may be able to push myself hard and perform a miracle, but the next day I'll be too sore to move.

I also have my limits in the context of work. For example, I can spend around half a day researching, analysing complex data or developing solutions to unique problems. After that time my brain starts to slow down and the quality of my work drops. On the other hand, I can immerse myself in design and artistic activities or process routine tasks as long as needed, sometimes even late into the night.

When you're setting out what you want to achieve in a day, you too should keep in mind how long you're able to work effectively on different tasks. Be realistic. As shown by research, most people can fully focus on mentally demanding tasks only for up to four hours in a day.

There are times to be ambitious, of course, but falling short of your targets over and over again could destroy your spirit. Under the pressure of a heavy workload, you might also think less rationally about how you should tackle your tasks. In contrast, when you feel your goals are achievable within the given timeframe, you're more likely to set the right priorities.

2. IDENTIFY THE SMARTEST ROUTE

Imagine you're walking across hills and valleys towards a spectacular lookout. You come to a fork in the path. On the left, you see a wide and smooth path gently sloping downhill. On the right, the path is narrow and rocky, leading steeply uphill. Which one do you pick?

Well, you'd better check the map or the signposts before deciding. Choosing the seemingly easier path just because it allows you to move faster for a little while would be a silly mistake, wouldn't it? With this approach, you'd risk making your journey longer and harder, and you may never even arrive at the lookout.

Yet, at work we're inclined to make this kind of mistake over and over again.

Moving fast and ticking things off is always very satisfying because we get the sense that we're highly productive and in control. Every time we finish a task we also feel a bit lighter, knowing we have one less item to worry about. In fact, we're hardwired to seek quick rewards, and to choose simple and easy tasks over challenging ones, even when they are not very important or urgent. Sometimes we can become so caught up in knocking things off a to-do list that we forget about the big picture. Ticking ten things off your list doesn't mean you've made progress if that list included 'sort my paper-clips by colour', 'count the number of pens in my drawer' and 'make sure my coffee mug is really, really, really clean'.

To avoid this common trap, you need to find a smarter way to measure your progress. I suggest you spend some time at the beginning or end of each day thinking about what you'd like to achieve next and what's the best way to get there. With a strategic approach, you should be able to reach your goals much more quickly than choosing tasks on a whim and following the easy path.

3. START ON THE RIGHT FOOT

I remember a walk in the mountains where I reached a lookout point only a few minutes after starting out. From that place, I could clearly see that I was already closer to my destination. I suddenly felt proud and unstoppable, even though getting to that point had been really easy.

The first few steps you take in the morning could set you up for success or wear you out. Starting on the right foot can be a bit tricky, but with a bit of practice, you'll soon get the hang of it.

First of all, you'll want to see some progress early on. As we've just discussed, defaulting to the easy path all the time is a counterproductive habit. None-theless, completing a few quick, straightforward tasks at the start of the day can be a great way to get into your groove. You don't need to overcome a major challenge to feel powerful. After you've reached some minor mile-stones, you should notice an improvement in your energy and motivation.

In contrast, it might be a mistake to attack a daunting project with no end in sight first thing in the morning, as you could quickly find yourself feeling overwhelmed. You also want to avoid those kinds of tasks where you might end up going in circles or getting lost in the woods. In my work, doing open-ended research or troubleshooting tech issues can send me down that path. I can spend hours exploring dozens of different avenues without finding what I'm looking for. And with a frazzled mind and shattered confidence, it's difficult to achieve anything meaningful for the rest of that day.

Also keep in mind that to gain a strong and lasting sense of progress, you need to spend some time on a project that's meaningful to you. Getting a step closer to a vision that excites you is more likely to fill you with optimism, energy and pride than, say, clearing out your inbox.

My final suggestion – which may sound a bit counterintuitive – is to start your day with something less interesting, and save the most exciting tasks for later. After enjoying a very interesting activity, it can be especially difficult to focus on a mundane job. You know what it's like when you walk in nature; you feel more motivated when the most amazing scenery is yet to be discovered.

Bringing it all together ... to get on a roll, pick a couple of tasks in the morning that are quick and easy to complete, and are supporting a meaningful goal, but are not overly exciting. Once you're up to speed, you'll feel more ready to plunge into bigger challenges.

4. TACKLE THE HARDEST CHALLENGE WHILE YOU'RE AT YOUR PEAK

When you need to jump over boulders or cross a wild river with 20 kilos on your back, you'd better be fully switched on. You have a much better shot at succeeding if you challenge yourself at the time of the day when you're at your strongest and sharpest. Having to exert yourself once you've used up your energy is not fun, and can even be dangerous.

Similarly, when you're at work, there are a few hours each day when your focus, energy and mood are peaking. Most people find they produce their best work in the morning, a couple of hours after waking up, while others ('owls' or 'night owls') are in their element in the evening or late at night.

Either way, whenever you get the chance, tackle the tasks that require intense concentration and deep thinking during your most productive hours. You'll find that your work reaches a higher standard, you deal with distractions more effectively, and you achieve more during your work time. (We'll look more closely at the optimal timing of different work activities in the next Choice.)

5. KEEP UP THE MOMENTUM

I love hiking across diverse landscapes where new scenery opens up at each turn. In anticipation of the next surprise, I often forget about the effort it takes to move forward. Still, I've had many wonderful nature walks where I was wandering through the same sort of terrain for very long periods. On some occasions, I descended into deep valleys for hours on end. At other times, I strolled along sandy shorelines for several days without anything breaking my rhythm. With every step I became more and more present, clear and connected to the world around me.

At work, I also enjoy focusing on similar types of activities for long periods of time, when I get the chance. I find it easier to get my head around complex topics and reach a state of flow when I don't need to put on a different thinking cap again and again. A business educator once taught me a technique to create momentum. Each morning you decide what kind of headspace you want to be in for the day, and then you choose tasks (as your workflow allows) that most benefit from this kind of thinking. You might explore creative challenges, focus on analytical tasks, or meet and collaborate with clients and team members throughout the day. I often use this technique, and it works well for me.

Batching similar tasks together is a well-known technique to maintain focus and boost productivity. It's easier to get on a roll and keep your energy high if you don't keep changing direction. On the other hand, mixing tasks could also help you find your momentum – after all, variety makes work more interesting and exciting. Alternating between various modes of thinking can also spark creative ideas and lead you to innovative solutions.

So the question is, how often should you switch activities and modes of thinking? It depends on your personality and the type of work you do. I know people who can quickly become bored doing the same sort of work for too long, and prefer to dive into vastly different activities every couple of hours or so, on an average day. Still, the same people can also spend a whole week or two on a single task; for example, preparing for a major presentation or writing a book or a paper.

How do you best maintain your momentum? Do you prefer to allocate certain hours in a day, or certain days in a week, for specific activities such as focused work, creative activities, emails and meetings? Or are you at your most productive when you focus on one type of task in the morning, and another in the afternoon? You might want to experiment with this. (Choice 4, 'How can I stay focused?', will also help you find the answers.)

6. FIND YOUR OWN PACE AND RHYTHM

I once went on a climb with a local guide in the Argentinian Andes. I expected it would take at least a couple of hours to reach the peak towering 1000 metres above us, and that I'd be huffing and puffing. I felt tempted to power ahead as I usually do, but every few minutes, my guide – who was watching me closely – told me to take a brief break. We kept stopping even though I didn't feel tired at all, which seemed to be a waste of time. To my astonishment, we reached the peak in just one hour, and there was not a single moment during the climb when I was out of breath. On that day, I realised how much difference it makes to rest at the right times.

We all prefer to walk at our own pace and rhythm on different types of terrain. For example, I tend to move relatively fast uphill and have frequent short breaks. When descending, I proceed more slowly and steadily and have fewer pauses. Interestingly, I often reach the destination at the same time as my hiking mates who walk in their own style. But in any situation, if I need to stick to other people's rhythms, I can quickly run out of juice.

We also have our natural pace and rhythm at work. How long can you engage in specific activities with your full attention, energy and smarts? How often do you need to take a breather? How long does it take for you to refresh your mind? There are no right or wrong answers, but you need to be aware of how you perform at your best.

For me, 90 minutes is usually a good amount of time to get on a roll and make good progress with writing reports or analysing data, and then I need to take a substantial break. But when I'm brainstorming innovative ideas, for instance, I'm in a very different headspace. I need to refresh my mind more often, but after a short breather – typically moving around and stretching my body – I'm usually ready to carry on.

You'll find it easier to maintain momentum throughout the day once you start taking restorative breaks, following a pace and rhythm that works for you. Plan your breaks in advance, which will make it more likely that you'll actually take time out for recovery when you need to. (We'll discuss the ins and outs of taking effective breaks in Choices 6 and 7.)

BONUS TIP: HONOUR YOUR PLAN

While bushwalking, it can be tempting to check out side tracks to nearby hilltops or lookouts. They are often only short distances away from the main track and promise spectacular scenery. However, good hikers know whether they have enough time and energy for these little side trips or if they should say no.

Likewise, you rarely see a seasoned hiker doing things half-heartedly. When they walk, they truly walk, with their eyes on the path ahead. When they rest, they truly rest, enjoying where they are, with their backpacks off. Just picture them trying to sneakily shuffle themselves a few metres forward during a break to feel that they are not wasting any time. Or can you imagine them leaving the track every few minutes as they walk, to check out what interesting surprises they may find in the area? That would be ridiculous.

Yet, we keep making the same kinds of absurd mistakes at work: multi-tasking, distracting ourselves, abandoning the task at hand when we should concentrate, and doing work when we should actually rest. These habits consume our time and energy, so why not make an effort to stop them?

With a good plan, you'll find it easier to stay on track and make the most of your time and energy. Honouring your plan doesn't make you rigid or boring. You can allow plenty of room for flexibility and spontaneity. But you have a much better chance of successfully responding to the unexpected if your eyes are on the goal and you know the possible pathways very well.

CHANNEL YOUR INNER ADVENTURER

Even if you're not a hiker, I'm sure at some point in your life you've ventured through difficult terrain and overcome mountainous challenges. And although you probably needed to stretch yourself to complete the journey, at the end you felt it was all worth it.

Next time you're faced with a difficult goal, put yourself in the shoes of your inner adventurer and think about what it takes to reach your destination through rain, hail or shine. The steps are simple. Know what you're capable of and set achievable targets. Identify the smartest route to your goals. Start on the right foot. Tackle the hardest challenge while you're at your peak. Keep up the momentum, and find the right pace and rhythm.

After making a killer plan for your day, you should be able to quickly get up to speed and have a focused, purposeful and fun journey.

INDIVIDUAL EXERCISES

Before starting work in the morning, make a list of the tasks you'd like to complete during the day. Then before you knock off, check how much you've actually achieved. Do you see a big difference? And how does it make you feel? Repeat this until you develop a knack for estimating what you can realistically fit into a day.

Experiment with tackling tasks in different orders. On the first day, start with something exciting, and then switch to a mundane job. The next day, do things in the opposite order. Then reflect on your experience. Which strategy was more enjoyable? And which one helped you achieve more? You could also play around with easy vs challenging tasks, or quick jobs vs monster projects, for instance.

TEAM EXERCISES

Discuss with your teammates your individual strategies for finding momentum, along with your challenges and counterproductive habits. What can you learn from each other?

Have a chat with your team about timing. What's everyone's natural pace and rhythm? How long can each of you focus on various tasks? How often do you prefer to switch your mode of thinking? And in light of all this, how can you organise yourselves better and work more effectively, both as individuals and as a team?

CHOICE 2

WHAT SHOULD I DO AT DIFFERENT TIMES OF THE DAY?

How can I align my routines with my circadian rhythm?

How can good timing improve my performance?

When should I dive into different activities to make the most of each day?

One of the first pieces of advice any productivity expert will give you is to organise your day around your body clock. The idea is simple. Over the course of the day, your alertness, mood and energy levels fluctuate. Different tasks suit different mental states, and if you can do the right tasks at the right times, you'll feel better and be more productive.

The importance of effective timing is becoming common knowledge, thanks to huge amounts of research. However, many individuals and teams are still sticking to their old routines, which is frustrating to witness. Lots of people blow their most precious hours on mundane tasks. They try to be creative when their minds are attuned to critical thinking. They tackle their most challenging tasks while unfocused and low on energy. And they make important decisions when they are too tired to think clearly and rationally. The consequences? A lot of time, brain power and emotions wasted. Mistakes and bad decisions that could have been easily avoided.

So let me try to answer some of your questions and help you reap the low-hanging fruit of smart timing.

'WHAT'S HAPPENING IN MY BODY?'

Many functions in your body operate in a 24-hour cycle, including your sleepiness and alertness, your appetite and digestion, your body temperature and your immune function. This orchestrated process – your circadian rhythm or body clock – is controlled by a tiny part of your brain called the suprachiasmatic nucleus, which responds to the changes in light reaching your eyes.

One of the manifestations of this daily cycle is the notorious afternoon slump. Some time after lunch your energy drops. You feel a bit flat and unmotivated, and you struggle to concentrate. The clock seems to be moving at a snail's pace and you may desperately need a caffeine hit to keep going.

Roughly 12 hours later, in the wee hours, you experience another, even deeper dip. This is the time of the night when you're programmed to sleep, and you find it most difficult to stay awake (assuming your internal clock is well tuned).

But the periods between these 'low points' are most interesting. For a few hours in a day, you should experience a peak when your brain is razor-sharp, your energy is high and your mood is pretty good. And you should also have another few precious hours on the other side of the cycle when, though you're a bit tired, you feel quite positive and ready to create something exciting.

'WHEN DO THESE VALUABLE TIMES OCCUR?'

The time of the day when you're most productive depends on whether you're a morning person, a night person, or somewhere in between. Scientists call this predisposition your 'chronotype'.

Around 14% of the population are estimated to be morning people – also known as 'larks'. Larks are early risers and have early bedtimes. Their minds are sharpest in the morning, and their most productive period starts an hour or two after waking up. Just like everyone else, larks are also hit by a slump later in the day. Once they have recovered, they experience a second wind, typically late in the afternoon, when their energy levels are moderate but their minds are most creative.

Around 21% of the population are night people – or 'owls' – who are inclined to wake up late and go to sleep late. Interestingly, the phases they go through during the day are in reverse order compared to larks. Owls are most focused in the evening, or sometimes late at night, and that's when they prefer to tackle their most challenging tasks. Earlier in the day, they find it easier to work on lighter tasks and creative challenges.

And the rest of us are what scientists refer to as 'third birds'. Third birds follow similar patterns to larks, but with a couple of hours delay.

'HOW DO I KNOW WHAT MY CHRONOTYPE IS?'

Chances are, you already know where you stand. If you wake up with the roosters, fresh and energised, and prefer to get things done early in the day while keeping your evenings free to relax, you're certainly a lark. If you're in your element in the evening or late at night when the rest of the world is already in bed, but find it a real struggle to get your head off the pillow early, you must be an owl. And if you can't identify with either of these, you're likely to be a third bird.

You've probably also figured out how some of your colleagues are wired. Sometimes it's easy to tell … One of your workmates is never quite with it at morning meetings, and rarely smiles before his first coffee. Yet, he keeps sending you eloquent emails in the middle of the night. Another of your colleagues always arrives in the office insanely early, and gets most of a day's work done by the time others are just getting ready to start. On the other hand, you can't expect much from her later in the day.

Unfortunately, traditional working hours have little regard for our individual circadian cycles, and so many of us need to get into gear at a time of the day when our bodies are not ready – either with the help of substantial amounts of caffeine or through sheer willpower. Family commitments can also wreak havoc on our sleep cycle. And if we get used to a daily routine that's dictated by others, it's easy to lose touch with our natural rhythm.

If you're unsure what your chronotype might be, just ask yourself: If you had the opportunity to go to sleep and wake up whenever you wanted, when would that be? What time do you wake up on holidays when there's zero pressure to get anything done (if you ever have the privilege)?

You can also find out which type of 'bird' you are by completing a simple online quiz.

Be aware that your circadian rhythm can change over your lifetime. Perhaps you were a lark or an owl at some point in the past, but your body might function differently now.

'WHAT SHOULD MY WORK HOURS BE?'

In an ideal world you'd be able to work when your body and mind are in the best shape, and take a break while going through a dip. For example, I'm a third bird, and my preferred working hours are roughly from 9 am to 1 pm, and then from 5 pm to 7 pm. This may seem like a cruisy day to you, but when my schedule is aligned with my circadian rhythm and I tackle the right task at the right time, I can get more done in six hours than on an average eight- to ten-hour day.

Of course, we all have constraints. We need to adapt to the schedules of our colleagues, clients and families. But work is becoming increasingly flexible, and hopefully you're able to negotiate the hours that suit your chronotype. Many collaborative teams set 'core hours' when everyone should be available, and allow members to organise themselves freely outside this time slot.

I've seen workplaces (both physical and virtual) that are never perfectly quiet. Even in the middle of the night, you can find at least one or two people working there. They are not there to catch up with their workload, but to produce the best results they can without wasting time and energy.

Unfortunately, managers don't always evaluate people fairly. Larks are often glorified for their apparent work ethic, since they are always the first in the office. On the flipside, owls can come across as unmotivated and lazy when evaluated superficially. But if you're not wired to be a morning person, acting like one won't help. You'll risk achieving less than you are capable of, while wearing yourself out. You're better off having a good chat with your teams and managers, explaining how you produce your best work.

Some professionals are burning the candle at both ends, trying to master both worlds. I know someone who regularly works at night, because that's when he's most productive, but then he wakes up early in the morning, because that's when he's expected to attend meetings. And sadly, he's frequently burnt out.

How does your current schedule suit you? Is the snooze button your best friend? Do you keep staring at your computer screen with glazed eyes while your brain is still booting up at the beginning of the day? Do you find that just as you're getting into your groove, your workday is over? … Or do you tend to be most energised and switched on well before you sit down at your desk? And do you often find yourself completely spent by the afternoon, feeling that those last couple of hours before you can clock off are never going to end? If any of this sounds like your story, you should consider making a change. With the right schedule, you'll not only be able to bring your best self to work, but also sleep better at night.

'WHAT SHOULD I WORK ON AT DIFFERENT TIMES OF THE DAY?'

During your peak hours, your energy and mood are high, and your head is clear. In this state, it's easy to block out distractions, focus on the task at hand, and think deeply. This is therefore the best time to tackle activities that require intense concentration and mental effort, such as strategic and analytical tasks. (You've probably heard the term 'deep work', coined by Cal Newport, computer science professor and author. Well, deep work refers to exactly these types of activities.) You also want to evaluate ideas, make critical decisions, and study new and complex subjects while at your peak.

I personally prefer to immerse myself in research, prepare presentations, and write reports, articles and difficult emails at this time. I tend to get into the groove quickly, and often find it surprisingly easy to solve problems that seemed daunting the previous afternoon. I also try to schedule planning sessions and critical meetings for the part of the day when I'm at my sharpest.

Going through a low point approximately seven hours after you wake up is inevitable. That's how your body functions. (Scientists call this phase the 'trough'.) Your energy drops, and you may feel a bit lethargic and flat. But if you're resourceful, you can still use this time productively. This is a good time to do administrative work and any other routine tasks that require less concentration.

I also often use this time to catch up with members of my network, which immediately lifts me up. Or when I can, I take a clean break from work. Perhaps I run a few errands, exercise, or go for a walk in a nearby park while allowing my mind to wander.

If you're a lark or a third bird, you probably notice that you become more upbeat later in the afternoon, as you're recovering from the slump. Your energy is still a bit low, and therefore you're easily distracted. But interestingly, this is a great place to be when it comes to generating new ideas. Your mind is open, and your thoughts are free to bounce around like a pinball, because thinking linearly and critically about your ideas just feels like too much hard work at this time.

If you're an owl, you experience this dreamy phase shortly after waking up.

This state of mind is great for brainstorming, creative design and artistic activities. You'll probably find that some of the best innovations are born in this phase. During my 'inspired hours', I also like to collect stories for my writing and my consulting work, and explore new opportunities with my partners and teammates.

'WHAT ABOUT TEAMWORK?'

When it comes to collaborative work, finding the ideal time for different activities can take some coordination, since people have different rhythms. So here's my suggestion: when you schedule a meeting or some other team activity, think about what you're aiming to achieve during that session, how your team needs to think and feel, and whether participants are predominantly larks, owls or third birds. Then find a time when most people are able to contribute their best.

In a typical team where third birds are the majority, you want to schedule training, planning and strategy sessions for the morning, and creative idea-generation sessions for the late afternoon. However, when the makeup of your team defies the norm, so should your schedule. If your team is dominated by owls, for example, it's best to explore new ideas at the start of your workday, and discuss complex problems and strategies in the evening.

Either way, make sure you don't just blindly follow the status quo. In the corporate world, meetings tend to be scheduled based on convenience and the availability of people and meeting rooms, without giving much thought to participants' mental states. Creative sessions are often held in the morning, when most of us are wired to think critically. Strategy meetings are often scheduled for after lunch, when no-one is able to concentrate or process information well. I'm sure you agree – we can all do better!

'HOW MUCH DIFFERENCE DOES TIMING MAKE?'

Research suggests that by working on the right tasks at the right time, you may improve your performance by up to 20% on cognitive tasks. At first glance, this is a startling figure. It's an extra day's worth of work in a week, without putting in additional hours or changing anything else about the way you operate. But all this makes sense when you understand that timing affects countless different aspects of your performance.

You know by now that when you time your tasks effectively, you gain access to your best thinking. You work faster and more accurately. You learn more and you come up with more creative ideas. Now, let me also give you a few other – perhaps less obvious – examples of why timing matters.

If you try to get into a mentally challenging task when your energy is low, you're more likely to procrastinate. In fact, a large proportion of chronic procrastinators are found to be owls, which is hardly a surprise. As they try to meet managers' and society's expectations by working traditional hours, they are often faced with difficult tasks at a time when their brain is not yet in top gear.

You approach decisions differently when you're fresh and when you feel tired. During your peak, you have the energy to evaluate risk and consider decisions carefully. When you're tired, on the other hand, you're more inclined to delay decisions or just rush into them. You may take unnecessary risks as a result, or you may avoid risk altogether by playing it safe. None of these strategies is a recipe for success. Sure, you want to follow your intuition, but in most situations, you'll make a better choice when you carefully consider the facts first.

The way you feel, which fluctuates throughout the day, can influence your communication and actions to a great extent, sometimes in unexpected ways. One fascinating study analysed the earning calls of thousands of public companies. (Earning calls are conference calls focusing on a company's financial accomplishments within a given period. They are typically attended by management, analysts, investors and the media.) The results of the study showed that calls held later in the afternoon had a more negative and irritable tone compared to those held early in the morning, and this had an adverse effect on the companies' stock prices.

When your energy is low, you're less disciplined. This is perfectly illustrated by two medical studies. One of them observed that healthcare workers who started their shifts in the morning washed their hands much less frequently in the afternoon, often violating their professional obligations. The other study found that doctors were more likely to prescribe unnecessary antibiotics in the afternoon – presumably because they were too weary to explain why the patients didn't need antibiotics and thus succumbed to the pressure of giving them what they wanted.

Of course, you can't change the fact that you will go through ups and downs during the day. But when you understand your limitations and organise your day accordingly, you will find it much easier to do a job you can be proud of.

'SOMETHING ALWAYS COMES UP – WHAT CAN I DO?'

Are your most productive hours often hijacked by others? Do your colleagues and clients keep sending you urgent demands and filling up your calendar with meetings that don't work for you? Perhaps it's time to have a chat with them. Tell them – or even better, show them – how you could create more value by maximising your brain power. It's also difficult to dispute the fact that the entire team will become more efficient when everyone's biological rhythms are respected.

I suggest you first work out with your teammates what the optimal times are for different team activities – including meetings, calls and collaborative sessions – and how you could all adopt a healthier and more productive rhythm. Then mark the hours in your calendar when it's the best time for you to concentrate on mentally demanding tasks, and do your best to protect these periods from unnecessary distractions. Even if you can only allocate 30 minutes to deep work at a time, it's a good start.

MAKE SURE TIME IS ALWAYS ON YOUR SIDE

A few years ago, I found myself in an odd situation when I needed to co-ordinate the renovation of a property located on the other side of the world. I was out of my depth, and stressful news kept coming each day. Because of the different time zones, I ended up talking to the contractors night after night, and consequently, I slept badly for months. To make things worse, when I woke up each morning, I couldn't resist the urge to read and respond to the distressing messages that landed in my inbox overnight, and the regular early-morning anxiety completely derailed my days. I was embarrassingly unproductive with my other projects during that period. There's no punchline to this story, but the lesson learned has been burnt into my psyche: timing alone can make a difference between staying on top of things and ending up in a heap. Looking back later, I realised that by organising my time more skillfully, I could have kept my sanity and handled the challenge much better.

These days I tend to protect my most productive hours like a tiger protects her cubs. I'm super selective not only about the tasks I focus on during this period, but also about the potential distractions and stresses I allow in my life. Of course, I'm not immune to curly challenges, but now I'm more conscious of when to deal with them, and as a result I usually manage to stay focused and effective.

So here are a few tips for you to make sure time is always on your side:

- Start each day with a clear idea of what you're going to work on in your peak hours, during the slump, and in your creative period. You might find it useful to prepare a separate to-do list for each phase.

- Be clear about which kinds of distractions and challenges you should say no to before and during your peak. Unexpected issues tend to come up all the time, but with well-defined boundaries you'll find it easier to protect your most valuable hours.

- Know when it's time to ease off. As your peak state winds down, give yourself the permission to switch to simpler tasks or just rest. You'll achieve more if you roll with the ride your brain takes you on each day, rather than fight against it.

In the following Choices we'll explore how you can maximise your mental energy and brain power. As you're learning to plan your days and manage your inner resources better, you'll spend less time in that sad place where moving forward is a grind, and more time in the zone where work is deeply satisfying and rewarding.

INDIVIDUAL EXERCISES

If your job allows, experiment with different working hours. How does the good ol' 9 to 5 suit your biological clock? Do you feel inclined to dive into work at dawn and finish shortly after lunchtime? Do you achieve more if you start later in the morning (or perhaps even in the afternoon) and work till late? Or do you perform to your best if you divide your working hours into two blocks, and take a long break in between?

Start developing your ideal daily schedule. Decide what kinds of tasks you'll work on each hour – and as you're getting through your day, pay attention to how you feel and perform. Are you able to concentrate? Are you making good progress? Can you find your flow? Or do you find it difficult at times to immerse yourself in what you're doing? Keep fine-tuning your schedule until it's just right.

TEAM EXERCISES

Get together and have a chat about how each of you are wired. Find out who is a lark, an owl, a third bird or perhaps something else – and how they work most effectively. Then work out how you should schedule different team activities, ensuring that everyone can contribute their best.

Experiment with holding different kinds of meetings – including training, project updates, creative sessions and strategy discussions – at different times of the day. Notice when the team is most attuned to the type of conversation you aim to have, and when these meetings are most efficient and successful.

CHOICE 3

HOW CAN I MAXIMISE MY MENTAL ENERGY?

What activities build my mental energy, and what activities drain it?

How can I nourish, protect and preserve my inner resources?

Why do I find myself mentally exhausted early in the day,
and how can I prevent this?

Staying on top of your work, day after day, is a relentless pursuit. To concentrate, communicate well, solve problems and make great decisions, you need a lot of mental energy. However, your resources are finite, and you're burning precious brain fuel whether you're being productive or doing something trivial or futile. In this Choice you'll find out how you can nourish, protect and preserve your mental energy, and achieve more while feeling strong and positive.

If someone told you that you must run a marathon in a month, how would you go about it? Would you show up on the day unprepared, hoping for the best? And would you sprint until you collapsed? Of course, that would be foolish. If you were serious about doing well, or at least finishing the race, you'd start building up your fitness and developing a strategy straight away. Then during the race, you'd aim to carefully manage your energy and run with the least effort.

These days, work often feels like a marathon. We pursue ambitious goals and targets, and the pressure is always on. We can never really slow down and take things easy.

To do well, we must always be fully focused and switched on. Our jobs require deep and intense thinking, but the brain can't perform at its peak all day long – just like we can't sprint through a long-distance race. Overwork and haphazard habits lead to mistakes, stress and exhaustion, and there's not much we can do with a fried brain. So we need to manage our mental energy carefully if we want to create genuine value while maintaining a healthy mind and spirit.

THE NATURE OF MENTAL ENERGY

It's not easy to put your finger on it, but you certainly know what it feels like when your mental energy is abundant.

At your peak state, it's easy to get into your flow. You have the mental stamina to focus on challenging tasks and block out distractions. You also have the willpower to do things you don't particularly enjoy, and to say no to temptations that won't do you much good, like watching cute cat videos when you have work to do or eating a huge slice of chocolate cake for a mid-morning snack.

When your mental energy is high, you tend to feel happier and more optimistic. You think more clearly and communicate more effectively. You can get your head around large amounts of information, filter out what's relevant and connect the dots with ease. You're ready to take calculated risks and to make rational, considered decisions.

But sadly, you're not superhuman. Your brain gets tired easily, and the consequences are palpable. You slow down and start making trivial mistakes. You find it increasingly difficult to concentrate and to learn anything new. Chances are you lose your sense of control, and become anxious and irrational. You set the wrong priorities, and make poor decisions or avoid making any at all.

Your mental energy is finite

Whether you're working productively, fighting distractions, procrastinating, or doing personal tasks like shopping online or messaging your friends, you're burning precious brain fuel. You're expending mental energy while getting things done and also while wasting time. However, at any given time, your resources are limited. If you use, say, 50% of your energy doing something unnecessary or futile, you'll have only 50% left for activities that matter.

Thinking, learning, listening and communicating all consume energy, just like switching your focus, working through negative emotions and adjusting to change. And in the modern work environment, energy-draining traps are lurking everywhere. It's too easy to become exhausted without making progress. Every bit of irrelevant information, distraction and stressful or disheartening news depletes your reserves, bit by bit. And after a few little, seemingly innocuous assaults on your headspace, you can only function at a reduced capacity.

Humans haven't evolved for heads-down, focused work

I'm sure you agree that getting in the groove at work is becoming increasingly difficult. To stand a chance of regaining your focus and energy, you need to understand that our modern lifestyles are very unnatural, at least in a biological sense. The human brain hasn't evolved to do deep intellectual work for hours on end.

You are easily distractible, for numerous reasons:

- To survive, our prehistoric ancestors had to be attuned to what was going on around them. You still carry this instinct, which means you likely find it difficult to ignore anything new or unexpected happening around you.

- High-level thinking consumes a lot of mental energy. However, your brain is wired to preserve energy. So while you're trying to focus on a challenge, part of your mind is actively seeking opportunities to tune out and rest.

- Your 'monkey brain' loves surprises and excitement, so when your work is not really fun or stimulating, you can easily get bored. And boredom is a painful place that you crave to get out of as soon as possible.

- Focusing on something dull is very hard, again because of your neurology. When you work on a challenging task, you typically pursue a future goal. However, the brain is attuned to look for immediate relief or reward – something easy and enjoyable to do. (This tendency of the mind is called 'present bias'.)

- You may try to use your willpower to stay focused and overcome distractions – and to resist the temptation to switch to something easier or more enjoyable – but there's a catch. Exercising willpower requires a lot of mental fuel, so as you're getting tired, you find it harder and harder to do the 'right thing'.

In short, concentration is an uphill battle, and therefore you have to be especially smart about the way you look after your brain.

Okay, it's time to explore how your choices can boost or deplete your mental energy, and what you can do to succeed in this marathon called work.

TAKE CARE OF YOUR BODY

When your body is in great shape, you should find that your mental energy budget is plentiful. While this might sound like a cliché, developing a powerful mind really starts with a **healthy body**. You know the drill: have sufficient, high-quality sleep, exercise regularly, eat well and stay hydrated. By looking after your physical state, you not only give yourself a better chance to live a long and healthy life, but you also make your work easier and more enjoyable.

Be mindful of possible **dips in your energy** during the day. For example, your mind could be a bit foggy after strenuous exercise. Unless you're a seasoned athlete, the best time to push your body to its limits is after work. If you're keen to exercise earlier in the day, choose a moderate-intensity workout instead, like a brisk walk, a light jog or a bike ride.

Your brain also demands some downtime after a hearty meal. It's best not to have critical meetings in the early afternoon (for a variety of reasons) but if you must, then stick to a light lunch. I'm sure you know what it's like when you're trying to innovate or make strategic decisions with a heavy stomach.

Remember your body's most basic need: **clean, fresh air**. You can't do much good with a cloudy brain that's starving for oxygen. Always work in a well-ventilated space – you don't want to compromise on this.

Severe **discomfort and pain** are extremely draining. Even your wardrobe makes a difference. Wear comfortable clothing, as your work allows.

Whenever you can, choose a comfortable environment with good-quality lighting, pleasant temperatures and ergonomic furniture.

Always maintain a **healthy, upright posture**. If possible, switch where you sit every few hours. Stand up often, move your body, and go for short walks during the day. All these will help reduce any discomfort or pain you might be experiencing. Holding good posture and keeping your body in motion should also trigger a positive shift in your mental state, making you feel more alert, energised and upbeat.

LOOK AFTER YOUR EMOTIONS AND INNER LIFE

Positive emotions are invigorating. When you get the chance, choose or create a workspace that inspires you and lifts your spirit. Natural light and pleasant views make a huge difference, for instance. In your free time, engage in activities that elevate your mood – perhaps listen to upbeat music, read something heartwarming or have a good laugh.

In contrast, **negative emotions** and unresolved conflicts can suck the life out of you. It can be incredibly difficult to get anything meaningful done after a confronting conversation, whether with a colleague, a family member or a complete stranger. Personally, when I'm feeling stirred up I find it very difficult to concentrate. My thoughts keep revolving around what I should have said or done differently, who is right or wrong, and how I could possibly repair any damage. Stressful or disappointing news can also take a lot out of me, whether a phone call from a confused client, an email informing me about a missed opportunity, or an article about a natural disaster.

If you can relate, the trick that works for me will likely be helpful for you too. When possible, simply avoid any **potential triggers** early in the day and during the hours when your work requires intense focus. Create a safe bubble for yourself, unplug if your work allows, and stay away from people who have the tendency to push your buttons.

I'm not suggesting you hide from negativity, but you want to be smart about when you face emotionally difficult situations. Try to only expose yourself to potentially stressful news and events when they can't ruin the best part of your day, and you're able to dedicate enough time and attention to addressing the issues.

Of course, it's also worth strengthening your **resilience and emotional intelligence**, so you can stay centred and calm amid adversity. And it goes without saying that when you're part of a trusting and caring team, conflicts are less frequent and are easier to handle. So nurturing your relationships is definitely a worthwhile effort.

Improve your relationship with your work

Working towards **exciting goals and opportunities** alongside inspiring people can really boost your energy. So if you feel a bit flat, tune into the purpose of your work and connect with your teammates. Engage in uplifting and stimulating conversations. Keep track of the progress you're making, day by day, and celebrate even small achievements and milestones.

Interestingly, experiencing **a bit of pressure** at work can also help. However, the way you deal with demanding situations is your choice – you may see them as obstacles, or as opportunities to learn, grow and achieve something extraordinary. If you can make friends with pressure, you'll find that many of the challenging situations which might have crushed you in the past will make you feel unstoppable. (We'll explore this further in Choice 32, 'How can I make pressure my friend?')

Too much pressure, on the other hand, can be debilitating. Do you constantly feel behind, stressed about tight deadlines, and overwhelmed by the amount of work ahead of you? Such **heavy emotions** could render you powerless. So put your to-do list and any project files you're not using out of sight, turn off your phone and close your inbox for a while, and focus on the task at hand. Concentrate on the next step only. There's wisdom in the saying, 'You can only eat an elephant one bite at a time'.

When you feel positively challenged, your energy can go sky-high. But what happens when you don't believe you have what it takes to succeed? Or when you can't stop thinking about your critics, or the consequences of making a mistake? This kind of negative head chatter can seriously deplete your energy and stop you from taking action. **Worry and lack of confidence** are among the main reasons people procrastinate.

To overcome this issue, I suggest you spend a bit of time observing your thoughts and feelings, and reflecting on how you might be standing in your own way. Awareness is the first step towards building your confidence and transforming your thinking. If you suffer from **imposter syndrome** (welcome to the club), you can find excellent advice from the experts. Getting better at what you do should also strengthen your self-belief, so keep developing your professional skills and knowledge, discussing your challenges with people you trust, and learning from your mistakes.

PROTECT AND PRESERVE YOUR ATTENTION

Without doubt, productive work is taxing. Processing information, making decisions, taking calculated risks, and even focusing on dull tasks all consume a lot of mental resources. If you'd like to save yourself from **unnecessary hurdles**, weed through your to-do list and remove anything that doesn't serve your individual or team goals. This is not poor work ethic but smart planning. You don't want to burden yourself with irrelevant information, unimportant decisions and unnecessary meetings. You should channel your efforts where they count most.

If you can immerse yourself in what you do, you'll be able to go a long way. On the other hand, if your attention is all over the place, you'll be ineffective and slow, and unable to find your flow. Think of running that marathon … To reach the finish line in the shortest possible time and with the least amount of exertion, you'll need to gain momentum. You won't do very well if you keep changing your speed and focus every few minutes. You won't be able to settle into a steady rhythm and get your **second wind**, which could help you run with less effort and pain.

I'm sure it's not news to you that **multitasking** is also a bad idea. Your mind can only focus on one thought at a time, and if you try to complete two incompatible tasks simultaneously, you'll end up switching your attention back and forth, rather than multitasking in the true sense of the word. (Are you skeptical? Try picturing a fluffy baby penguin while adding 17 and 29 in your head.) And this is a costly habit. Each time you shift your focus, you're burning precious mental fuel, as your brain needs to load information into your working memory about the context of whatever you're doing or thinking about. If you shift your focus every few minutes or even seconds, your brain has to transfer information between its different compartments over and over again, which can drain you very quickly.

What does multitasking mean to you? Taking a call while writing an email? Reading a report while participating in a meeting? Even when you just think of something irrelevant to your task, you're essentially multitasking. Let's say it's a gorgeous day outside … When you look out the window, you see the glistening blue sky and the birds having a jolly time. Don't you wish you could enjoy this beautiful day outdoors, rather than sitting at a desk? The truth is, many people are measurably less productive when the weather is especially nice. Digest this for a moment. Isn't it fascinating how your **wandering thoughts** – even those most innocent – can disrupt your concentration?

Is this the story of your life?

You probably switch your attention way more often than you're aware.

You sit down in front of your screen, ready to jump into work. You have a quick glance at your web browser with a dozen tabs open, and you're immediately reminded of a pile of articles you want to read, podcasts to listen to, and other commitments to follow through on.

As you try to get some work done, your eyes land on your mobile phone on the desk, and you can't help thinking of the calls you're expecting. But when the phone doesn't ring for a while, and there are no new messages, you're a bit concerned that you might be missing out on something. *Should I check what's going on in the world?*

You scroll through your social feed and quickly evaluate every single update before deciding if they're worth more of your attention. As you're reading a few updates and comments, you wonder how some people can be so inspiring while others seem rather narrow-minded.

You suddenly remember an interesting video from your favourite artist that you were planning to watch. *Should I do it now?* You know it's a bad idea, but it's hard to resist. You give in and watch the video – but all the while you feel guilty and stressed, well aware that you're supposed to be working instead and those deadlines are looming.

You receive a text message. Your mind quickly runs through the story behind this message, and although you decide not to respond just yet, you already start to formulate the answer in your head.

It's time to join your team's regular videoconference call. You're wondering if you look okay on camera. The meeting feels a bit slow, so you decide to write an email while others are talking. You keep switching your attention between the call and the email. You're also a bit worried that your teammates may notice you not being fully present, or that you're missing out on an important part of the discussion.

You finally manage to concentrate on your job, but a colleague soon interrupts, asking you to help her out on an urgent project. You now try to focus on this new task, but your mind keeps jumping back to the one you've abandoned. *What will I need to do when I get back to it?*

Strengthen your mind – weaken the problem

It's no surprise that your brain is exhausted after switching focus a zillion times. And you can't expect that the world is going to slow down, distractions will decrease, or that people and platforms will stop fighting for your attention. If anything, the trends are pointing in the opposite direction.

If you'd like to maintain control over your attention, there are two things you can do.

First, you can train yourself to concentrate and be present, taming your monkey brain. Here are just a few tips:

- Concentration is like a muscle; the more you exercise it, the better you get. Commit to a specific period when you will focus on a single task – whether for 5 minutes or 30 minutes – and just do it. Say no to any distractions. When the time is up, take a break, and then repeat. After a few days' practice, you'll notice that staying on task will become easier, and that you can focus for longer periods than before.

- Get used to boredom. When you have a quiet moment in your life, just stay with it, instead of seeking stimulation. Spend some time each day unplugged, alone with your thoughts. No screen. No music. No snacks. You'll eventually learn to find joy in simple activities and to immerse yourself in tasks you previously struggled to get into.

- Consider practising meditation or mindfulness, which are both wonderful for building concentration. This is why Buddhist monks are so great at focusing at will, even in busy environments. (Scientists studying the brain images of monks who had been practising meditation for years noticed something extraordinary: even when not meditating, their gamma wave activity – indicating deep concentration – was significantly more powerful compared to people with little to no experience in meditation.) However, you don't need to be a meditation master to see results. Even if you can only commit to daily five-minute sessions, you'll notice some benefits.

And here's my second piece of advice to manage your attention:

- Learn to get on a roll. Create habits and environments that help you stay on track, and eliminate those sneaky traps that could derail your attention. There are a lot of useful tips and tricks to share in this area, so I'm dedicating the next Choice to showing you how you can achieve this.

LET'S TACKLE THIS CHALLENGE FROM ALL ANGLES

Work in many ways is like running a marathon. You can only succeed if you look after your body, emotions and mind. With any weak links, you have little chance of reaching the finish line, let alone performing well or enjoying the race.

Human evolution hasn't prepared you for channelling your energy into deep, intellectual work, so you must tackle this challenge strategically from all angles. Invest in yourself by strengthening your mental fitness and emotional intelligence. Develop powerful habits, and reduce or eliminate any negative influences from your environment that could drain your inner resources.

Your mental energy is your currency for success. Nourish, protect and preserve it with great care, and you could achieve more than you ever thought possible.

INDIVIDUAL EXERCISES

Commit to three simple actions you can do daily, for at least three weeks, to improve your physical and mental health. You have plenty of options: perhaps have a walk or exercise, drink enough water, have heathy snacks, limit caffeine and alcohol, use a gratitude journal, meditate, or go to bed at a reasonable hour. Do you notice any change in your physical and mental energy by the end of the three weeks? Do you find it easier to stay on top of work? Is it worth continuing with your chosen routines? And can you perhaps also develop some new ones?

Try to catch yourself every time you're switching attention – whether you're multitasking, flicking between apps or software, responding to interruptions, or daydreaming when you're supposed to work. Remind yourself each time that you've just burnt a good dose of brain fuel. Stick to this habit as long as you feel you have room for improvement … Are you getting better at noticing these moments? And are you becoming more conscious about preserving your attention?

TEAM EXERCISES

Organise yourselves in groups of two or three. In each group, share with one another what kinds of situations and challenges (if any) tend to bring down your spirit or shake your confidence. How do negative emotions, stresses and worries affect your ability to work? What advice can you give, and how can you support each other?

Put your heads together to identify which team activities tend to drain your mental energy (perhaps long meetings in windowless rooms, discussions about daunting goals and deadlines, brain-frying project update sessions, or sugar-fuelled company events). Also gather a list of team activities that can boost your energy (which might include walking meetings, inspiring conversations about new opportunities, and social catch-ups involving fun games, music, exercise or laughter). Where can you make improvements? What should you do less of, and what should you do more often? Commit to some changes, and get together again in a month to discuss the results.

HOW CAN I STAY FOCUSED?

What do I need to do to gain control over my attention?

How can I overcome procrastination and self-distraction?

What does it take to work effectively in a distracting environment?

Work can sometimes feel like a wicked game designed to test your focus. However, it's still in your power to control your attention and work effectively. The key is to understand the inner workings of the habits that don't actually serve you, and strategically replace them with new ones that allow you to make conscious, empowered choices throughout the day. Once you get this right, you'll almost forget how to waste your energy and time.

'TRAINS OF THOUGHT'

Derren Brown, a world-renowned mentalist and illusionist, is a true master of the human mind. In the popular video 'Trains … of thought', you see him get on a London underground train and ask random strangers, 'Can I ask you what stop are you getting off at?' Passengers answer in an instant. But after Brown blurts out a few hypnotic phrases and makes some confusing hand gestures, many of his perplexed subjects immediately forget the answer. They are travelling on a train with no idea which station they are heading to.

It's difficult to believe that this kind of memory lapse could happen to us. How could we forget something as obvious as our destination, especially when we're already on our way? Well, I'm sure you know what it's like when your mind goes blank mid-conversation after being interrupted. Or when you need to get something from another room, but by the time you get there you've forgotten what it was.

We perform many activities in our lives from routine, without consciously thinking about what we're doing. Our 'trains of thought' serve a purpose: they help us complete simple repetitive tasks efficiently and with little mental energy, allowing us to focus our attention where it's most needed. We would get things done incredibly slowly if our brains had to make well-considered decisions about what to do next in every waking moment. However, when these unconscious processes are distracted midway through, we can easily find ourselves in limbo.

What drives our everyday routines?

Neuro-linguistic programming (a field of psychology, also referred to as the 'language of the mind') can help us understand how our 'trains of thought' guide our decisions and actions. This insight might be the key to gaining control over our attention and working effectively in this distracting world.

We store much of our knowledge and memories in our minds as images, sounds, sensations in our bodies, and the words we tell ourselves. Many of these 'memory bites' are closely connected in our brains, forming well-defined chains of thoughts and feelings. When we function on autopilot, we tend to recall every single element of a specific chain, and always in the same order. As soon as the first element in a sequence pops up in our minds for whatever reason, it automatically triggers the next one, and that triggers the next one, and so on. It can all happen very rapidly. In a fraction of a second, a dozen images, sounds, words and sensations can flash through our minds like frames in a movie.

In the language of neuro-linguistic programming, a specific sequence of such interlinked thoughts and feelings is called a 'strategy'. We construct a myriad of them through our life experiences, and replay them over and over again, usually unconsciously. We have strategies for all sorts of habitual activities, like getting out of bed, shaking hands, speaking our native language (or a foreign one), becoming terrified of whatever terrifies us (whether it be heights, spiders or 'the boogie man'), and even falling in love. We also have our own strategies for remembering things, and this is what Derren Brown interrupted with his hypnotic words and gestures.

THE DOMINO EFFECT

Strategies are also present in our work lives, in many different shapes and forms. Have you noticed that on some days you can cruise through your tasks without a hitch, and on others you keep hitting obstacles? You may feel you have lucky and unlucky days, but in truth, you probably play out different strategies at different times.

When you're on a roll, you're riding a wave of powerful thoughts and emotions. As you complete even a small step towards an important goal, you experience a sense of progress. This boosts your mood and your motivation to complete the next step as quickly as possible. You focus relentlessly, you move fast, and seeing your results further strengthens your sense of progress.

And what about those times when everything seems to move backwards? Something happens during the day that sets you back a little, and you unwittingly respond in a way that creates more problems. As you try to dig yourself out of that hole, adopting *ineffective* strategies, you sink deeper and deeper.

Let me share three common pitfalls where one bad decision leads to the next. Are any of these familiar?

The procrastination pandemonium

You sit down at your desk to tackle that challenging project. You're already behind schedule, and uncertain if doing your best will be enough. The task ahead of you is less than exciting. You crave something a little more rewarding, and suddenly you hear your inner voice: *Why not tidy up my desk first, answer a few easy emails, or browse the web for a bit? Should I check what my social network is up to?*

You give in. At the same time, you're fully aware that you're procrastinating, thus making your own life more difficult. Instead of finding relief, you're experiencing frustration and guilt. You know you'd better get into that task ASAP. But by now, with this cocktail of emotions and a frazzled mind, you can barely concentrate and you feel even less motivated than before. So you can't help looking for an escape again, asking yourself, *What can I do now that's easy and fun?*

The distraction disarray

You'd love to focus and work productively. At the same time, you feel you need to be on top of things. *Everything.* And you must always be available for your colleagues and clients. You keep your phone on your desk, check your inbox every few minutes, and have many app notifications turned on. Not surprisingly, calls and messages keep coming. You immediately assess what's urgent, respond as needed, and then try to regain focus.

But you're starting to feel scattered and frustrated. You find it increasingly difficult to prioritise things and ignore irrelevant messages. Even the slightest noises and movements irritate you. Whenever something derails your attention, you tell yourself, *Oh well, I'm already off task, so I might as well mess around a bit longer before getting serious again.*

Ironically, you now also start looking for distractions yourself. You can't help it; you're stressed and spent, and your mental power has been exhausted. *Time to fix that dripping tap in the kitchen? Sure is. Haven't spoken to grandma in a while? Better call her right now. What movie are we going to watch this Friday evening? Let's get that sorted …*

The multitasking misery

You have a lot on your plate. To get everything done in time, you intend to 'optimise' every minute of your day. You read reports and articles during meetings. You keep working on that monster spreadsheet while taking phone calls. And you jump back and forth between urgent tasks.

You're trying hard to concentrate on whatever you're doing, but your mind is becoming cluttered. Unfinished tasks are haunting you. You're not sure why, but you also start to feel quite sad and anxious. Mental fatigue kicks in. You struggle to remember even basic information, and you can't really judge anymore what's urgent and relevant. As soon as you face a minor difficulty, you abandon what you're doing and switch to something simpler. You just can't put in the effort to think. (Gregory Ciotti – an expert in productive work and human behaviour – aptly calls such moments 'ah-screw-its'.) Eventually you realise that you're making a lot of errors and wasting loads of time. Now you're really under pressure to up your game.

How can you avoid these traps?

Perhaps you've noticed that these grim situations often start with good intentions. The decisions you make about how you deal with the challenges coming your way may seem logical, or at least innocent. But what is really happening? You're jump-starting – and then rolling with – a chain of reactions that only creates a mess.

Procrastination, distraction, self-distraction and multitasking are huge problems in the workplace. They can destroy your performance, along with your spirit, as also shown by research. And the more you give in to these deceptive habits, the harder it becomes to break them.

How can you avoid these traps? You need to gain and maintain a healthy control over the way you work, rather than constantly reacting to distractions and setbacks. You need to start your day on the right track, stay on that track, and when you find yourself accidentally heading in the wrong direction, you need to be able to jump tracks.

1. GET ON THE RIGHT TRACK

The morning is naturally the best time to set the course for your day. Your mind is still fresh and your willpower is strong. Your mood (perhaps after a coffee) is relatively high and the day is full of possibilities. So you want to use this time wisely and determine your own direction, rather than simply reacting to what comes your way.

Protecting your headspace early in the day is critical. Avoid activities that can clutter your mind with irrelevant information or make you feel frustrated or stressed. You'll feel more empowered if you kick off with a powerful routine, compared to spending a long time answering emails, scrolling through your social feeds or reading the news.

If you find your mind is already too busy – perhaps you feel a bit overwhelmed about everything going on in your life, worried about the state of the world, or agitated by an argument – spend a few minutes putting your thoughts on paper. After emptying your mind, you'll feel more at peace and better able to focus.

Make sure your environment supports what you're planning to do, and the resources you need are in easy reach. Be proactive about distractions. Before tackling a challenging task, perhaps ask your teammates not to interrupt you for a couple of hours. Find a quiet spot a safe distance from colleagues who are allergic to silence. Close the door, if that's an option.

You also need to look at the way you use technology, and create some breathing space for yourself. Close all apps and software you don't need. Do you have dozens of tabs open in your browser? I'm guilty of this too. But you can easily save all links and then close those tabs without losing information, or use one of the many apps that are designed to help manage your browser. Turn off unnecessary notifications. Put your phone out of sight, and on silent, if possible.

Find your focus

It's worth spending a moment reflecting on the purpose of your work, and what motivates you. What will be the rewards for achieving your goals? Knowing that you've changed people's lives for the better? Proving yourself? Making your team proud? Learning something valuable? Being able to connect with amazing people? … You want to make sure that the pull towards your goals is stronger than the push towards procrastination. In other words, you need to find a better reward than escaping hard work.

This is the moment of truth. When you're ready to dive into your first serious task, don't check 'just one more interesting thing'. Sure, you may spend a little time in the morning frolicking around, but once that door is closed it should stay closed. You want to draw a clear line between work and play. You might find it helpful to use different devices, software or apps for work-related tasks, and for social activities and entertainment. This way you can simply close or put away everything you don't need for work.

Immersing yourself into a difficult task takes effort, of course. Before you reach a state of flow, you might be tempted to quit. Here's a trick I find particularly powerful in this situation: I simply review some of the work I've already completed – whether it's a design or research project, consulting advice or a written piece. This helps me get into the right headspace while giving me confidence and a sense of achievement. Once I'm up to speed, it's much easier to jump back into the deep end.

2. STAY ON TRACK

The reality is that your attention will be tested, and you may be knocked around over and over again, even after the most careful preparations to stay in your zone. This is the nature of work. So you need to be ready to respond skillfully to a variety of hurdles, and to stay on track even as you're riding out a storm.

When you're under pressure, you might feel inclined to tackle several tasks simultaneously in an attempt to progress faster. The truth is you can only focus on one thing at a time. When your brain needs to alternate between tasks, you run out of energy fast and become highly distractible. You slow down and produce lower quality work. (Studies show that when multi-tasking, people waste up to 40% of their time and make up to 50% more mistakes.) Over time, habitual multitasking also reduces brain density in the area responsible for attention, motivation and problem solving (the anterior cingulate cortex). Not a winning strategy, is it? The solution is simple. Focus on one thing at a time. Finish one task before starting the next, whenever possible.

Each time you switch between tasks – and ways of thinking – your mind is challenged. However, today's jobs are complex. You may need to complete lots of vastly different tasks in an average day – perhaps brainstorming ideas, researching, running calculations, preparing presentations, meeting clients, answering emails, doing administrative chores, or troubleshooting tech issues. You might need to be playful and adventurous in one moment – say, when exploring disruptive innovations – and put on your analytical hat 10 minutes later when preparing a formal report.

To preserve your mental energy, avoid taking too many sharp turns. Group similar types of activities together, and switch between work modes only when necessary. I'm a fan of this technique, as I find it much easier to tackle creative challenges, complete analytical tasks, read documents and answer emails in large batches, compared to mixing things up too much. (You can tell, just by looking at my calendar, if I've had a successful day. When it looks tidy, filled with a few large blocks of activities, you know I was on top of things. And when my calendar is littered with dozens of short, mixed entries, it shows that my attention was all over the place.)

It's also worth batching meetings. One study observed that people were 22% less productive during the one to two hours prior to meetings, compared to other times with no upcoming meetings. By grouping them together, you not only make it easier for yourself and your teammates to stay on a roll; you also minimise the unproductive periods when, in the shadow of impending 'interruptions', you are reluctant to dive deep into work.

Switch your attention skillfully

When you need to switch between different ways of working, watch out: this is a critical moment when you could easily go off track, as you're particularly vulnerable to distractions and the temptation to procrastinate. After completing a task and before starting a new one, you might want to spend a few minutes clearing your head.

This can be a good time to take a refreshing break. Maybe go for a walk, listen to music, catch up with your workmates or just daydream a little. But once you're ready to continue working, do not waver. You need to get back on the right track. Consider moving to a new location in your workplace, shifting your body posture, or using different tools and technologies from what you just used. These tricks could help you reset your thinking and focus on the new activity with all your attention.

Distractions can occur in any environment, and bouncing back can be tricky. Once your attention is hijacked, you're more inclined to get in your own way – say, by starting an exciting but non-urgent task, browsing the internet, or reaching for your phone to check your favourite apps. Before you know it, you're heading down the rabbit hole. Be mindful of this risk. After an interruption, I suggest you spend a couple of minutes gathering your thoughts, and then return to your task straight away. Make this a habit, and distractions will take much less out of you.

At certain times, you might find that focusing is nearly impossible. Maybe a loud colleague is on a call right next to you. The fire alarm is being tested. Vehicles are beeping out on the street. And my pet hate while working from home: those leaf blowers! When way too much is going on around you, it's best if you either pick a really easy task, or just stop, whether for five minutes or half an hour. You're better off losing a bit of time than getting exhausted and stressed, which could affect you for the rest of the day.

3. JUMP TRACKS WHEN NEEDED

As we touched on earlier, channelling your energy into high-level work is a challenge that evolution hasn't prepared you for. Even if you work with outstanding ethics, you may still find yourself off track once in a while. I know incredibly disciplined and productive professionals who sometimes struggle to get into the groove. This is human nature. But they are highly self-aware, and are ready to change their approach as soon as they catch themselves wasting time and energy.

It's certainly possible to jump from the wrong track to the right one at any time, but it's important that you notice early when you're caught up in an unproductive pattern. This will save you a lot of frustration and make course correction easier. If you sit down at your desk to get some serious work done and after 15 minutes you're still fiddling with unimportant tasks, you're probably on the wrong track. And if you actually start working on that important job straight away but your mind keeps wandering to places even half an hour later, something still needs to shift.

Once you realise there's a problem, you need to make the conscious decision to stop what you're doing immediately, even if it's somewhat inconvenient. Doing 'only one more' irrelevant thing will keep you in the loop for who knows how long. It's best to start again with a clean slate.

Make a fresh start

Reset your physical, mental and emotional state – your options are endless. Meditate for a few minutes. Stand up. Move your body. Go for a walk. Listen to music. Laugh. If your environment allows, sing, jump or dance. Have a shower ... Do whatever helps you think and feel different.

Are you up for a little game? Picture yourself from an outside perspective as you're sabotaging your day. You can see now that you're doing some strange things, can't you? Some of your choices are quite absurd, and even ridiculous. You're trying to avoid hard work and stress, but you're actually creating more of both! You're escaping negative feelings, but end up feeling even worse. What a joke! ... The point of this exercise is not to criticise yourself, but to forge beneficial neurological shifts in your brain. Give it a go, and you'll probably find that the temptations to avoid hard work become weaker, and the distracting internal voices quiet down.

When you get back to your task, you don't want your attention to be hijacked again, and changing your way of working will help avoid this. Maybe stand up if you were previously sitting. Switch to a pen and paper to jot down your ideas if you were using a computer earlier. Find a fresh environment. Perhaps walk to another spot in your workplace, or to a nearby library or cafe. Those few minutes it takes to move to a different, more supportive location will certainly be time well spent. I keep hearing the same kinds of stories from my colleagues and friends: when they can't find their flow in a certain location and they move to a more stimulating or more peaceful place, their productivity often skyrockets.

There might also be times when your best option is to change your plan for the day. Perhaps your mind needs a rest from a certain kind of challenge, and you'll make more overall progress if you focus on a different project for a while. You may find, for example, that you're in a better headspace to deal with facts and figures, rather than coming up with creative ideas. Check with yourself whether it's your monkey brain trying to derail your plan or you genuinely need to pick a new 'destination'. You'll know the right thing to do.

FORGET HOW TO WASTE YOUR ENERGY AND TIME

The distracted mind can be a sneaky beast – it can lead you down all sorts of dark alleys. And you can't win this battle with self-discipline and willpower alone. You need to break unproductive habits and develop new ones that are stronger and smarter than those holding you back.

Is your mind roaming free when you need to focus? Create smart routines to get into the right frame of mind. Is your attention easily derailed? Avoid sharp turns, and perfect the habit of jumping back on track without hesitation whenever you're interrupted. Do you sometimes find yourself heading in the wrong direction? Stop what you're doing, shake it all off and restart afresh.

Derren Brown has taught us that breaking all-too-familiar patterns is very much possible. Put simply, by overriding unproductive strategies with powerful ones, you can intentionally forget how to waste energy and time.

INDIVIDUAL EXERCISES

For one week, record all your work activities in a diary. Also rate your overall effectiveness, energy and mood each day. What do you notice? Do you see any correlation between your work patterns and the way you feel and perform?

Pick an unproductive habit you would very much like to change. Observe for a few days how exactly that habit plays out. What triggers it? What's your immediate response to that trigger? And what happens next? Which link in this chain is easiest to break? Can you avoid the trigger? Or do you need to respond differently?

Make a plan for what you will do when you drift off track. How will you notice when there's a problem? What will you do to regain your focus? And how will you approach your task differently?

TEAM EXERCISES

Have an honest conversation with your teammates where everyone shares their challenges and triumphs around focus. Who is often tempted to procrastinate, distract themselves or multitask? (Who *isn't*?) What tricks do each of you use to stay on task? And what can you learn from one another?

Play this fun game as a team: one person should act out their most troublesome habit, step by step, and the rest of the team should copy it closely, but spicing it up with humour. Who can make the centre player laugh at their own habit first? Take turns until everyone has played both sides.

CHOICE 5

WHEN AND WHY IS IT A GOOD IDEA TO WORK UNPLUGGED?

What happens to my mind when I try to stay connected to everything?

Why is it a problem if I make myself available all the time?

How can I block out digital distractions?

What difference can it make to put away my phone,
turn off notifications, or block the internet?

The digital world is constantly demanding your attention, with dire consequences. Every single email, phone call, app notification or visit to the internet can erode your spirit and brain power. Even when you try to ignore digital distractions, your mind is affected. The solution might sound radical, but is certainly effective: work in a bubble for a couple of hours a day. Simply pressing the 'off' button might be your best chance to preserve your energy and sanity.

Unless you're living the dream, you probably have a certain part of your job that you find particularly challenging and involving. You might be very good at it and enjoy it once you're on a roll, but getting into it is often just hard work … So which tasks make you want to run in the opposite direction?

For me, I must admit, it is writing; composing complex emails, reports, articles and business collaterals. Once I get in front of my laptop, I often need to push myself to stay on task for a good half an hour before things start to flow. (Since I've written books, you may assume that writing comes easy to me. But just ask any author, and they will probably tell you a lot about their love–hate relationship with words.)

When facing such demanding tasks, I often find it difficult to say no to the enticing escape routes offered by my apps and the internet. Every minute spent clearing my inbox, checking my social media and chat accounts, or getting up to date with 'essential' news can feel like a refuge from the hurdles ahead … but work is still impatiently waiting.

Even after I finally get into my task, the internet often lures me into unproductive habits. For example, whenever a question pops into my mind, I tend to immediately look up the answer. I know too well that multitasking and constant fact-checking are the enemies of creativity and flow; however, I just can't discipline myself when the information I'm looking for is only a click away.

Well, I'm certainly prone to make my life harder than necessary – but I know I'm not alone.

RADICAL STEPS ARE NEEDED

Your work probably looks very different to mine, but when it comes to mentally demanding tasks, you and I possibly experience similar challenges. We're likely both hindered by external distractions and self-sabotaging habits to some extent that have something to do with our phones and the internet.

So, what's the solution?

Here's my strategy to get around these problems. Before starting a challenging and perhaps daunting activity, as long as my work allows, I simply turn off the Wi-Fi on my laptop. When I'm in my home office I even unplug the router. I also put my phone on silent or flight mode and leave it in another room. Essentially, I put myself in a bubble. These are radical steps I know, but they work wonders for me.

Creating your own bubble, at the right times, could help you find your flow too. (If you've ever worked on a plane and noticed how easy it was to get things done, you'll know what I mean.)

YOUR BRAIN DOES EXACTLY WHAT EVOLUTION 'DESIGNED' IT TO DO

You have no reason to feel guilty. You may just expect more from your brain than it can reasonably handle – as most of us do in the information age.

It all comes down to your neurological wiring. The amount of energy available to your brain is finite – it consumes around 20% of your total calorie intake, on average. Now, when you engage in activities that require intense focus and critical thinking, such as planning, analysing and prioritising, your brain needs to burn fuel like there's no tomorrow.

To sustain itself, your brain tries to preserve energy, and therefore has a natural inclination to escape from persistent hard work. This is why you might find it tempting to avoid or drop a difficult task, and to do something easy instead, even when you feel fresh. And when you're mentally tired, it's particularly difficult to focus, because your brain is running on empty. So instead of staying on task, you're prone to procrastinate, multitask and look for escape routes.

The human brain is also notoriously susceptible to distraction, for reasons rooted in our evolution. Our ancestors constantly had to stay in tune with their environment to survive. So even today, we have a natural instinct to pay attention to what's happening around us and to respond to the unexpected. This means that if you want to successfully ignore distractions, you need to override your nature, which certainly requires energy. And when your mind is already overworked, this can be mission impossible.

To sum up, we have a tendency to demand too much from our brains, expose ourselves to temptations and distractions, and then fight against them in an uphill battle. This creates exhaustion, stress and anxiety. Try to control your attention when feeling exhausted, anxious or stressed, and you'll find yourself on the road to failure.

HOW DISTRACTED ARE WE?

In the 'good ol' days', before everyone had a mobile phone, receptionists and personal assistants vetted calls. Faxes landed in the copy room and you decided when to collect them. When someone wanted to talk to you, it was perfectly acceptable to say, 'I'm unavailable'.

So, what does our reality look like now? In this 'always plugged in' work culture, how do our apps and devices influence our habits?

Let's look at some statistics from the last few years:

- The average office worker checks their inbox 30 times an hour.

- The average employee uses 10 different apps in a day to get their work done, and toggles between them up to 10 times an hour.

- In the UK, 45% of office workers read news websites during work hours, for 65 minutes a day, on average.

- People in the UK check their smartphones every 12 minutes, on average.

- Smartphone users in the US receive 46 push notifications a day, on average.

- Office workers are distracted or interrupted (often by themselves) every 3 minutes and 5 seconds, on average.

This issue has probably become even worse since these statistics came out – but you only need to glance at your own chat and web browser history to get a sense of your patterns.

When I scroll through my Google search history at the end of a hectic and unproductive day, it always looks terrifying. I also know how awful I feel when I lose my sense of control over my day. So for me, preserving my focus, energy and sanity is top priority.

YOU CAN'T **NOT** BE AFFECTED

Perhaps you have exceptional discipline and willpower, and you believe you're great at ignoring emails, calls, texts and notifications when you need to focus. Well, you might be interested in hearing about a research study which looked at people's performance while working amid these kinds of distractions and 'ignoring' them.

The study found that when participants were bombarded with emails and phone calls while they were trying to solve problems, their IQ dropped by an average of 10 points. This is despite the fact that they didn't respond to any of the messages and kept working. (Interestingly, men were affected to a greater extent than women.)

What exactly does it mean to lose 10 IQ points? Your ability to focus and solve problems is reduced just as much as if you were missing out on a night's sleep, and twice as much as if you were smoking cannabis. Essentially, the distraction caused by unopened emails and unanswered calls reduces your mental sharpness. And while resisting the temptation to respond, you're also weakening your willpower.

Another experiment revealed fascinating insights about how keeping your smartphone nearby could affect your thinking and performance. Before taking a series of tests that required concentration, participants were divided into three groups. They were asked to place their phones on their desks (face down), to keep them in their pockets or bags, or to leave them outside the room. All phones were turned to silent.

People who left their phones outside performed far better than those who placed their phones on their desks, and slightly better than those whose phones were in their pockets or bags. The vast majority of participants were under the impression that the whereabouts of their phones had no effect on their performance. Well, it appears they were wrong.

These results might seem surprising, but certainly make more sense once you learn about what scientists call 'continuous partial attention'. This is a mental state when you don't want to miss anything, and so you keep staying alert and reachable. You're on constant lookout for updates and opportunities, and available to respond as needed.

When you're trying to stay connected to everything, in truth you can't be fully present with anything you do. Even when you receive no calls or alerts, or when you don't respond, you feel somewhat uncertain and tense. Spending a lot of time in a state of suspense is likely to leave you anxious and overwhelmed, and also dissatisfied.

ACTIVATE YOUR CONE OF SILENCE

You have several options to shelter yourself from digital distractions, and even from your own nagging thoughts of anticipated interruptions. You can turn off notifications on all your devices – including email, chat, social media and other apps – block access to certain websites, or disconnect from the internet. You can silence your phone, put it in flight mode or switch it off – and leave it out of sight and out of reach. Perhaps you can also find a place to work with poor or non-existent mobile network and internet access (many authors' dream).

The point is you need to stop relying on your willpower and discipline to stay focused while the digital world is demanding your attention. There are times when you need to cut yourself off from this environment completely to preserve your focus, energy and spirit.

It's best to disable every single source of interruption for those few hours in the day when you want to maximise your brain power. If you wish to pick and choose, you'll still see some positive results, but you may want to check with yourself first:

- 'Why is it so important for me to stay connected?'

- 'What am I afraid of missing out on?'

- 'Do I really need to be contactable all the time?'

After creating a communication etiquette and ensuring that your teams and clients are on the same page, you should be able to carve a few hours out of your schedule when only you decide where to direct your attention.

No matter where you are in the food chain, you must be able to find a time when your headspace and the quality of your thinking are top priority. Many successful business leaders and CEOs are using this strategy to take control of their days and access their best thinking. And if they can get away with putting themselves in a bubble for a little while, why couldn't you?

If you're still hesitant, I suggest you experiment just for a single day, as a start. You may find it an enjoyable and rewarding experience and get hooked. You won't be the first person this has happened to.

INDIVIDUAL EXERCISES

Try working offline for the most productive hours of your day, or block access to the websites that stand in the way of your productivity. (There's a vast array of apps available to help you with this.) What difference do you notice? Are you enjoying the experience? Do you find it easier to get into the groove? Do you work more effectively?

Install a time-tracking app on your devices to get a better sense of how many hours in a day you spend productively. Work as usual for a few days, and then start experimenting with the different strategies discussed in this Choice. How much time do you save when you implement one or two of these strategies? And what happens when you go all the way and unplug completely?

TEAM EXERCISES

Agree with your teammates on the times when everyone is allowed – or perhaps even encouraged – to be unreachable each day. Work unplugged during the agreed times, and meet again after a couple of weeks to discuss your experiences. Fine-tune your schedule if needed.

Organise a 'device-free' meeting: tell participants to keep their laptops closed, and to put their phones in flight mode or to switch them off. Have a quick debrief after the meeting. Did you notice any benefits? How did the conversation flow?

For the second part of this experiment, make sure your next meeting is truly device free; all laptops and phones should be left outside the room. What was your experience this time? Were you and your teammates more present and switched on than usual?

CHOICE 6

WHEN SHOULD I TAKE A BREAK?

Should I take lots of short breathers or a few longer ones?

Why is it so important to take effective breaks?

Why should I plan my breaks in advance?

When it comes to taking time out, should I just follow my instincts?

Well-timed, restorative breaks are good for you, helping you feel positive, energised and switched on. This is common knowledge. Still, most people are quite lousy at taking breaks. What's going on? The challenge is that your body and mind often send you mixed signals: they tell you to take a break when you shouldn't, and to stay on task when you should actually stop. So, let's explore how you can overcome this deceit and create a healthy routine.

You're no doubt aware that taking quality breaks during the day can help you up your game. Not only athletes and physical labourers need to recharge from time to time, but anyone whose job involves prolonged mental activity. By 'sharpening the saw', you can quickly make up for the time away from work.

When you get it right, a good breather can replenish your energy, clear your mind and sharpen your focus. It can enhance your brain function, your creativity and your ability to learn. Tuning out of work for a little while should also leave you feeling more motivated, positive and relaxed.

After your break, with renewed energy and a fresh mind, you naturally approach your job more intelligently. You're more conscious of your goals and purpose, and better at setting priorities. And since you have stronger self-control, you also find it easier to block out distractions and cultivate productive habits. Put simply, you become more efficient as well as effective.

WE'RE NOT VERY GOOD AT TAKING BREAKS

These benefits are common knowledge, or at least common sense. Yet, most of us don't take enough breaks, or we don't take breaks the right way:

- We take breaks too late. When we're exhausted, our work performance has dropped already, and from this state it's much harder to recover.

- We take breaks too early, before getting the chance to immerse ourselves in what we do. In other words, we quit before reaching a state of peak performance.

- We take fake breaks. We escape our tasks on a whim when they become a bit challenging, and seek momentary pleasure on our phones or on the internet. We jump back and forth between activities, and as a result, we end up scattered, exhausted and consumed by guilt.

- When we're on a 'break', we don't allow ourselves to switch off and relax. We keep putting pressure on ourselves – we continue to do work-related tasks, we talk about work, we think of work or feel guilty about not working.

It's all a bit counterintuitive

Why do we make such a mess of something that should be really simple? Surely, 'not working' can't be rocket science … Well, one of our challenges is that the right time to step away from work is not that obvious.

It feels counterintuitive to just drop what we're doing when we're on a roll. However, the truth is breaks are most effective when we stop working *before* we get tired.

In his brilliant book *How to Stop Worrying and Start Living*, Dale Carnegie tells the story of an average physical labourer, Mr Schmidt, who was selected to take part in a productivity experiment. He was required to follow the instructions of a supervisor who told him exactly when to work and when to rest, using a stopwatch. Mr Schmidt ended up working approximately 26 minutes in an hour and resting for 34 minutes, so he rested more than he worked. Yet, he managed to load almost four times the weight in a day than other men who were doing the same job but were not taking the same breaks. His exceptional performance, which he was able to maintain for years, was attributed to the fact that he always rested before the point at which he would otherwise get tired.

This strategy also applies to mental work. And while quadrupling your productivity is probably a long shot, you'll likely notice amazing results if you give it a try. But be aware that the ideal time to rest depends on your task and how you're wired. There's no scientific consensus about the optimal work rhythm, so you need to work out for yourself when to work and when to rest, paying close attention to the signals of your body and mind.

Unfortunately, the signs of an overworked mind are not always evident. You may not catch yourself yawning and dozing off. Instead, you might become irritable and easily distracted. You possibly struggle to think creatively, and start playing too safe. You might begin to make inferior decisions, and to give in to unproductive habits such as multitasking. Perhaps you find it difficult to resist temptations such as checking your emails too often, or surfing the web for entertainment when you've got work to do. Or maybe you keep reaching for snacks even when you're not hungry.

A couple more twists

Do you know the feeling when every cell in your body is aching to get away from what you're doing? I bet you do. It feels like you're overdue for a break. However, in this situation the best strategy could be to press on, since you might be just minutes away from getting into the zone.

Depending on what you do, you might need to push yourself to stay on task for half an hour or more before you get into the right headspace. Moving beyond this phase can be gruelling, but quitting – as suggested by your instincts – would usually be a mistake.

And here is a final conundrum. Taking breaks at the right time (and in the right way, as we'll explore in the next Choice) requires discipline and willpower. Simply giving in to the confusing signs of your body and mind could send you off track. But when you most desperately need a well-deserved breather your mental resources are already depleted, which means your discipline and willpower are probably also a bit weak.

As a result, you might end up making the easiest and most convenient choice rather than the most logical one. This explains, at least in part, why most of us fail at taking well-timed, effective, restorative breaks during our workdays, and why we keep making those nonsensical mistakes we talked about earlier.

SO HOW CAN YOU TELL WHEN IT'S THE RIGHT TIME FOR A BREAK?

Whenever you find yourself wondering whether you should step away from a task or continue, ask yourself:

- 'Have I given myself enough time to get into the zone? Does it make sense to take a break at this time? Have I expended much of my mental energy? Will my brain and body really benefit from resting right now? Am I ready to take a proper break, put work aside and do something that will refresh me?'

- 'Or am I acting on an impulse? Is work just a bit too hard or boring at the moment? Am I trying to escape the challenges ahead of me, and craving some entertainment?'

After contemplating these questions – and being honest with your answers, of course – you'll know what you need to do.

FIND YOUR NATURAL PACE AND RHYTHM

It's worth exploring your own natural pace and rhythm: how long to stay on task, when to take breaks and for how long. There are a number of different techniques recommended by scientists and experts:

- Scientists have discovered that our levels of energy and alertness fluctuate in approximately 80- to 120-minute cycles – not only while we sleep but also when we're awake. This is called our bodies' 'ultradian rhythm'. So, if you work in 90-minute blocks, followed by 20 minutes of rest, you can stay in sync with your natural rhythm, which could help you maximise your performance.

- Other experts recommend that the length of your work sessions should be somewhere between 50 and 90 minutes. One study suggests that the recipe for peak productivity is to work for 52 minutes at a time and then to rest for 17 minutes.

- The Pomodoro Technique, developed in the late 1980s, involves 25-minute intervals of intense work, separated by 3- to 5-minute breaks. Every fourth work session should be followed by a longer, 15- to 30-minute break.

- If you're unable to take frequent breaks throughout the day, you'll probably find that taking a decent lunch break as well as two 15-minute intermissions in a day can still help. It's best to take a break mid-morning, and one at around 3 pm when you're most likely to be hit by the afternoon slump.

- In certain situations it's important that you don't cut your focused sessions too short. When you're learning a new skill, for example, you'll remember more if you can power through a 40-minute study or practice session either with no breaks or with frequent short breaks. If you take a long break before the 40 minutes learning threshold or end your session early, you might not retain as much, as shown by research.

I suggest you experiment with these techniques, trying out each for a few days and checking with yourself at the end of each day to see how much you've achieved. You might also want to combine some of these ideas and develop your own unique schedules. You'll probably find that shifting your rhythm depending on what you do and how you use your brain helps you maximise your performance.

For me, 90 minutes is a good length of time to get on a roll and make good progress with writing reports or analysing data. Then I need to take a substantial break. On the other hand, when I brainstorm or engage in other creative tasks I need to refresh my mind more often. However, after a brief break – typically moving around and stretching my body – I'm usually ready to carry on with revived energy and clarity.

TIME TO PUT THINGS INTO PRACTICE

Relying on your self-discipline and willpower to take breaks at the right times is not sustainable. It's therefore best to schedule breaks in advance – based on the understanding of your natural rhythm – and to put these breaks into your calendar. Alternatively, you might want to set an alarm or use a suitable app to keep yourself in check.

You might be surprised how much you can achieve once you get this right. I know people who are able to engage in mentally demanding tasks all day long, staying focused and energised, because they have mastered the art of taking breaks. Their productivity seems superhuman. But ironically, the key to their success is the very fact that they know their own limits, and they make the conscious effort to look after themselves. I'm sure this is something you can do too.

INDIVIDUAL EXERCISES

Pay attention to the fluctuations in your mental energy, focus and mood. How long does it usually take for you to get into the zone? How long can you stay fully immersed in challenging tasks, and in easy ones? And when do you start losing your focus? Once you better understand the cycles of your mind, you'll have a clearer idea of when to take breaks.

For one week, keep track of the number of hours you spend each day on work-related tasks (perhaps using a time-tracking app), and on genuine breaks. At the end of each day, calculate the amount of time you spent on activities that were neither work-related nor restorative, and also rate how much you achieved (on a scale from 0 to 10). Check your notes at the end of the week. When were you most effective – when you worked with minimal breaks or when you took plenty of time out? Or was it somewhere in between?

TEAM EXERCISE

Try out various techniques together as a team, practising each one for a half day or a full day. Agree on your schedule before starting, and make sure that everyone in the team takes breaks at the same time. Hold each other accountable, ensuring no-one works through a break or takes a break during the work session. Have a debrief at the end of each experiment. Did the technique make it easier to focus and to work effectively? Or was it perhaps a bit disruptive or unnatural? Was it helpful to work in sync as a team and to be held accountable?

CHOICE 7

WHAT SHOULD I DO DURING MY BREAK TIME?

What are the best ways to recharge my batteries?

Do I really 'deserve' a break for my hard work?

Why do I feel more tired after taking a breather?

How can I make it easier to get back on task after taking some time out?

We know that restorative breaks are essential for our wellbeing and performance, and that activities like meditating, exercising or socialising are great for us. Yet, we often opt for 'pastimes' that only leave us demotivated and depleted: we think about work, overload our brains, or engage in addictive habits … You deserve better: taking true breaks that are not only enjoyable but also make it easier for you to excel. Once you learn to recharge, everything improves, including your focus, ideas, conversations and relationships.

When you take a break from work during the day, whether for five minutes or an hour, what do you usually do?

If you're anything like me, you're inclined to do something useful. Perhaps you try to tick off some easy items on your to-do list – send a few quick emails, catch up on admin or read a few articles from your ever-growing 'to read later' library. Or maybe you have a quick chat with a colleague and – guess what? – yes, you talk about your work and your team.

Okay, so when you *do* stop working, how do you spend your time?

Personally, I'm a sucker for online logic puzzles and word games, and I also love tuning into fascinating interviews and talks on YouTube. I actually enjoy playing games and watching videos simultaneously. And until I learned what I'm about to share with you, that's how I often spent my breaks.

The reality is that most of us routinely seek stimulation and entertainment online. We can spend hours each day checking our personal emails, reading the news, dipping into social media, or playing addictive games …

This is understandable. It's fair to claim that you earn your breaks through hard work. They are your reward, and therefore you deserve to spend them however you feel. After a focused session of analysing data, solving problems or writing reports, you naturally want some excitement, pleasure and fun. And this is exactly what the online world promises: little surprises, unexpected news and messages, beautiful pictures, funny stories, and a cocktail of interesting ideas, opinions and snippets of wisdom.

But how effective are these breaks? Well, let's see what science says about true restoration.

WHAT MAKES A BREAK RESTORATIVE?

To give your brain the chance to recover from the mental workout your job requires, you need to stop challenging yourself the same way your work does. This makes perfect sense. How could you possibly restore your inner resources while draining them at the same time? You don't see athletes running around in between training sessions.

This means you shouldn't do any work – including easy tasks or light work – while on a break, or discuss work-related issues with your colleagues. Ideally, you shouldn't answer emails, even personal ones, or run any errands that might be mentally demanding, stressful or tiring.

It's also advised that you refrain from experiences and platforms that may scatter your attention, bombard you with information, or prompt you to solve problems or make lots of decisions. You already have to deal with these kinds of mental demands while doing your job.

Put simply, you need to allow your brain to relax.

How can you achieve this? Take a clear break from work, in every possible sense. As a starting point, get out of your chair and walk away from your desk. If possible, leave your phone behind – you need to get your eyes off the screen. Find a space, either in your workplace or outside, that looks and feels different from your usual work environment. Do something that will take your focus away from work and help you be present in the moment.

To sum up the outcomes of extensive research:

- You recover better if you can tune out from work completely, rather than keeping one eye on your duties.

- You gain more from going offline, as opposed to staying plugged in.

- Breaks are often more restorative when you move your body, compared to when you sit or stand.

- When you get the chance, it's better to spend your break outside, in a natural environment.

- You likely benefit more from social activity – and here I'm talking about meeting others in person, not virtually – than from passing time by yourself.

WHAT YOU CAN DO DURING YOUR BREAKS

When it comes to choosing what to do in your free time, your options are abundant. You could catch up with your colleagues or mates, play a fun game or have a relaxed chat. A lively conversation or a good laugh can be truly energising. You could also spend time on a hobby you enjoy, or listen to uplifting music.

Or you may find a peaceful spot and simply allow your mind to wander. When you daydream or contemplate, your brain is in a different mode compared to when you're focusing on your work and approaching problems consciously and systematically. This is an incredibly creative state. You've probably noticed that brilliant insights and solutions to tricky challenges often come to the surface when you let your mind roam free.

However, when you consider their restorative power, four activities stand out: napping, meditating, walking and exercising. The benefits are impressive and all-encompassing.

Evidence shows that each of these four activities can:

- improve your brain function and cognitive flexibility

- improve your memory and your ability to learn

- increase your focus and alertness

- help you work more productively

- boost your creativity

- help you find better solutions to problems

- help you make smarter decisions

- lower your stress

- improve your mood

- help you feel energised

- strengthen your immune system.

With the possible exception of napping, they can also help you sleep better at night.

Let's look at each of these four activities in a little more detail.

Napping

You don't need to sleep for a long time to feel refreshed; a 10- to 20-minute nap can be very effective. In fact, you don't want to nap longer than 20 minutes; otherwise you could wake up feeling groggy, due to a phenomenon called 'sleep inertia'. It's best to take a nap at a time of the day when you naturally feel a bit drowsy, which is probably at around 2 or 3 pm. You'll find it easier to nap if you make it a habit and have a regular nap time.

Some productivity experts passionately promote the idea of the so-called 'nappuccino', which combines the power of napping and caffeine. Now, I'd personally never turn to caffeine – or any other substance – as a performance booster, but you might choose to give it a go. The idea is that you have a coffee just before taking a nap. The caffeine will take about 25 minutes to fully kick in, so when you open your eyes you'll feel wide awake and energised.

Meditation

Similar to napping, even very short meditation or mindfulness sessions can alter your state of mind. If you can practise for just five minutes at a time, that's a great start. Regular meditation can change your brain, making and strengthening connections and increasing the density of your grey cells. With regular practice, you'll be able to better manage your attention and emotions. You'll also increase your self-awareness, resilience and self-control – the very qualities you need to meet the ever-changing challenges of work.

Walking

My favourite pastime … Again, even a brief, five-minute walk could leave you refreshed. If you're pressed for time or your options are limited, just stroll around in the building you work in. Perhaps walk to the cafe or say hello to a colleague who sits in a distant corner. The key is that you move your body. However, when possible, have a walk outside, ideally in a natural, green space. As we all know, nature has an incredible restorative power.

Exercise

There are different views about the best time to exercise. With a morning workout, you'll start your day strong. If you exercise at lunchtime, you'll reap the benefits all afternoon. And if you exercise in the late afternoon, you'll sleep better at night. To boost your grey matter, moderate-intensity cardio is best – anything that makes you sweat but allows you to speak normally, such as walking briskly or riding a bike. Activities that are mentally challenging or require coordination are especially potent, like ball games, dancing, yoga or Pilates (which I've lately become hooked on).

Beyond the health benefits, physical exercise has amazing psychological effects. A strong, flexible and balanced body provides the perfect home for a strong, flexible and balanced mind.

ARE YOU READY TO DO WHAT'S GOOD FOR YOU?

Well, all this may sound convincing … But in all honesty, many of these restorative activities are a bit unexciting. So if you haven't already learned to enjoy, for example, napping, meditating, walking, exercising, or even just unplugging – despite the well-known benefits – a few logical arguments may not suddenly persuade you to change your habits.

If you're genuinely committed to improving your performance and well-being by taking smarter breaks, you might need to trick your brain.

Why you find something exciting or boring

We naturally gravitate towards activities that make us feel good. However, the human brain especially loves experiences that offer frequent random rewards. This is why it can be so difficult to resist checking the news, engaging with social media, or browsing your favourite video channels whenever you get the chance.

These activities release large amounts of dopamine in your brain. This hormone creates immediate pleasure and also regulates your cravings for further experiences. Regardless of whether an activity is good for you, if it gives you momentary pleasure, or even just the promise of instant reward, you can quickly develop an appetite for it.

Just think about this … When you visit your favourite online platform, how often do you find disconcerting news, atrocious attitudes, and updates that fill you with anger, regret or self-doubt? All this negativity can leave you agitated and exhausted. However, there's always that promise of pleasure and surprise, and therefore the temptation to revisit this space over and over again.

Scientists often compare our search for constant stimulation to playing slot machines all day. Once you're hooked it's difficult to stop, even when you're losing, because you think you might be about to win.

When you indulge in these activities excessively, your brain eventually gets used to the unnaturally high dopamine levels. It becomes desensitised, and you essentially develop an addiction to constant stimulation. Subsequently, you lose interest in activities that offer less excitement and no immediate reward – and thus a smaller dopamine hit to the brain – such as doing hard work and pursuing your goals. In this state of mind, you feel no desire for true relaxation either, like napping, meditating, walking or exercising.

This is a vicious cycle. Every moment you spend with overly stimulating, high-dopamine activities increases your unhealthy cravings while simultaneously reducing your motivation for being present and getting things done.

The effects are both short and long term. For example, if you spend too much time with feel-good activities in the morning or during the day, you could find it more difficult to focus on your work later on or to enjoy what you do. In the long term, if you allow your cravings to take over, you could develop some physical and mental health issues. Your social skills could suffer, along with your relationships. You can probably see some sad examples of this in your own circles.

How you can break the cycle

The good news is that even simple experiences can release some dopamine, like listening to birds chirping or feeling the breeze on your skin. So with a bit of effort, you could learn to enjoy many of those activities you currently find a bit dull. One of the strategies experts recommend is called 'dopamine detox'. The idea is that if you can refrain from highly stimulating activities for a period of time – say, for a day, a week or a month – your brain will adjust and you'll soon be able to find pleasure in activities where you previously couldn't.

It's important to note that not only online activities contribute to this issue but also any routines or habits you may fall into when you're hungry to engage your senses and instantly fill any void in your life. These could include listening to music, watching TV, gambling, eating comfort food and indulging in other physical pleasures. So, if you want to restore a healthier balance in your brain – and your life – you need to be able to say no to any of these temptations at certain times, and make friends with the present moment.

You can always exercise, go for a walk, meditate, have a nap, have a healthy snack, catch up with your mates (without your phone), or allow your mind to wander … You get the idea. These activities are not only restorative but could also reduce your desire for unproductive, unhealthy and potentially addictive habits. The more you do them the more you'll love them, and the pull towards escaping the here and now will wane.

CHANGE HOW YOU THINK ABOUT BREAKS

You might also want to sort out your beliefs around breaks. Do you see them as some kind of benefit or compensation? And is this helping?

Let me share my experience. When I noticed that my old views fuelled several counterproductive habits, I decided to turn my thinking around. I stopped seeing my recovery time as a reward. I don't believe anymore that I deserve a few moments of easy entertainment for my hard work. What I actually deserve is the opportunity to nurture my body and mind, and to allow myself to excel. I deserve the chance to make work easier for myself and the people I work with, not harder.

(I still watch entertaining videos and play my favourite games, but I now do these much less, and usually at the end of the workday.)

If you're prepared to change your thinking, you'll see the rewards, without doubt. You'll find it easier to get into your groove, and quite likely surprise yourself with what you can achieve. And few things are more gratifying than making progress towards a meaningful goal and seeing the difference you create.

It's of course up to you to decide where you look for rewards. Do you opt for fleeting pleasures that can eventually exhaust and demotivate you? Or do you get a high from becoming the best version of yourself and kicking goals?

WORK INTELLIGENTLY

Workplace designers and change managers tell me how difficult it can be to get people to move away from their desks. The benefits of frequently walking around or moving between different settings in the office are sound and clear, yet most workers seem to be glued to their desks for hours, if not for the whole day. What could be the underlying issue? Most people know a lot about productive work, but unfortunately their habits around taking breaks seem to weigh them down.

Once you start taking effective, restorative breaks, your work experience will inevitably transform. You'll also become more switched on, motivated, energised and agile. Could this be the missing piece of your productivity puzzle?

INDIVIDUAL EXERCISES

When you take a break, do something different to what you'd normally do. After your break, check how you feel. Are your body and mind refreshed? Do you feel energised, motivated, and ready to get back to work? Keep experimenting with new break-time activities until you find your groove.

Say no to counterproductive breaks for a whole day. When you take a time out, tune out from work, go offline – and move your body, catch up with your mates or just rest. Then reflect at the end of the day. Did you notice any change in your focus, productivity, energy levels and motivation? Was it a difficult 'challenge'? Are you up for doing it again … and seeing how much easier it gets?

TEAM EXERCISES

Share with one another how you usually spend your break time. What are your favourite activities? What do you default to when you don't want to make any effort? What helps to recharge your batteries, and what doesn't? Are there any common threads within the team?

Take some time out together. Go for walks, play fun games, have coffee or share a lunch. Have lighthearted conversations – feel free to share good ideas as they come up, but don't dwell on work-related problems. What do you notice? Do you enjoy these breaks? And do they leave you recharged?

35 SMART CHOICES

CHOICES

PART II

PART II

HOW CAN I COLLABORATE BETTER WITH OTHERS?

Effective teamwork is the beating heart of creative, knowledge-based work. It allows you and your teammates to play to your strengths, inspire and learn from each other, and solve complex problems together.

Yet, teamwork can be very challenging. In fact, the more diverse your team is – and therefore the greater your potential – the more challenges you're likely to face. Aligning different views, perspectives and work styles can take a lot of effort and patience, but with the right tactics, you can make collaboration much smoother and more rewarding.

In this Part we'll look at teamwork from different angles. **When** is it a good time to interact with others, and when are you better off getting things done by yourself? **Who** are the best people for you to work with – or next to – and how can you find common ground with almost anyone? **Where** and how should you meet to ensure your team session is successful? **What** does it take to build better relationships and stronger connections? And **how** can you bring more personality, humour and fun to work?

After reading this Part you'll hopefully find that underneath all the complexities, the foundations of great work relationships and effective teamwork are actually quite simple: get to know your teammates, stay open and present, show your true self and have a great time. The tips and strategies you'll learn will help you and your team to live and breathe these qualities, and to create a positive, transparent and dynamic environment where collaboration thrives.

CHOICE 8

WHEN SHOULD I WORK ALONE, AND WHEN SHOULD I COLLABORATE WITH MY TEAM?

How often should we meet and communicate?

Is it possible to interact too much?

What's the rhythm of successful innovation?

Collaboration and innovation are critical factors in any organisation, but one aspect gets little attention: the *rhythm* of teamwork. If you don't see the fruits of your innovation efforts, chances are you communicate too little, too much, or at the wrong time. To turn things around, try thinking of your team as an orchestra. Make sure that everyone plays in sync, and is ready to switch between quiet and dynamic activities just when the time is right.

You may have all the ingredients you need for successful collaboration and innovation: smart team members, exciting ideas and detailed plans ... But the way you organise your team is critical. You need to know when it's the right time to meet and when it's better to work apart – otherwise you may struggle to see the results you're looking for.

DO ANY OF THESE SCENARIOS SEEM FAMILIAR?

You start with a bang

Once or twice a year all members of your team, department or perhaps the entire organisation are brought together to discuss big-picture strategies and make exciting plans for the future. You explore opportunities to innovate, brainstorm ideas for improved products or services, and seek ways of working more effectively. You and your colleagues then walk away with rough action plans, including roles and responsibilities for getting these promising projects off the ground.

Over the following months, you periodically check in with each other about how you're progressing, but everything is same old, same old. The team is still eager to work towards the vision you've dreamed up, but those plans are yet to be followed through, as churning out deliverables and meeting deadlines take priority.

Your workplace is buzzing with ideas

Collaboration and innovation are central elements of your team's strategy. You and your teammates often try to outdo each other in coming up with exciting new ideas for improving how you work and delivering new solutions. The office walls are covered with whiteboards and sticky notes capturing the never-ending flow of ideas. Your team spends several hours every day working together in meetings and collaboration sessions, and you also regularly hang out with each other in your free time.

The office has the vibe of a busy cafe, with questions and ideas constantly flying back and forth. Those who need to concentrate are allowed to put on their headphones, but you operate with an 'open door policy', and as such, everyone is expected to be approachable at any time. Countless innovation projects are in motion ... However, the results are often underwhelming. Despite all the energy and buzz, you rarely see real breakthroughs.

You plan and follow through diligently

You already know that innovation seldom happens without careful planning, diligent follow-through, and time carved out for implementation. You're also well aware that creating something new and valuable requires the skillful coordination of individual and team activities. With your team, you refresh your strategy and map out innovation projects at least a couple of times a year, perhaps review priorities and milestones monthly, and discuss immediate tasks and issues weekly, if not daily.

In your workplace, teamwork is organised around well-defined goals, and follows a clear structure. At the same time, you and your teammates have plenty of flexibility to work in ways that suit you best, and to approach problems creatively. Put simply, you're committed to becoming truly agile … But somehow you still can't see the results you're hoping for.

WHAT COULD BE MISSING?

Powerful teamwork and collaboration have similar qualities to performing a captivating piece of music. For your team to successfully innovate time and time again, people need to work together a bit like an orchestra:

- All members should play in sync, creating a symphonic experience.

- Dynamic, more intense parts should alternate with quieter, softer parts.

- The performance should have a naturally flowing rhythm.

Let's explore what these artful strategies can look like in practice.

EVERYONE PLAYS IN SYNC

To work together like an orchestra, everyone in your team needs to be on the same page about what exactly you're doing at any given time. In the same way that musicians use sheet music to produce beautiful harmonies, you can develop an action plan to ensure your team works in sync. At the start of your collaboration, you should agree how you're going to coordinate tasks and balance priorities. For example, each member needs to know when it's time to think creatively and embrace risks, and when they are expected to work accurately and efficiently, following tried-and-tested processes.

Unless you all understand good timing, a lot of potential will be wasted. When most people are in an analytical headspace, ideas will die quickly. Just watch what happens when you throw a radically new idea into a rushed conversation focused on efficient delivery, perhaps during a structured team meeting or conference call. Chances are that the idea will be quickly shot down without receiving the consideration it deserves – not because your teammates are seasoned critical thinkers and safe players, but because in this particular conversation they are attuned to think critically and to play safe.

On the flipside, in an environment of incessant creativity, projects won't get finished. Your team will find it difficult to turn innovative ideas into systems, products or services if certain members keep going off on tangents. Equally, you'll struggle to make headway on technical or analytical tasks, or to concentrate on complex calculations or difficult reports, for example, if some people keep asking 'what ifs'. At certain times, everyone needs to hold back on suggestions that could bring the project back to square one and preserve them for the next innovation session.

Consider using different settings for different activities, to make everyone's life easier. Once you get into the habit of brainstorming in the 'brainstorming space' and planning in the 'planning space', for instance, there will be no ambiguity about what's expected from the team during a particular session. In addition, the physical environment will make it easier for you to get into the right frame of mind – boosting your creativity or helping you focus on the details, as needed for the task at hand.

QUIET AND HIGH-ENERGY WORK ALTERNATE

The alternating dynamics of quiet, peaceful sections and high-energy, fast-paced sections can make music really powerful – and that's no different for innovative teamwork. With extended quiet periods between interactions, members may lose touch with the team's goals. And with too much com-munication and collaboration, it's difficult to make progress with individual tasks. But if you can switch between different modes of work at a healthy pace, you'll be well set up to make impressive progress.

However, it's critical that team members know exactly when it's the right time to tackle tasks by themselves and when it's best to approach work collaboratively.

In any business, the majority of tasks can be divided into two categories:

Clearly defined, routine activities that produce predictable results

These are straightforward tasks you can usually complete by going through the motions, such as answering recurring questions, preparing standardised documents, or reviewing and organising data. You know exactly what you're aiming to achieve and how to get there, and you have all the pieces ready to get things done. Minor issues may still arise, but you can easily deal with them by following set processes. I call this the 'mechanical mode'.

There's no point approaching these tasks collaboratively – that would only waste time and test everyone's patience. (We've all been there at some point, having to sit through frustrating meetings where speakers were just citing straightforward facts and the rest of the team had absolutely nothing to add or learn from the conversation.) Put simply, you're better off tackling such clear-cut tasks by yourself without too much fuss.

Clearly defined, routine work can often be automated or systemised. Nonetheless, if the system has some hiccups or doesn't deliver the expected results, you need to find a creative solution – which is a job that belongs in the second category, and therefore calls for a different approach …

Unique tasks and challenges, unclear goals and objectives

When a system or a process you've set up needs improving – perhaps because there are too many mistakes or delays – you're facing a unique challenge that requires innovative thinking. Sadly, this is not the sort of problem you can solve by simply following a manual.

There are of course many other types of challenges where you don't have a defined path to follow. You might be looking to create something fundamentally new; for example, launching a new service or developing a customised solution for a client with unusual needs and circumstances. Or you're facing a problem there's little precedent for, and which can't be processed by your systems. (We all faced countless issues like these in the early days of the COVID pandemic, when we needed to rethink how to collaborate and to serve our clients in a radically different environment from what we'd been used to.) I call this the 'dynamic mode'.

Maybe you're not exactly sure what a successful outcome will look like, or there are differing opinions among your team or peers. Perhaps you're also dealing with conflicting interests or priorities, or trying to work with incomplete or ambiguous information ... If only you had a crystal ball to see into the future.

In his latest book *A Promised Land*, Barack Obama gives a vivid illustration of the complex nature of the decisions he had to make as President. And even though my job is a little less demanding, his description really resonates with me. Obama writes:

> *... I was constantly dealing with probabilities: a 70 percent chance, say, that a decision to do nothing would end in disaster; a 55 percent chance that this approach versus that one might solve the problem (with a 0 percent chance that it would work out exactly as intended); a 30 percent chance that whatever we chose wouldn't work at all, along with a 15 percent chance that it would make the problem worse.*

Can you relate to any of this?

Whenever you're faced with such a tricky situation, it's a good time to get together with your team to explore options collaboratively, taking advantage of the team's collective knowledge and intellect. Trying to tackle these kinds of tasks alone will likely slow things down and lead to mistakes or unresolved issues.

THE TEAM PERFORMS WITH A NATURAL RHYTHM

Beautiful things can bloom from a team that moves to a natural rhythm. Each phase of an innovation project has an important role – just like each movement in a symphony. But when the different pieces all come together in the right way, that's when true magic happens.

As your team solves one problem after another through creative collaboration, many initially challenging tasks eventually become mechanical.

And as you keep developing your systems and processes to complete routine tasks more efficiently, you always find new opportunities for improvement – which, again, calls for dynamic teamwork.

Your team will need to find its own pace and rhythm. Sporadic collaboration can hinder innovation; this is no news. But too frequent communication – which can be easy to get caught up in, especially with an abundance of online chat platforms at our fingertips – can also have negative consequences. Apart from distracting people from focusing on their individual tasks, it can actually stand in the way of brilliance. As suggested by research, constant communication can yield a lot of average (and largely similar) ideas, but may hold your team back from coming up with extraordinary, game-changing solutions.

Once you find your groove, things should start to accelerate. Individuals will get the chance to find their own creative flair, and to arrive at team sessions well prepared. And during those sessions, everyone will have ample opportunity to find inspiration and learn from each other, even the creative stars in the team.

ORCHESTRATED WORK

I suggest you experiment with different communication and collaboration strategies, and fine-tune your routines as you go. You and your teammates will certainly notice if you interact too much, or not enough.

You'll need to think about how you organise yourselves for individual projects, and how you discuss your day-to-day progress and challenges. You'll also need to work out how frequently you need to get together to review your big-picture goals and milestones, and discuss emerging opportunities.

Switching between different types of individual work and group work at the right time is a valuable (though rather underrated) skill. By honing this skill as a team, you'll be able to work more productively and solve problems faster. You will become more responsive and at the same time more efficient. Ultimately, innovation will become an integral part of your work, as opposed to a set of standalone projects which may or may not get off the ground.

INDIVIDUAL EXERCISE

Think about the tasks and challenges you routinely try to tackle yourself, but which would actually benefit from your team's wisdom and experience. What would it take for you to get the help you need?

TEAM EXERCISES

Share with each other how your work calendar would look if you had absolute freedom to manage your time. When would be your quiet, focused periods? When would you run team meetings and collaboration sessions? And what periods would you leave open for spontaneous communication and unexpected issues? Looking at everyone's ideal schedule – do you see any common threads? How can you organise yourselves so that everyone wins?

Have a team chat about routine (mechanical) and non-routine (dynamic) work activities and problems. What can each of you successfully handle by yourselves? And when is it useful – or even necessary – that you discuss the issue with each other and address it collaboratively? Which discussions can wait, and which are really urgent?

Review your typical (daily or weekly) team meeting agenda together. Does everything on the list need to be talked through with the whole team? Are there any topics – recurring challenges and unresolved issues – missing from the agenda that call for a collaborative effort. And are there any items that should be discussed more frequently, or less often?

HOW SHOULD WE RUN MEETINGS TO ENSURE PROBLEMS ARE ACTUALLY SOLVED?

What kind of meeting should we have – formal or informal?

What do successful collaboration sessions look like?

What does it take to unlock the team's collective intelligence?

How can we get into the right frame of mind to tackle difficult challenges?

Some meetings go amazingly well while others flop miserably. What makes the difference? Having the right people in the room is only a part of the story – whether they can bring their best selves to the table is equally important. Some environments and meeting styles only kill engagement and creativity, while others activate the very behaviours and attitudes that fuel thriving collaboration. To give your team the best chance to solve difficult problems, you need to keep things high-energy, informal, and a bit messy.

We've all been there … It's meeting time. Your team has come together to solve some tricky problems. You're all swamped with work, so it would be great to run this meeting as efficiently as possible. However, the energy in the room is low. Some people are checking their emails or social media feeds; others are zoned out. A few are engrossed in debates, but not everyone is ready to share what's on their minds. One person has fallen asleep in the corner. Those who speak up are mostly defending their points of view rather than seeking common ground. The team is running in circles, unable to make meaningful progress or to commit to clear, actionable decisions.

It would have been more productive for you to spend the time throwing office furniture at each other.

We know what true collaboration looks like. Everyone is participating passionately, focusing on the agreed goals and respecting each other's perspective. Each team member is adding something valuable to the conversation; even the quietest person in the room is joining in. Ideas are bouncing around, and exciting, innovative plans are emerging. At the end, everybody leaves the meeting pumped, eager to jump into action.

Why do some meetings turn into a total train wreck while others run like a dream?

There's no doubt that for a successful discussion, it's essential to have the right people in the room, with the right knowledge and intentions. But the other question is whether participants are able to bring their best selves to the table – and this largely depends on the physical environment, as well as the way the meeting is run.

THE ENERGY IN A ROOM IS CLEARLY VISIBLE

Let me invite you to play a quick game. Imagine you're walking through your office, and stop outside one of the meeting rooms. You can't hear what's being discussed inside, but you can see what's happening through the glass wall. You can observe people's body language, and whether they are sitting, standing or moving around. You see the tools and technologies they are using and the way they communicate. You can also sense the vibe of the room, since all the furniture and decor are clearly visible.

And here is what you see …

People are reclining on uniform, expensive-looking executive chairs around a large table, facing each other. Some are fidgeting a little, but no-one is standing. A large wall-mounted screen is displaying images and charts. The space is sleek, clean and tidy, but lacking personality and character. There are pieces of paper, laptops and mobile phones on the table, but nothing seems out of context. People are taking turns speaking, and the meeting looks very orderly. There are very few laughs.

You have no way of knowing what's being discussed; however, you've seen enough to get a sense of how this meeting is playing out. So you continue walking until you find yourself in front of another room, where you're greeted by a very different sight …

The activity in this room appears quite messy at first glance. People are frequently standing up and moving around while engaging in fast-paced dialogue. They are scribbling on whiteboards and putting sticky notes on the walls, windows, and even the glass wall you're peeking through. Some participants are standing side by side, completing each other's notes and sketches. Others are sitting at the edge of their seats. Even though you can't hear a thing, you get a fairly clear idea of what the conversation is about, just by looking at all the notes and drawings. The room itself is a bit messy too. The furniture arrangement is somewhat ad hoc, and many objects appear to be out of place. Yet, the space has an air of authenticity, and feels friendly and welcoming.

The question is, if you had a creative challenge to solve with your team, which kind of meeting would you rather be a part of?

I hope you picked the second one.

Yes, I'm well aware that myriad factors can make or break the success of a collaboration session. But I'm sure you'll agree that just from seeing a space and the way people act you can tell a lot about the energy in the room, the dynamics of the conversation, and even the quality of ideas being discussed.

Let's explore this in more depth …

A **PICTURE** OF THRIVING COLLABORATION

Effective collaboration and problem solving requires a certain frame of mind:

- **P**urpose-driven: You focus on your shared purpose, rather than your differences.

- **I**ncluded and inclusive: You know that you're heard and valued, and you make sure that others also feel the same way.

- **C**reative: You think expansively, and you're keen to explore uncharted territory.

- **T**eam-spirited: You see your teammates as trusted partners rather than as competition.

- **U**pbeat: You are positive, excited, energised and optimistic.

- **R**eceptive: You think openly and flexibly, embracing different perspectives.

- **E**ngaged: You are committed to the goals of the team.

The space where you meet, the tools you use, and the way you interact with each other can activate every one of these thinking patterns. They can engender a sense of purpose, facilitate inclusion, make you more receptive to different ideas, boost your creativity, raise your team spirit, help you feel upbeat, and enhance engagement. This means that the choices you make about where and how you run a creative session can make a world of difference to what your team will achieve.

Let's have a look at the different strategies you could employ.

Use tactile tools – and work with your hands

We all have a natural inclination to handle ideas in ways similar to how we handle physical objects. Our language reflects this tendency beautifully. We dissect, sort and build ideas. We pull apart and reverse-engineer concepts. Perhaps we go in circles for a while. We then organise our thoughts, weigh the pros and cons, and get things straight.

Because our brains are wired for a more potent spatial memory than short-term memory, we are in fact much better at working with the visual or physical representations of ideas than processing abstract concepts in our head. So, if you want your team to solve problems quickly and effectively, you need to make it easy for them to capture ideas in two- or three-dimensional form and develop them using their hands.

This is one of the many reasons whiteboards, sticky notes, butchers paper, coloured markers and 3D modelling materials are such popular tools for creative problem solving. Tactile tools also allow team members to work side by side and develop an idea together, expanding on each other's suggestions. (We'll explore the ins and outs of different work tools in Choice 24.)

Drawings and physical models deserve special attention. They represent a universal language; everyone understands what they mean. When you draw or build something, you can put any pieces together without preconceived notions. You could even use LEGO pieces for solving real-life problems. Who cares that they are designed to be toys, as long as they help your team innovate? I've tried using LEGO pieces for exploring serious issues and gained amazing insights.

Use the right seating – and hold an upright posture

The way we hold ourselves during a collaboration session can influence our behaviour and enhance or dampen our engagement.

A study found that when participants sat on comfortable sofas, at a low height, they felt physically settled, and so they rarely stood up. But interestingly, they were settled in their opinions as well, and contributed less to the idea generation process. They were inclined to critique other members' ideas rather than developing them further or sharing their own thoughts.

In the same study, sitting close to each other on floor cushions, in a cosy space, also made it difficult to develop ideas. This setting actually made people feel uncomfortable; the closeness and intimacy felt unnatural. To make things worse, members found it difficult to get up and share ideas, while those standing were towering over the rest of the team. The interaction was slow and lacking flow.

On the other hand, when participants had no seating options and could only stand or lean against something, they moved around more. Not only were they more energised and physically active, but they were also better team players. They engaged in animated interplay, and came up with a large number of great ideas.

Of course, it's not necessary to remove all chairs from your meeting spaces. But when you're running an idea-generation or problem-solving session, you want your people to hold an upright posture and be able to stand up easily. In addition, you want to make sure that no-one in the room feels small. So, consider using tall, bar-stool-type seating for these sessions. And if there are comfy chairs and sofas in the room, suggest to your teammates that they lean against the backs or half-sit on the arms, instead of sinking into those soft cushions. Now, this may not be an elegant look, but watch the results!

Stand up, move – and engage in active collaboration

So, why does it matter so much whether you're sitting, standing or moving around? And why is it a good idea to stand up and move your body when you have problems to solve?

First and foremost, your brain functions better when you're active. You're sharper, you remember things better, and you're more present, flexible and creative. You're more engaged, both mentally and emotionally … The benefits are endless. (In Choice 23 we'll explore how standing and moving can be the keys to peak productivity and creative breakthroughs.)

But when you also physically interact with the objects and images associated with the problem, your performance is taken to another level. You can immerse yourself in the issue more easily and work through it more successfully. (In schools it's already common practice to explore concepts through physical movement. As shown by research and experience, students in active learning environments tend to be more engaged, have better results, and develop more positive relationships with the subject.)

Here is an intriguing technique you could use to develop more empowered relationships with the problems you're looking to solve. Take a problem and create a physical representation of it – say, a mind map, a drawing or a model.

Put it wherever you want it to be in the room, and just play with it. You can choose to stand close to it and face it head-on, turn your back to it or distance yourself from it. You'll probably find that you feel less confronted by the challenge than you would be otherwise, and more in control.

Interestingly, whether you and your teammates physically stand on the same side of the problem or on opposite sides can also alter the dynamics of the collaboration. If you're standing on opposite sides, you're more likely to adopt a critical stance. But if you're on the same side, you're more inclined to think along the same lines and expand on each other's thoughts. So decide which side you need to be on to come to the best solution.

Playing with a problem like this can be an exciting game where you see innovative solutions emerge with ease. This is not smoke and mirrors; expect to see real results once you give it a try.

Create a fluid environment – and make everyone feel equal

Team members tend to share their thoughts more openly when they know they have an equal voice. Even when people have different levels of authority or experience, during a creative session everyone should feel they have a fair chance to participate.

How a room is furnished can promote a sense of inclusion or make some people feel marginalised. For example, participants sitting at the head or in the middle of a long rectangular table are typically perceived, even subconsciously, as more influential than those sitting at the corners. Similarly, people sitting at a higher level – for example, on tall chairs or on a platform – are assumed to have greater power than those sitting closer to the floor.

A straightforward option to create a non-hierarchical setting is to place identical chairs in a circle, and use a round table (if a table is at all necessary). However, this set-up can be limiting at times, and is also a bit dull.

Here's a more interesting and agile option. Mix and match different types of furniture and configure them in a variety of ways; for example, town-hall style, small circles, large circles, or random patterns. The point is you need to give participants the freedom to move around, rearrange furniture and choose where they sit. Isn't this true inclusion?

As an added benefit, a fluid environment promotes a more open and flexible mindset: you don't own your chair, and equally, you don't own your ideas.

Providing a variety of seating options also allows team members to change their posture as they wish. By moving from one spot to another, they can refresh their thinking and get into the right frame of mind at different phases of the creative process, including exploration, idea generation, evaluation and reflection.

Create an inspiring ambience – and tap into the team spirit

In a collaboration space that reflects the identity of your team, you can expect to see greater engagement and team spirit.

How can you create such an environment? If you're lucky enough to work in a place that reflects the personality of your organisation, you already have a head start. Otherwise, think for a moment about your workplace culture, values and purpose, and what motivates you to contribute to this business. Do what you can to create an inspiring space that feels authentic to your organisation. Remember, every single element of your environment – including furniture, fittings, decor, plants, wall colours and lighting – will affect the vibe.

If you have a dedicated team space, you might as well make it a real hub where you feel you belong. What's unique about your people? What makes this a champion crew? And what makes you proud to be a part of this team? In your team space, highlight those qualities that mean the most to you and your colleagues. You might personalise it with your messages, drawings and photos, along with posters, artworks and personal items – showcasing your ideas, achievements and passions. Have fun with this 'makeover', and create a space you'll all love.

You don't have your own team space? If possible, use the space of another crew. Interestingly, even in a room that feels like foreign territory, people may perform better than in a lean space, as suggested by research. Using a room that echoes the spirit of another team or organisation, for example, could spark a sense of healthy competition, inspiring members to pull together – whereas the kind of barren, soulless conference rooms we know all too well only suck the life out of creative collaboration.

Always keep in mind that the physical environment offers endless opportunities to trigger powerful mental states and spark positive emotions. In fact, as I pointed out earlier, the right ambience can stimulate every single thinking pattern that drives effective collaboration and problem solving. It completes the whole PICTURE, making you and your team more *purpose-driven, included and inclusive, creative, team-spirited, upbeat, receptive* and *engaged*.

RUNNING IN A DIVING SUIT?

I'm not suggesting that this is the end of the formal meeting and meeting space. You don't need to be in a highly energetic and creative state to analyse facts and figures, discuss status updates or provide objective feedback, for example. If anything, too much buzz could disrupt progress.

Different environments suit different activities. Lounge-style spaces with sofas can be great for social catch-ups, relaxation or reflection. And in cosy, campfire-type settings you might find it easier to have deep, personal discussions. (The next Choice is all about meeting spaces.)

In short, you have a wide variety of choices and strategies available to bring out the best in your teams in different situations. But when planning a meeting, you must be clear about the kind of attitudes and dynamics you want to see in the room, and choose the space, work tools and activities that support your goals. Putting people in a cold and static environment and expecting them to tap into their creative genius is like dressing someone in a diving suit and asking them to run a 100-metre sprint.

An informal meeting doesn't mean chaos. You still need to follow certain rules and processes, and keep an eye on the agenda. But to conquer creative challenges and innovate successfully, you need high energy, inspiration and flowing collaboration.

So, if you want to create the best conditions for finding winning solutions, think informal. Think physical. Think messy.

INDIVIDUAL EXERCISE

Go on a quick mental journey before you start organising a collaboration session. Imagine that the problem your team is facing is already solved. How did that happen? How did they draw out the best in each other and find that winning idea? What made their collaboration so powerful? Where did they meet, how did they act, and what tools and devices did they use?

TEAM EXERCISES

Have a discussion with your team about what 'successful collaboration in action' looks like to each of you. In what kinds of spaces do you feel most motivated and energised? What helps you connect with each other and think outside the box? What inspires you to speak up, and what can turn you off? Then, based on what you've learned about each other, come up with new ideas to take your collaboration to the next level.

Experiment with holding collaboration sessions in different environments and in different ways. For example, use a space with tall chairs only (or no chairs at all). Try using physical tools only, no digital devices. Hold one session in the room of another team. Have a meeting where everyone is expected to change something about the space … What do you notice? Which strategies are worth sticking with?

WHERE SHOULD WE MEET?

How can I choose the best environments for different team activities?

What do great meeting spaces look and feel like?

How can the right settings help us achieve our goals?

We think, communicate, and approach problems differently in different environments. As such, the qualities of a meeting space can determine to some extent if a meeting will be a success or a flop. So if you find that your people are not the most inspired or engaged when you get together in the 'usual' places, try new locations. Think about what it will take to achieve the goals of your meeting, and choose a setting that will help people get into the right frame of mind.

Picture this place … It's a bit run-down and creaky, with a low ceiling and an underground feel. It may well be in a basement. You see black walls and raw brick. The lights are dim. There's a stage in the room, and the rest of the floor is tightly filled with chairs facing the stage. No tables. No empty spaces. Some chairs are also placed on the side of the stage. There's nothing posh about this room, and it's not the most comfortable either. It seats a few hundred people, but you can curtain off part of the space for smaller audiences.

According to comedians, places like this make excellent comedy venues. They work very well both for the audience and for the performers.

Just put yourself into the picture … As you enter this dark and secretive space, you sense that you're going to be part of something illicit. Nothing is too sacred here; rules will well and truly be broken. You sit close to other audience members, and you feel you're in it together. Yet, the stage is your main focus. You're connected to the comedian, and he or she is connected to you. It's an intimate experience which allows everyone to drop their guard and participate fully. In this space, you and the comedian feed off each other. The laughter is trapped inside and bounces around the room. The real world seems far away; yet, this exciting place down here feels more real than anything.

If you grasp this scenario, you also understand why it's so important to choose the right space for any sort of group activity and event. A great comedy club is designed to give you a fun time and to keep you from taking yourself too seriously. But it would be a terrible venue for corporate training, for example. And vice versa; running a stand-up night in a traditional corporate training room probably wouldn't go down too well either.

SETTING THE TONE FOR CONVERSATIONS

Comedy clubs, churches, cafes, beer gardens, community centres and so on all support different kinds of interactions and experiences, just like conference rooms, innovation spaces and training rooms. And there are also huge variations even when comparing apples to apples.

Spaces send signals about what the rules are and set the tone for conversations. Perhaps you've noticed that you engage with people differently in various settings. You talk about different subjects, use different words, come up with different ideas, and show different parts of your personality. In certain environments you might ask questions, tell stories and share wild ideas that you otherwise wouldn't.

Put simply, the design and vibe of the space determines to some extent how the meeting or event will unfold. If you choose to get together with your friends or your colleagues in the right place, you'll have a head start towards achieving what you planned, but if you make the wrong choice, your gathering is more likely to be a flop.

I've attended meetings in sleek conference rooms where many people were reluctant to speak their minds, simply because the space felt intimidating. As a result, we couldn't discuss innovative ideas or solve problems effectively. I've also been involved in collaboration sessions where everyone was prepared to share valuable knowledge yet the conversation didn't flow. It was difficult to connect with each other because we were sitting too far apart, and the enormous, cluttered meeting table stood as a barrier between us.

Thankfully, I've also had many positive experiences, including strategic planning workshops where the inspiring environment brought the team together and sparked new innovations. And I've attended stakeholder meetings where I was immediately put at ease because the relaxed and transparent setting made it clear that the people I was engaging with had nothing to hide.

A FRESH APPROACH TO MEETINGS

As a bottom line, a meeting or collaboration space needs to function well. This means that the layout and furnishings need to support the type of interaction you'd like to see. The space also needs to have appropriate communication technologies, and provide the required levels of security and privacy.

I'm sure you're already conscious of these factors when organising a team activity. And as part of your preparation, you're probably checking: How many people will need to be seated? How should the tables and chairs be configured? Will you need a digital screen or a whiteboard? Will you use videoconferencing? Does the room need to be soundproof? ... And then, from the available spaces, you pick the one that ticks most of the boxes – perhaps a meeting room in your office or a table at your favourite cafe.

But there's so much more worth considering. In my experience, the intangible aspects of the environment receive much less attention than they deserve.

After an unsuccessful meeting, people rarely blame the vibe of the meeting space. It's easy to come up with other, more 'plausible' explanations ... The weather is draining. We're all too tired after staying up late last night watching the tennis final. People's minds are on other projects or on their holidays. And so on. It may be hard to recognise that the physical space can make such a difference and actually be responsible for draining the energy and creativity from the team.

So, if you find that your people are somewhat jaded and passive when meeting in the usual places, I suggest you try new locations and see the difference for yourself.

I know of teams whose weekly meetings took on a whole new dynamic after they switched from traditional conference rooms to exciting and energising places. And I've talked to consultants who managed to build trusting collaborative relationships with their new customers more quickly and easily after they started meeting them in casual and homely environments.

KNOW YOUR EXPECTATIONS AND OBSTACLES

Meetings and team activities come in many different flavours. There are times to seek out new ideas, and times to select the best one from several options. Sometimes you want to openly discuss an issue, and at other times it's best to just listen to an expert who can teach you a tried-and-tested solution. Every so often you and your team get together to create new strategies, and later on to check in with each other how you are tracking. You meet new people to build relationships, and you get together with colleagues you already know and trust for feedback and advice.

Some meetings are serious and formal while others are more playful and casual. Some are loud and dynamic; others are quiet. Conversations can be spontaneous and free-flowing, or thoroughly planned. They can be truly enjoyable, but some of them might be difficult and emotional. And different interactions call for different environments.

Before you make a choice, it's worth asking yourself a few questions: What's the purpose of the meeting you're planning? And how should people think and interact to achieve the goals of the meeting? Do they need to be playful or serious? Courageous or cautious? Conforming or revolutionary? Imaginative or critically minded? Direct or tactful? Big picture or detail focused?

And here's the power step: look even deeper beneath the surface. Teamwork has its challenges, and sometimes emotional or mental barriers can stand in the way. So, I encourage you to ask yourself what could possibly hold people back from contributing their best …

- Worrying about upsetting others, looking silly or being criticised?

- Thinking that their ideas won't be taken seriously?

- Sensing the weight of the hierarchy in the team?

- Feeling scattered and distracted?

- Being overly stressed, impatient or risk averse?

- Feeling uninspired and disengaged?

Being clear about what you're expecting from your team and what could stand in their way will make it much easier for you to make excellent choices. A great meeting space should help everyone get into the right headspace and give them the inspiration and support to contribute fully.

YOU HAVE PLENTY OF OPTIONS

The majority of modern workplaces offer a wide array of formal and informal settings for social and team activities. Flexible furnishings are increasingly common, which allows you to adapt the space to your needs. And of course, you can also meet people outside the office – say, in a cafe or a park.

You might find it useful to pull together a list of spaces in your workplace and its surrounding areas that could accommodate your team, partners and clients. Try to identify a suitable location for each type of conversation and collaborative activity you frequently engage in.

Let me share a few suggestions, just to get your ideas going:

- **Blue-sky thinking:** Look for expansive, outside-the-box spaces that stimulate people to think freely. A bright, sunlit, spacious room with open views, high ceiling and simple furnishings could offer plenty of space for new ideas. Avoid settings that may remind your team of the day-to-day challenges of work.

- **Innovation sessions:** Find a place that gives people permission to experiment, break the rules and make mistakes. This could be a creatively decorated, colourful and playful space with flexible furnishings and a relaxed, non-precious vibe. When you're stuck on a problem, you could also try using a place that feels new to you. An unfamiliar environment can stimulate you to see things from a fresh perspective and to explore new solutions.

- **Brainstorming:** You want to find a place where nothing feels off limits, and where the impossible feels possible. Your team should feel comfortable sharing ideas that may appear ridiculous at first glance, knowing that they won't be judged. A moderately noisy, buzzing, casual, cafe-style space might be just the right environment to get the creative juices flowing.

- **Team building:** Find a place that you and your team can make your own. It may be a dedicated team room or a workshop space with easy-to-move furniture and lots of interactive surfaces. Co-creating a space is a great team-building activity in itself, and you'll end up with a hub that feels like the team's home.

- **Deep personal conversations:** The space should offer great privacy, and have a gentle and peaceful ambience, helping everyone to feel safe and open up. Look for a comfortable, cosy, dimly lit room with warm colours and soft finishes.

- **Technical and analytical discussions:** You want people to stick to the agenda and focus on the details. This might not be the time to shake things up or challenge the status quo. Look for a low-key, simply decorated and traditionally furnished meeting room with cool colours and hard surfaces. Stay away from distractions. A quiet, soundproof room is best.

- **Status updates:** Your mission is to keep everyone engaged and ensure that the meeting doesn't drag on and on. If possible, find a space suitable for standing meetings – with a tall table and no chairs. The space should be well lit, and have an energising vibe. In this situation, interactive technologies and tactile tools are your friends.

- **Collaborative sessions:** Everyone should feel they are an equal and valued part of the team, knowing that their thoughts and ideas count. Find a comfortable and friendly room where you can sit in a circle – or in any other configuration you wish, as long as no-one has a prime spot. If you're adventurous, you may also run your session in a game room where playing a round of pool or foosball can help break down hierarchical barriers.

- **Meeting a client or a partner you don't know very well:** Consider seeing your new clients and partners at their own workplaces. Just by looking around and (respectfully) checking out the furnishings, design and vibe of their offices, you'll find out a lot about how they think and work. Even the decor tells many stories – those photos, books and knick-knacks all serve as great conversation starters, helping you to learn more about them and subsequently collaborate more effectively.

- **Planning the future:** While developing a vision for the future and talking about exciting new opportunities, you want your team to feel motivated, optimistic and connected to the world outside. If possible, choose a room with large windows and sweeping views, or a lively roof-top cafe. Or you may walk to a beautiful, green outdoor space and hold your meeting on the lawn.

YOUR TEAM'S WARDROBE

You'll probably find that the best meeting spaces embody at least a few attributes you wish to see in your people. Whether your team needs to demonstrate, say, agility, boldness or imagination in a particular situation, spaces with these kinds of qualities will help put you all in the right frame of mind. (It goes without saying that a meeting space – and in fact, any space intended for human interaction – should also help people feel well, think clearly and connect with each other with ease. We'll dive deeper into the secrets of inspiring and nurturing spaces later in the book.)

Your preferred meeting spots could look quite different from mine. But if you pay attention to how different environments influence the flow of ideas and the dynamics of teamwork, you'll soon figure out what works best for your team and your clients.

Think of your list of gathering spaces as your team's 'wardrobe'. You become a different person when you change your environment, just like when you change from formal attire to t-shirt and jeans – perhaps before heading to a comedy club. But whatever your plans are, you want to end up with a smile on your face at the end of the day, rather than a frown.

INDIVIDUAL EXERCISE

Think of a recent meeting where you gave 100%. How did you feel? What helped bring out the best in you? Also think of a meeting where you felt flat and withdrawn. What went wrong? Do you think that in these meetings, the vibe of the physical space might have had something to do with your motivation and mood – and with the energy of the team?

TEAM EXERCISES

Have a chat with your teammates. How do your team meetings usually go? What's going well and what could be improved? Are you all focused and engaged? Do you work through issues and solve problems efficiently? Also discuss how you could take your meetings to the next level, and what kinds of environments could help you achieve this.

Experiment with a few different collaboration spaces. In each space, complete a set of different tasks as a team: perhaps a creative task (e.g. brainstorm ideas for a new product), a people-focused task (e.g. discuss opportunities to improve your workplace culture), an analytical task (e.g. develop a project timeline), and a decision-making task (e.g. pick a winning idea from a range of options). Do you find that different kinds of conversations flow better in different environments? Do you find it easier to complete certain tasks in certain spaces?

CHOICE 11

WHO SHOULD I SIT WITH IN THE OFFICE?

How can the right neighbours inspire me to lift my game?
How can a smart seating arrangement bring out the best in everyone?

In a diverse work community, learning opportunities are everywhere. In fact, you and your colleagues can all help each other to grow without anyone missing out. Here's a simple strategy that requires next to no time or effort, yet makes everyone a winner: sit near people with complementary strengths. Smart seating arrangements and strategies are not only for school kids. Just wait till you see the results.

You're probably familiar with the popular notion, 'You are the average of the five people you spend the most time with'. This idea seems to make sense ... well, sort of.

Yes, the people you surround yourself with can change how you look at life and how you grow as an individual. You've known this since childhood. I'm sure you've noticed how your closest friends and colleagues can draw you into their worlds, shape your views and shift your moods. If you're lucky, they're fun to be around and they inspire and support you to excel. Or perhaps some of them can drive you crazy at times and drag you down.

But no, you're not destined to blend in and lose your edge or become any sort of 'average'. The richness of your thinking, your ability to solve problems, or the extent of your creativity, for example, are not capped by the limits of your environment. Moreover, the collective power of your team can be much greater than the sum of the qualities, strengths and weaknesses of the members. You can bring out the best (and sometimes the worst) in one another. As a thriving team, you can conquer new territories and come up with ideas and solutions that none of you would be able to achieve individually.

A TRUE WIN-WIN

There are many techniques to improve individual and team performance, but this one is too often overlooked: sit close to people who are positive influences on you, and whom you can influence positively. None of you needs to be a superstar; you just need to complement each other's strengths.

Maybe get together with your team, work out who would be the best 'buddies' for each other, and create a seating arrangement that suits everyone. I know, this idea might sound a bit childish at first – after all, we're not in school anymore. But I suggest you give it a go; you might be surprised at how well it works.

Alternatively, you can decide who you sit (or stand) next to when you come to the office. Still, you need to know who can bring out the best in you at any given time or situation.

But before jumping into action, it's a good idea to think through how your current arrangement is working for you. Who do you usually sit close to in the office? What are your relationships like? Do you support each other to do your best work? Or do you perhaps make each other's lives more difficult?

WHO ARE THE PEOPLE IN YOUR NEIGHBOURHOOD?

Thankfully, employees these days are rarely seated together based on their status, except in a few very traditional organisations. In a modern business, this arrangement has little benefit on individual or team performance.

In your workplace, you and your colleagues might be grouped by discipline, or perhaps you're part of a multidisciplinary project team that sits together. Either way, you have plenty of opportunity to exchange knowledge and learn from your neighbours. When you have a question, someone nearby might know the answer. Or you can just listen in to conversations near your desk and learn something relevant to your expertise or project.

If your workplace allows you to sit wherever you wish, you probably gravitate to people whose company you most enjoy. And this certainly has some upsides; you can discuss anything under the sun, motivate one another and give each other emotional support during challenging times.

At the same time, you naturally try to avoid being too close to people with vastly different temperaments. If you need peace and quiet to concentrate, you won't appreciate listening to the jokes of the larger-than-life 'resident comedian' all day. On the other hand, if you thrive on passionate, animated conversations, you won't want dead silence just because the nerdy analyst nearby can't handle the slightest noise.

In a well-designed office there should be opportunities for everyone to approach work and express themselves in their own unique way without disturbing others. But in a flexible environment, distractions and conflicts can still occur when colleagues who rub each other the wrong way share the same sandpit. And why would you want this kind of stress? Mixing with like-minded people makes life so much smoother.

But here's the issue: teammates with similar expertise, project focus, attitudes or mindsets won't always bring out the best in you. Sometimes you need people around you who will stretch your thinking and inspire you to grow.

IMPROVE THE SPEED AND QUALITY OF YOUR WORK

Superstars who consistently produce top-quality work at top speed are practically non-existent. Everyone has some strengths and weaknesses, but weaknesses can often be improved upon. And sitting with the right people can make a real difference here.

Research suggests that when you sit in close proximity to a person who works faster or produces higher quality work than you, your performance could measurably increase. And interestingly, the other person won't be negatively affected; in this scenario there are only winners.

This means that if you're a fast worker and you sit close to someone who produces excellent-quality work – or vice versa – both of you will benefit. You will improve on your weaknesses while your strengths will remain intact. The slower person will speed up while continuing to achieve high standards. At the same time, the faster worker will increase their quality of work and still maintain good speed.

So, what counts as 'close proximity'? If you can't reach someone by flicking a rubber band at them, you probably won't have that many spontaneous conversations. To enjoy the positive influence of an inspiring colleague, you should try to stay within around eight metres of them. However, you'll get the greatest benefits if you can work at neighbouring desks.

In one study where employees with complementary strengths worked alongside each other, many of them improved their weaker sides by close to 15% after about a month.

Now this is an impressive result ... But keep in mind that this strategy might work better in situations when you aim to improve a hard skill – for example, using a particular software program, analysing data or managing projects – and you have clear targets to strive towards. Seeing another person doing what you do – only better or faster – will nudge you to up your game. Playing alongside Michael Jordan made everyone on the team better.

CREATIVITY IS A DIFFERENT BEAST

When it comes to creativity, the story is very different (though equally promising). Creativity is multifaceted and limitless, and thus every person in your circle, regardless of their knowledge or background, might be able to elevate your ideas to the next level.

When you'd like to boost your imagination, I suggest you get together with people who have roughly similar levels of creative talent and experience. You don't want anyone grabbing the lead or dominating others, and in an inclusive little group (or pair) you should be able to inspire one another and run with each other's ideas more easily.

Of course, this doesn't mean you should all think alike. You'll see greater results if you can mix with people of different personalities and mindsets. Colleagues who approach challenges differently to you can help you see things from fresh perspectives and shed light on your hidden knowledge. Working with them might not be the easiest, but if you can debate issues with open minds and respect, together you could redefine what's possible.

Just think of the creative exchanges between John Lennon and Paul McCartney. Similar levels of experience. Different skills and knowledge of music, different temperaments and different artistic flair. While they certainly had some personal differences too, they were able to work as equal partners and maintain great respect for each other. As McCartney said, they 'never had a dry session'. Even after they stopped co-writing songs, they continued to shape each other as musicians. And boy, did they change the world!

A QUICK WORD ABOUT PEOPLE YOU REALLY WANT TO AVOID

Hopefully there's no-one in your organisation who drags you down. Some of your colleagues may challenge or annoy you, which is part of the workplace experience. But toxic personalities can do real harm. They can spread toxicity incredibly quickly, and very far.

Unlike people who work slowly or do less-than-excellent-quality work, colleagues with intolerable behaviours can affect you negatively, weakening your integrity. Studies suggest that sitting near someone who will eventually be sacked for their behaviour will increase your chance of doing something atrocious and thus being sacked yourself. On a positive note, once they are gone, their negative effect quickly vanishes too.

PROVE THE SMARTYPANTS WRONG

So, who should you sit with when you arrive at the office? This depends on which aspect of your performance you'd like to improve:

- Do you need to learn the ins and outs of the project you're involved in? Sit with your project team.

- Do you need to deepen your knowledge in a particular area? Find someone who has the experience and answers you need.

- Would you like to master a hard skill? Work side by side with a colleague who does what you do, just a bit better or faster.

- Or do you wish to boost your creative talent? Get together with someone who can expand your thinking and draw out your ideas.

Of course, you want to become a well-rounded professional, but you can't improve everything at once. So pick your priorities.

Now, I understand that organisations are complex systems. Your company might already have strategies in place to keep departments or teams together, limiting your flexibility to pick your neighbours. When teamwork requires that you sit with certain people, you don't have much choice either. And if members in a team have different ideas about how they should buddy up, this whole strategy could turn into a mess.

But on days when you're not tied to specific people or teams – when you could perhaps even work from home if you wanted to, but you prefer to go to the office to be around people – hopefully you can play with this idea. Try it and see how much difference it makes. Chat with your colleagues about how you could all work smarter together. If you get the hang of it, your whole team will shine. And I'm sure you'll soon be able to prove all those smartypants wrong who claim that you are just some sort of an 'average'.

INDIVIDUAL EXERCISES

Think about your professional development goals. Which technical or hard skills would you like to further develop? Specifically, which aspects of these skills do you wish to improve? And who in your office has already achieved the level of mastery you're aiming for? Write down your goals along with the names of colleagues you see as inspirational. Use this list as a reminder, and spend as much time near these people as possible.

For a few days, sit next to someone you don't know very well, and pay attention to how they work. Is there anything you can learn from them? Did they demonstrate a skill you wish to improve on, or inspire you in some way?

TEAM EXERCISES

Get together with your team and have a chat about your individual strengths, weaknesses and aspirations. Then create a seating arrangement that will support everyone's professional growth. Stick to this plan for about a month, and then have a discussion about how it worked. If your experiences were positive, perhaps create a new learning/seating plan for the next month. Keep doing this month after month, as long as you notice the benefits.

Experiment with different ways of forming neighbourhoods in the office; for example, based on project, discipline or work activity. Also see how it works when you mix things up completely (everyone has to pick a different spot each day), and when you can all sit wherever you wish (it's okay to keep the same spot for many days in a row). Run each experiment for at least a couple of weeks, and then have a debrief. Do any of these strategies seem to work better than others?

WHAT KINDS OF RELATIONSHIPS SHOULD I CULTIVATE AT WORK?

Should I always work with people who are easy to collaborate with?

Is it important that I like all my teammates?

How can different types of work relationships shape my performance?

What are some of the qualities of effective teams?

It's fun to mingle with like-minded people, but this is not the best recipe for effective teamwork. While you must agree on the fundamentals, it actually helps if you have different views on certain matters. You'll achieve more if you embrace your differences rather than avoiding any friction. Sure, work relationships are inherently complex – but if you know how to nurture them, your collaboration will soar.

If you're fortunate enough, you know how nice it is to work in a team where everyone's on the same wavelength and you treat each other like family and friends. You and your workmates understand one another really well – so much so that you can even finish each other's sentences at times. When a challenge arises, you find it easy to agree on the best course of action. Everyone is kind and polite, careful not to hurt others' feelings, and in this amicable environment conflicts are sparse.

But just think about this … What's the right culture for you to be your natural best? Can you truly thrive in a team where everyone thinks like you, harmony is sacred, and individual differences are seen as obstacles?

I've worked in companies where collaboration was really smooth, because most of us had similar cultural backgrounds, world views and personalities. Some members were even proud of the fact that they had identical personality profiles. Sure enough, when it came to following established processes, we were super productive. On the other hand, we were not very inventive. Sometimes we tweaked our standard approach to solving problems and delivering services, which in this steady environment felt like real innovation. But in truth, we rarely produced anything groundbreaking. And when tension eventually arose between members, we had no idea how to handle it. We just avoided the issue, and naturally, the trust in the team started to erode.

COLLABORATION SHOULD BE BOTH EASY **AND** HARD

I love the notion that when we do what we love and we're good at, work is easy and effortless. At the same time, personal development and productivity experts are telling us that to reach our potential we must be willing to work hard and be uncomfortable – which also makes sense. But isn't this a conundrum? When my job feels easy, does it mean I'm playing small? And when work is difficult, is this a sign that I haven't found my natural flow?

I used to battle with these seemingly opposing ideas, but after a lot of thinking and research, I realised that there's no conflict here. To make the most of your talent, certain aspects of your work need to be effortless while others should be difficult. This also applies to work relationships. A modern, creative team will only thrive when collaboration is both easy and hard. Let me explain.

WHAT NEEDS TO BE EASY

Here are some important aspects of teamwork that make life smoother and more enjoyable for everyone.

Positive relationships

Trust, care and respect … These qualities are cited over and over again in conversations about effective teamwork, but let me just spend a moment summing up why they are so incredibly important.

Game-changing solutions often start with outlandish and even ridiculous ideas. However, some of the best ideas might never see the light of the day unless you all feel safe enough to share them, knowing that no-one will shoot down your idea, embarrass you, or even worse, criticise you behind your back.

Pursuing big goals is a courageous act, since you need to take risks and explore uncharted territory. At times you need to make yourself vulnerable to succeed. All this can be terrifying when you're left to your own devices and you're not sure who to trust. In contrast, as part of a close-knit and supportive community, plunging into the challenge can be exciting and fun. Even when you're going through a rough patch, your caring teammates will be there to motivate you and help you keep your spirits up.

A culture of helpfulness

In high-performing teams, members are keen to help each other out rather than focusing on their own gains. It's really inspiring to work in an environment where you know your teammates want you to succeed and are happy to lend a hand anytime you need it.

Working with people you can rely on should also boost your confidence. You don't need to have all the answers and be a master of all trades. You can play to your strengths, reassured that when you come across a question or hit an obstacle, you'll get help. In a culture where everyone's success is celebrated, it's a real pleasure to do great things for each other.

Aligned values

Experience and research tell us that the way people work together is just as important to team performance as the skills and qualities they each bring. In other words, even when your team has some skill and knowledge gaps, you might be better off focusing on improving collaboration rather than trying to bring in the most qualified and experienced people. However, when it comes to personal and professional values, assembling the right team is critical. To effectively solve problems together, everyone needs to be aligned with what's important, what's unacceptable, and what success looks like.

You can usually reconcile different ideas and beliefs by sharing knowledge and experience on a subject. On the other hand, incompatible values are very difficult to overcome and can lead to corrosive conflicts. Even with the most brilliant minds in the team, collaboration is doomed to fail if members pull in different directions. When tackling a project, you want to focus on making meaningful progress rather than arguing about where you're heading and what's right or wrong.

WHAT NEEDS TO BE HARD

Now, let's look at those aspects of teamwork that can sometimes be challenging to deal with, but which are still critical to your team's success.

True diversity

Do you wish to learn, grow and expand your thinking? Surround yourself with people who challenge your views with their unique knowledge and perspectives. There's not much point ruminating over ideas with people who think just like you.

You've probably noticed that you're more creative and your ideas can reach greater heights when you're part of a diverse team. In fact, studies show that teams with members from a wide variety of educational, cultural and professional backgrounds tend to be more innovative and successful than homogenous groups.

The reality is, working in a diverse team is far from easy ... Beth loves numbers while Jonathan is more interested in the artistic aspects of work. Martin is an avid fan of the latest technology but Jen is drawn to the human perspective. Robert only believes in science, yet Leah's most trusted advisor is her intuition. Sylvia prefers to keep things safe while Benny can't help coming up with game-changing ideas. Jim thinks work should be fun, though Dwight believes the office should be run with an iron fist.

I'm sure you appreciate that in a team like this, getting from A to B is rarely straightforward. To find common ground, you need to consider differing views and let go of old beliefs, which take self-awareness and effort. When there's a clash of ideas or opinions, it can be tempting to respectfully disagree and just move on to keep the peace. However, if you give in, you miss out on the very benefits that diversity can offer.

Passionate debates

To create magic together, you actually need to have debates and encourage each other to reassess their views, which can sometimes feel uncomfortable and unproductive. It takes time and patience to understand people who think, work and communicate differently to you. During open and passionate discussions, conflicts are also more likely to occur, and you need to be prepared to resolve them skillfully. But if you shy away from these challenges, you limit what you and your team can achieve.

In many ways, teamwork is similar to physical exercise or playing computer games. The more effort you invest, the better the results. To build your stamina and develop muscles, you need to push through some pain. To get to the next level of the game, you need to overcome hurdles. And in either of these domains, you'll only get a real sense of achievement if you're prepared to expand your limits.

As shown by research, teams that celebrate diversity and embrace the difficulties and uncertainty inherent in this type of collaboration produce better outcomes – not despite the challenges but because of them. Put simply, if you're willing to stretch yourself and accept some discomfort, you and your team have a much better shot at reaching the stars.

DARK TERRITORY

In specific circumstances, even some 'dark' behaviours and personality traits you'd otherwise want to steer clear of can be beneficial.

Raw feedback

Taking on feedback can be hard work, even when delivered constructively and with the best of intentions. Many people prefer hearing about their shortfalls through level-headed conversations, but some respond better to performance evaluation that comes without a filter.

In an interesting psychological study, participants were asked to complete a creative task, after which they received a (staged) evaluation that was delivered either in a neutral or in an angry manner. Participants then received a second task. When researchers looked at how the participants' performance changed after the feedback session, they found something really interesting. People with specific traits became more motivated, engaged and creative after facing an angry evaluator, compared to those with similar traits who received the even-tempered assessment.

Facing an angry manager or teammate can of course also be a real turnoff, and I personally do my best in any situation to be relaxed and gentle when discussing issues. However, it seems this isn't always the most effective approach to helping others excel. Certain people, under certain conditions, tend to put in even more effort when their frustrated colleagues don't try to hide their feelings.

So, what's the best way for you and your team to give and receive feedback? We'll come back to this in a minute.

Difficult personalities

We naturally gravitate towards virtuous people who are a delight to be around: generous, optimistic, considerate and kind. At the same time, we do our best to stay away from self-centred, arrogant and judgemental jerks. Why wouldn't we? Life is so much smoother and more enjoyable when we can share it with awesome, inspiring people, and what is there to like about those who drain our energy and spirit?

Well, life is not black and white, and neither are people. We all have some light and some dark traits in different measures. And interestingly, when it comes to work, some negative personality traits can prove to be beneficial. For example, people with egocentric, narcissistic tendencies often find it easier to promote their team's capabilities and accomplishments, and to recover from criticism.

On the flipside, certain positive traits can turn out to be problematic. Highly conscientious individuals, for instance, tend to worry more about making mistakes and upsetting others, and can more easily get caught up in small details. When they are put into unsuitable roles, their efforts to get things right can sometimes slow down innovation and change.

While it's great to have a few close friends in your team, you want to work with people who get the job done. Of course, it's essential that you're all able to work together and maintain a healthy culture. You certainly shouldn't tolerate any toxicity. But sometimes the best individuals for a role are those you would never invite over for dinner.

THE GOOD NEWS

Here's what I find most exciting about investing into work relationships: all you need to do is focus on making collaboration easier, and the rest will take care of itself. Develop trust and respect in your team. Nurture a culture where you and your teammates are more excited about helping each other than competing for personal gain. And make sure your values are aligned.

Many things that are difficult about collaboration will become more constructive and exciting as a result. Debates will be frequent and tension will still arise, since in a positive environment you'll feel safe to share your honest opinions and address sensitive issues. But you'll have fewer fruitless arguments and more constructive debates.

You'll more likely see your differences as an opportunity to create something extraordinary, rather than an obstacle to collaboration. And just imagine what you and your team will be able to achieve by adding to each other's strengths rather than playing 'tug o' war'.

In an engaged and relaxed environment, you'll be naturally kinder, more considerate, and more sensitive to the vulnerabilities of others. However, you won't need to sugar-coat your feedback. On the occasion when you do need to show someone tough love, they will know that you only want to help them excel, rather than make them feel small.

You'll take more risks and thus fail more often, but will bounce back more swiftly. You'll also become more open to engage with personalities vastly different from yours, because they will be less likely to push your buttons. And these relationships could open new doors for you.

So, where should you start? How can you cultivate positive work relationships? It all comes down to one simple act: getting to know your teammates very well – not just their professional persona, but who they really are. In Choice 14 I'll show you how you can develop solid, thriving work relationships through simple decisions and habits. Are you ready to take that step?

INDIVIDUAL EXERCISE

Contemplate the achievements you're most proud of. What did it take to succeed? What personal challenges did you need to overcome? What did you need to change in your thinking? Also ask yourself: who were your 'partners in crime', and how did they inspire and bring out the best in you?

TEAM EXERCISES

Have an open discussion with your team about some of your recurring disagreements and collaboration challenges. What hidden assumptions and beliefs might be responsible for these ongoing issues? What do you all agree on? And how can you turn your differences into a unique advantage for the team?

Organise yourselves into pairs for a role-play. Each pair should pick one tricky subject to discuss. Every person should also choose a specific role (or archetype) that they feel close to; for example, scientist, humanitarian, economist, artist, peace maker, entertainer or innovator. Debate your topic from your chosen perspective, with respect and an open mind. Then swap roles and argue the other person's viewpoint to see what it's like to be in their shoes.

Discuss the unwritten rules and values that guide your work, and do your best to find common ground. Focus on frequently arising questions that don't have obvious answers, for example: Should we give clients the type of advice they expect or what they really need for solving their problems? When is it a good time to innovate and when should we stick to tried-and-tested solutions? If a decision needs to be made urgently but a crucial piece of information is missing, should we wait or go ahead? What should we do when we face unforeseen problems or find ourselves behind schedule?

CHOICE 13

HOW MUCH PERSONALITY SHOULD I BRING TO MY PROFESSIONAL LIFE?

Is it a good idea to bring my whole self to work?

How can I open up and make my personality shine?

How can I encourage others to drop their guard and show their true selves?

In open and inclusive environments where team members bring their true selves to work, we see stronger relationships, higher performance and more fun. Unfortunately, it can be difficult to know where the boundaries are, and to express ourselves without inhibition. Keeping a low profile and fitting in may feel like the safer option – but in truth, everyone will miss out. In this Choice we'll delve into how you can create an environment where personalities are free to shine. The results can be transformative.

I vividly remember the last evening of high school. We knew we may never see each other again. The risk of saying something controversial and then living with the consequences was gone. So under the summer sky, my mates and I finally asked each other some difficult questions and expressed truths that had been suppressed for years … 'Why have you been avoiding me?' The answer which came surprisingly quickly is burnt into my memory.

Many of us shared secrets and deep feelings, and confessed loving or painful thoughts for the first time. Words were flowing effortlessly. We felt more connected than ever.

I also felt a tinge of regret, after realising that we would have spent a very different four years together had we reached this level of honesty and openness while we were still school mates. We could have repaired broken friendships.

As teenagers, we certainly made life quite complicated for ourselves in an attempt to feel safe and accepted, adjusting our own behaviours to fit into a group. So, what's different now that we're older and – supposedly – wiser? The way I see it, not a lot. Many of us have carried our insecurities into our working lives.

Thus history repeats. On several occasions, I've had fascinating discussions with colleagues about delicate topics we both felt very passionate about, just days before a final goodbye. We talked about spiritual beliefs and personal interests which we had thought would be laughed at or brutally judged in a corporate environment. But as things turned out, we were on the same wavelength all along. The connection between us grew stronger, just as our working relationship was about to end. Yet again, I wished I could have turned back time.

A COUPLE OF NAGGING QUESTIONS

'How much of my personality should I bring to work? And what should I leave at home?'

These questions have followed me throughout my career. Naturally, I like to be accepted by the teams I'm a part of, and to mesh with their culture. At the same time, I want to stay true to myself, shake things up as needed, and use my life experience to create a difference. It should be possible to achieve both, but in some workplaces it can be hard to know which ideas and behaviours are seen as professional, and which are perceived as eccentric.

And here is my conundrum. I don't feel comfortable raising these questions with my teams unless I already know that they are open to such 'out there' conversations. I'd love them to invite me to speak my mind, rather than me having to ask if it's okay.

Maybe I'm not alone. The way I see it, most of us want to be part of an authentic and transparent culture where no-one needs to wear a mask, and where we feel understood and accepted for who we are. We also prefer to work with enthusiastic teammates and clients who are curious to hear our ideas and can think outside the box.

However, not everybody knows how to invite others to show their true selves, or how to engage with unusual ideas and approaches. And despite their best intentions, some people send mixed messages to their teams about what they expect.

There were times in my life when my colleagues did exactly that; on one hand, I was invited to show my whole self, and on the other, I had to fit their mould. For example, whenever I came up with innovative solutions to work-related problems that were inspired by my personal interests and side projects, I was met with raised eyebrows. The ideas that reflected my personality were seen as too 'far out' – not because they didn't work, but because they didn't have a corporate feel.

A SMARTER, MORE ENJOYABLE WAY TO WORK

These days I'm consciously looking for colleagues, clients and partners who don't see a huge divide between the professional and personal realms, and are genuinely curious about the people they collaborate with. They want to have relaxed, insightful conversations, and to develop friendly, informal relationships – knowing that it's not just a nicer way to work but also good for the whole team as well as the business.

In open and inclusive cultures where team members express themselves freely and honestly, we see stronger social connections and higher performance. We see greater trust, commitment and cohesion, as well as more flowing communication and collaboration. Members work more productively, and innovate and solve problems better. And of course, they also love their work more.

Setting the intention to create a culture where personalities are free to shine is a great start, but it takes skill to make this a reality. Not everyone can drop their guard and open up just because they are allowed to do so. We all have a colourful personal history, perhaps including some embarrassing or regrettable experiences, as well as a fair amount of societal conditioning to overcome. Thus, most of us find it easier to come out of our shell in relaxed environments where we're surrounded by easy-going, non-judgemental people who genuinely want to see who we really are.

TIPS TO CREATE AN ENVIRONMENT WHERE PERSONALITIES ARE FREE TO SHINE

You can encourage people to let their personalities shine – and give yourself the nudge you need – in many different ways. Let me share a few ideas:

- Find **opportunities to play** as a team. You can use play as an ice-breaker or integrate it into constructive work. (We'll dive deeper into this topic very soon.) A good game helps you to forget about society's conditioning – what's 'wrong', what's 'right' and what's 'expected' of you – and to engage parts of your personality you tend to shut down when you're immersed in serious, focused activities. Play also entices you to push existing boundaries and let your imagination fly.

- Few things break the ice faster than **humour and laughter**. I'm sure you agree, personalities tend to shine while you're bouncing jokes off each other and discussing issues with a lighthearted spirit. In a culture where humour is appreciated, you'll find it easier to express yourself openly and authentically. You can certainly enjoy humour and still take your job seriously and work productively.

- While it's great to work in a positive environment, don't expect every-one to always have a happy face. Conversations about difficult topics can trigger raw emotions. If you'd like your teammates to fully engage in such discussions, you need to create a **safe space**. In some work-places I know of, members frequently get together after work, in small groups, to discuss personal and professional challenges. During these sessions people are able to have candid, down-to-earth conversations about issues that are meaningful to them but they wouldn't normally talk about.

- Use **interesting, fun collaboration tools**. You may find it easier to scribble bold, provocative ideas on a giant, lime-green sticky note, for example, compared to a plain whiteboard. Some creative consultants hand colourful crayons and sharpies to their corporate clients during collaboration sessions, which gives them permission to unleash their inner child and express themselves without filters.

- Even when you collaborate remotely, your choice of technology matters. When it comes to authentic self-expression, not all **online tools and platforms** are created equal. Check with your team how they feel about different applications. I notice that I'm usually more cautious and guarded when chatting on certain platforms, and more relaxed when sharing ideas on others – even when it's the same person at the other end of the line. (We'll explore more about the digital world in the coming Choices.)

- The **space in which you meet** can set the tone of your conversations, as we saw earlier. A comfortable and cosy place helps you relax. A casual and friendly ambience invites you to act more naturally. And a playful environment may put you in the mood to play with crazy ideas. Innovative teams often decorate their workspaces with offbeat artwork and quirky objects. Such spaces send the message that it's okay to be different – you don't have to fit the mould.

- Your body needs to know too that it's time to loosen up. You and your teammates spend hours each day sitting in office chairs, evaluating pros and cons, following protocols and working towards deadlines. A **different posture** should help you snap out of your usual work mode, which probably has a flavour of responsibility and urgency. You might have noticed that you're more chilled and straightforward when sitting on a sofa, a bar stool or a floor cushion, for example, compared to an office chair.

- You could also have a **standing meeting**, or when you only meet one or two people, **go for a walk** together. You'll likely notice that raising your energy will help the conversation flow more naturally. When you have different opinions about an issue, walking side by side will also feel less confrontational than facing each other, and thus sharing your honest points of view will be easier.

- You can of course also hold certain types of meetings in **public places**. You might enjoy catching up with your team, say, in a hip cafe or restaurant, or in a lush garden. And what about getting together and exploring ideas somewhere unusual, like at an art gallery, zoo or aquarium?

In a close-knit team where members know each other very well, it's easier for everyone to drop their guard – so it's certainly worth spending time with your team getting to know each other. Solid personal relationships are also the foundation of a thriving workplace culture. (In the next Choice I'll share a few ideas on how you can develop stronger connections in a relatively short time. There are so many other ways to connect with people than the good ol' Friday drinks.)

But even when you work with people you don't know much about, you can still help them – and yourself – to open up. With a bit of creativity and attention, you can encourage people to show a side of themselves they may otherwise keep hidden.

Simple tricks like those I've just shared can be used in a wide variety of environments. In an interview, Emerald Fennell, director of the brilliant movie *Promising Young Woman*, talks about one of the challenges she faced during shooting. There were many actors on set with small roles, who didn't know the cast and the crew very well. Yet, they were put in a vulnerable position where they needed to give a human, imperfect and 'textured' performance. Emerald wanted these actors to feel safe to experiment and not worry about screwing up. And to support them, she made sure that the set was 'incredibly lighthearted and fun and supportive'.

NO REGRETS

Are you concerned that exploring the boundaries of 'professionalism' is awkward at best and dangerous at worst? That your colleagues will take you less seriously once they get to know the real you? Or that your team's work ethic may suffer?

You're more likely to find that collaboration becomes more powerful and enjoyable when you all bring your whole selves to work. Your people will trust and respect you (and each other) more, and contribute with a greater passion. Sure, the elephants in the room will come to light, but isn't it better to deal with them than pretending they don't exist?

And when the sad day comes for one of you to move on, you won't be saying goodbye with a sense of regret, because you won't be wondering how things could have been different if you'd allowed each other to see your true selves.

INDIVIDUAL EXERCISES

Explore your emotions around opening up. Do you have any concerns about expressing yourself authentically at work? Have you got yourself in trouble in the past – perhaps in your childhood – for wearing your heart on your sleeve, or for sharing your ideas without censoring yourself? Do your old defence mechanisms serve you in your current environment? Are your fears grounded in reality, or just products of your imagination?

Reflect on the past achievements you're most proud of. Which parts of your personality did you need to bring to work in order to succeed? Where did you find inspiration for your winning ideas? Did you conform to the norm or cross some boundaries?

Think of a challenging project you're currently working on, and explore solutions from various angles. Ask for advice from different parts of yourself – your inner child, adventurer, philosopher, fighter, peacekeeper, magician and so on. Do *they* have the answers you're after? Are *they* able to bring you closer to the solution? (You could also complete this exercise as a team.)

TEAM EXERCISES

Have an open, candid conversation with your team about 'personalities in the workplace'. Explore what's appreciated, what's accepted, and what's considered distracting or inappropriate in different situations. Make sure everyone participates. Encourage everyone to ask any questions on their minds.

Experiment with running different types of meetings and team activities in different environments. Also try out different ice breakers. What do you notice? How are people's behaviours and ideas influenced by the environment, and the activities you engage in? When is it helpful to let personalities play out in full, and when is it more productive if people hold back a little?

CHOICE 14

HOW CAN I BUILD BETTER RELATIONSHIPS AT WORK?

How can I develop stronger connections with my teammates, clients and partners?

What are the best meeting spaces for personal conversations?

How can I get to know a lot about people in a short time?

The formula is simple: when you get to know someone better, your personal connection deepens. And when you feel close to someone, you also work better together. The question is, how can you invite others to share aspects of their personal lives, views and passions in a professional environment? Choose the right meeting spaces and follow a few common-sense suggestions, and you'll find that you can learn a surprising amount about your teammates and clients, even in a short time.

I met Clara through LinkedIn. After exchanging a few messages and talking once on the phone, we discovered that we share many interests. So we decided to catch up in person to get to know each other better and explore opportunities to help each other out. Since we both lived nearby, we agreed to meet at the cafe in Melbourne's Royal Botanic Gardens.

When we arrived, we found that the seating area of the cafe was closed due to COVID restrictions. So we grabbed our drinks, found a nice grassy patch under a tree overlooking the lake, and settled there. Not on a bench or a blanket, but right on the grass. Was I worried that my brand new jeans may get some grass stains? Not really. Being in the moment was more important.

Clara and I had a long and lively chat. We touched on all kinds of topics, from travelling and art, through family life and romance, to design and social issues. We quickly found ourselves diving into sensitive subjects and sharing delicate stories. A few wicked jokes also bubbled to the surface. We spoke our minds freely, without worrying about being judged or misunderstood. As it turned out, we didn't talk business, but we learned a lot about each other and had some good laughs. Our trust in each other grew quickly and naturally.

Our conversation certainly would have been different had we sat in a cafe, and very different again if we had met in a traditional office. It could have taken many meetings to develop the same level of connection that we created on that sunny afternoon – in just a couple of hours that seemed to pass in the blink of an eye.

PERSONAL CONNECTION CAN UNLOCK THE MAGIC

Some people choose to keep their professional and personal relationships separate, and in certain domains this may make sense. But in creative knowledge work where you tackle complex problems each day and create personalised solutions for unique clients, it helps to really know the colleagues and clients you collaborate with.

I'm not talking about understanding the skills and intelligence they bring to the team. And I'm not talking about becoming best friends with everyone either. Somewhere in between, there's a level of personal connection that can unlock the magic in collaboration. This is such an interesting aspect of teamwork ... Learning about others' passions, interests, pet peeves and opinions can make it so much easier to get on the same wavelength and conquer challenges together.

As you get to know a person better, you naturally find it easier to relate to them and see things through their eyes. You're also likely to grow to trust and respect them more, and become more open to learning from them, even if they have different views about certain issues.

When you feel close to your teammates and clients, teamwork is much more effective and enjoyable. You're happy to help each other out, and you prefer to cooperate towards a shared goal rather than compete for personal gain. Few things are more motivating than joining forces with a caring and loyal crew who truly get you.

The benefits of strong personal connections are proven by a large body of research. Studies also show that to improve teamwork, spending time with your mates and getting to know them can be just as effective as team-building exercises. But sadly, many organisations are missing out because members only know each other on the surface. Either they are 'too busy', or they simply find it pointless or awkward to engage in non-work-related 'chit-chat'.

THE RECIPE FOR A MEMORABLE CATCH-UP

Getting to know people takes time and effort, but perhaps not as much as you might think. You don't need to put yourself in awkward situations or go out of your way to strengthen your relationships. You can discover new sides of people through social catch-ups and quick informal chats that fit into the natural course of your day.

When you find the right tone, you can learn a surprising amount about others in a short time. Of course, building rapport largely comes down to your interpersonal skills, but the physical environment and the way you act can also make a great difference to where the conversation leads.

While sitting across from someone, say, in a polished and echoey board-room, under artificial lighting, you'll probably reveal less about yourself compared to when you meet in a laid-back and soulful place. I can testify that the lawn overlooking the Ornamental Lake in Melbourne's Botanic Gardens works like magic … but you don't need to go that far.

In my experience, it's really easy to have an engaged and memorable catch-up with someone when you both:

- are relaxed and comfortable

- feel accepted for who you are

- feel safe to speak your mind

- are able to listen to and understand each other

- share some emotions and feel things in your body.

Let me share a few ideas on how you can tick these boxes and subsequently deepen your connections.

Help everyone feel relaxed and comfortable

For a casual chat, look for a meeting space that's not too noisy or too quiet. The ideal place also has plenty of fresh air, pleasant temperatures and good-quality lighting that's gentle on the eyes. In a noisy, stuffy and badly lit room, you'll find it difficult to be fully present and have a relaxed chat. Distractions and discomfort can take a lot out of you and bring your mood down.

Many people feel a bit guilty about having a social catch-up during work hours, and feel the urge to wrap up the conversation quickly. A laid-back, informal setting may give you permission to take enough time away from work to get to know the person in front of you. A casual vibe and comfortable, soft furniture will also help put you at ease.

A lawyer once told me that when she first meets her clients, she prefers to welcome them in a lounge-style room with comfy couches and creative artwork, rather than in an old-fashioned, stark meeting room. She wants her clients to see her as a trusted and supportive friend, as opposed to a rigid authority figure sitting on a high horse, and she finds that in a homey environment it's easier to start the relationship on the right foot.

Make sure everyone feels they are in the right place

A few times during my career I worked in bleak, institutional-looking offices where I felt I didn't belong. It felt safer to check my personality at the door and just go through the motions at work. In these environments, my social connections developed quite slowly. I actually had the best chats with my colleagues on the rare occasions we caught up outside the office.

In spaces with an authentic vibe people tend to come out of their shells more easily. Of course, every business and team has a different take on what an authentic environment looks and feels like. How would you describe yourself and your team? What are your personalities like? Maybe playful, adventurous, dreamy, old soul, peace loving, smart, classy, eccentric, tenacious, rebellious or somewhat outrageous? I suggest you look for social spaces that resonate with you, and where you and your people feel 'at home'.

You also want to bring your unique personal qualities into your conversations. This may take a bit of time, since most of us tend to be polite and cautious when getting to know others, at least initially. But as the relationship develops, it gets easier to show our whole selves, including our messy sides.

Your team sets the rules for what behaviours are acceptable in your circle. Do you want to be kind and polite to each other all the time? Or do you enjoy teasing each other and swearing at times? Nothing is wrong with this if everyone's on the same page. In fact, playful insults and name-calling can be signs of camaraderie and belonging. Most people only let their tongues loose when they feel safe in the team, knowing that no-one will take it the wrong way – so when you hear someone mischievously swear, there's a good chance that they genuinely trust you and feel connected to you.

Make people feel safe to open up

As you're getting to know others, you probably find that you can comfortably talk with them about a growing range of topics. But the reverse is also true. When you have conversations about things you deeply care about – for example, about what inspires and energises you, what scares or hurts you, and what makes you jump out of bed with enthusiasm – your relationships grow stronger.

Some leaders and managers purposefully build workplace cultures where it's normal to feel vulnerable. They lead by example – talking openly about their personal challenges – and encourage others to do the same. We live at a time when many people feel lonely, scared, or lost in some way, and it's reassuring to know that we are not alone. This may sound touchy-feely, but moments of vulnerability do bring us closer and help create a culture of camaraderie.

However, most of us are not ready to expose our soft underbelly at the snap of a finger. If you'd like to engage in deep, emotionally charged conversations, I suggest you look for a place that feels calming, peaceful and safe.

Listen to each other

It goes without saying that it's only worth catching up with someone when you can listen to and understand each other. But there are different levels of listening and understanding. If you can read between the lines, sense what the other person is going through and show empathy – even if they only tell you a part of the story – your connection will become much stronger.

To get to that point, you need to be completely present with the other person and pay full attention. Catching up face to face, rather than virtually, will give you a head start. (We will explore the power of face-to-face interactions in Choice 16). Maintain healthy eye contact – hopefully this comes naturally to you. This is not just common courtesy; eye contact triggers positive emotions and increases attention, as also shown by studies.

To be fully present, you also need to tame internal distractions, including your nagging thoughts and head chatter. So, take your mind off your responsibilities and worries while listening to the person in front of you. It's best if you can meet in a place that doesn't remind you of work. Switch your phone off or set it to silent and put it away – or even better, leave it behind.

Do your best to build rapport. Here is a great little trick: try to become attuned to the other person's conversation style, pace and mood. This will not only make your catch-up more friendly and enjoyable, but will also help you see things through their eyes and get on the same wavelength.

Most importantly, what you need for developing well-connected relationships is emotional intelligence. Thankfully, we can all improve on this – for example, by keeping our habits in check. Interestingly, limiting your screen time, putting your phone away during conversations, and noticing other people's feelings are some of the routines that will help you become a more empathic and emotionally attuned person. Put simply, when you make a habit of being present with others, your emotional intelligence evolves, and in turn, you become even better at building relationships.

Have some laughs, get goosebumps, grab a bite

It's up to you if you're looking to have a fun catch-up or a deep heart to heart. Or you may go with the flow and see where the conversation takes you. Whatever happens, embrace the emotions that come up. Shared emotions and experiences create lasting memories and help build closer relationships.

When you'd like to have a great time, just go for it. You don't need a reason to enjoy yourselves, but isn't it nice to know that having fun together actually strengthens your connections and thus improves your teamwork and performance? (We'll look deeper into this in the next Choice.)

You can have a good laugh pretty much anywhere under the sun. But you might find that a playful environment can help set the mood and invite people not to take themselves too seriously. A lively room in your office, perhaps with bright colours, quirky furniture and humorous imagery, can be an ideal place for a lighthearted catch-up. Or you can pick an exciting venue outside the office. I'm not suggesting you meet at a theme park, but I know people who have actually done that, and the mood was as high as the Ferris wheel.

Food is often called 'social glue', and for good reason. Eating together always helps the conversation flow. You might also want to share a few plates (as health regulations allow), rather than just having your own food. Even such a simple experience can enhance your relationships. (An interesting study suggests that eating together can support increased cooperation and better negotiation outcomes, especially when people share bowls or plates.)

You can also strengthen your connections with others while exchanging very few words – for example, by enjoying sport, music or arts together. You must know what it's like to be a part of a crowd that cheers for the same team or sings along with a band. Goosebumps. But even in a small group, when you share your passion through listening to or playing music, singing, cheering, or just being part of a special moment, you may realise that you have more in common than you thought.

Let me just remind you, hopefully without ruining the fun … While your little group is having a great time, please be mindful of those around you, especially if you're in the office. Distracting your colleagues repeatedly or invading their personal space – even by accident – could hurt those relationships, which is the last thing you want to happen.

TAKE YOUR WORK RELATIONSHIPS TO ANOTHER LEVEL

Work relationships can be incredibly complicated. They can be a source of endless grief and stress, but also immense inspiration and satisfaction. However, the simple, everyday choices you make about where and how you meet people can make a real difference.

You're already spending a lot of time with your teammates, and possibly also with your clients and partners, doing some amazing work together. You have plenty of opportunities to get to know these people better and take your collaboration to the next level. Expect that your work will also become more exciting, and you might also make some new friends.

INDIVIDUAL EXERCISE

Reflect on what your teammates know about you, and what they don't know. What's the reason you don't talk about certain things at work? What would need to happen for you to feel comfortable and inspired to share more about yourself? And what do you think might be holding your teammates back from sharing more about themselves?

TEAM EXERCISES

Experiment with catching up with your teammates in different places; for example, in the office lounge, a friendly cafe, a buzzing pub and a lush park. Do you notice any difference in the tone of your conversations? Where do you find it easiest to build rapport and learn about each other?

Get together with your team and ask everyone to make a list of their personal interests and passions. These could be anything: hobbies, sports and teams, music genres, the arts and artists, books, TV shows, movies, travel destinations, branches of science or technology, periods of history and so on. Then start to mingle and see if each of you can find something in common with everyone else in the team.

Have a chat about artworks with your colleagues. You may talk about the paintings, photos and posters in your workplace (if you have any), visit a restaurant that features artwork, or check out a nearby art gallery. Which pieces do you like? What messages do they give you? Which pieces do you dislike, and why?

CHOICE 15

HOW CAN WE DO GREAT WORK AND HAVE A GREAT TIME?

How serious do we need to be?

How can we use humour and play to increase performance?

Can we have too much fun?

What can happen if we occasionally stop acting like grown-ups?

You're committed to working effectively and ethically – and you expect the same from your team. At the same time, you'd love to have some fun. How can you find the right balance? Well, it doesn't need to be a trade-off. Strategic play, humour and laughter can improve many aspects of performance – including communication, innovation, motivation and trust – as long as you respect the boundaries. So let's explore how you can use fun as a superpower.

'I want my teams to enjoy coming to work. I want them to have fun – but within limits. After all, they've got work to do.' I often hear this sentiment from team leaders. And many team members are also of the opinion that mixing work and play creates murky territory.

So, how much fun is too much? And how can you strike the right balance?

Well, if you're asking yourself these questions, you probably believe – on some level – that working efficiently and having a great time are mutually exclusive. That productive work is not much fun, and thus when you're enjoying yourself, you can't be very productive. This notion has been hammered into our minds since primary school, and throughout our working life.

Perhaps this is why many professionals – including some truly adventurous and free-spirited people I know – are somewhat wary of the idea of celebrating laughter, humour and play in the workplace. Leaders are concerned that their teams' work ethics and performance might suffer, and members fear that their commitment and contribution might not be taken seriously.

Thankfully, we see ever-growing evidence demonstrating how everyone can benefit from a fun workplace. Here are just a few insights.

LAUGHTER CAN HELP YOU FEEL **AND** WORK BETTER

A good laugh relieves stress. It lightens your mental load and relaxes your body, making it easier for you to deal with difficult situations. It also helps you connect with others and build better relationships and friendships.

Laughter naturally makes you feel happier, and happiness can transform your performance.

I'm sure you've noticed that in a positive state you tend to work smarter, communicate better and produce greater results. On the other hand, you'd also know what it's like when you feel stressed, upset or bored – you may procrastinate badly, communicate poorly, and sometimes make a real mess of your work.

HUMOUR CAN HELP YOU FEEL **AND** WORK BETTER

Humour and creativity stem from similar frames of mind. You need to think beyond boundaries and combine distant concepts in new ways. At the same time, you need to keep an eye on reality. A creative idea only has value if it solves a real-life problem, and a joke is only funny if it reminds us of real life. Given these similarities, it's no surprise that humour can open up our creative side, as also shown by studies.

However, I find it especially intriguing how using humour – teetering at the edge of reality and absurdity – can help us communicate better. Sometimes a wicked joke or metaphor is all you need to illustrate a complex idea simply and clearly.

Many people enjoy talking about news they've learned from comedy shows or performances. This is because messages conveyed with humour tend to capture attention while also engaging emotions, which is how you create lasting impressions and memories.

Interestingly, some of the best comedians are seen as trusted sources of news, and for a reason. A news-based comedy act needs to be bold and well-researched to resonate with a wide and educated audience. Jokes based on false information are rarely funny. This is something we can all learn from; to ensure our jokes land well among our peers, we need to understand the truth.

Using humour in the workplace also has myriad other benefits, of course. Don't we all enjoy working more with colleagues we can crack jokes with, and who don't take themselves too seriously? (Studies show that professionals who use humour at work are seen as more desirable teammates, and are also paid more.)

Humour inspires and motivates, and contributes to an inclusive and engaging culture. It creates a relaxed ambience for collaboration, inviting people to express their personalities and share their wacky ideas. It helps build trust and diffuse conflict, and makes it easier for those with different backgrounds to connect with each other.

PLAY CAN HELP YOU FEEL **AND** WORK BETTER

We're hardwired to play. This is how we learn about the world around us and about ourselves as children. But our desire to play doesn't stop as we grow up; we continue to be drawn to activities with elements of play. (This is why computer and mobile games are so addictive, and why so many service providers – including cafes, gyms, supermarkets and airlines – offer some sort of a gamified platform where you can collect points, earn badges or reach different levels.)

While the *wrong* sort of play just kills time, the *right* sort can assist you and your team to kick goals.

In my experience, playing is the fastest way to get to know a person. I've attended company events in the past that incorporated fun games which transformed my relationships with my colleagues. We might have been close workmates for years, but when we were playing frisbee in teams or racing go-karts, I saw a side of them I hadn't seen before.

The workplace also offers plenty of opportunity for playing. For example, some creative businesses frequently start their team meetings around a foosball or pool table. Team members are naturally tuned to tackle challenges and speak their minds when playing games. During these informal conversations, ideas flow freely and solutions to work-related problems often come to the surface.

When we play, our minds are highly receptive to new, unconventional ideas. We tend to focus on the goal of the game, rather than what could go wrong, and so we're not afraid of making mistakes. This makes it easier for us to immerse ourselves in the creative process and be open to where it takes us.

For this reason, games are often used strategically in innovation. In fact, some of the most innovative organisations expect their members to adopt a playful approach to solving problems, and credit much of their business success to this strategy.

And as we see in so many areas in life, playing is a wonderful motivator. When you approach a challenge as a game, you become more committed and resilient. You handle setbacks and obstacles better, learn more and achieve more.

SETTING BOUNDARIES AND CROSSING THEM – BOTH ARE IMPORTANT

Contrary to the common myth, having fun at work doesn't mean chaos. Any team needs guidelines around what's acceptable and useful, including rules for how and when to play.

In the early phases of the creative process when you generate lots of new ideas (in other words, when you use divergent thinking), playfulness is especially useful. But when you select and develop a specific solution (using convergent thinking), or engage in technical or strategic discussions, you generally need to be more focused and serious. A bit of humour can break the ice, but making a witty comment on every item on the agenda won't help you progress.

To bring your best to any situation, you need to be able to transition fluidly between different states. When we were children, we moved in and out of play all the time. And while jumping into play was easy, we didn't really want to stop. However, as grown-ups, our biggest challenge is getting into it. We are more self-conscious and worried about the opinions of others. Therefore, we too quickly judge our out-there ideas as useless or embarrassing, and this can hold back innovation.

In his TED Talk 'Tales of creativity and play', Tim Brown – then CEO of the global design firm IDEO – tells the fascinating story of a study conducted in the 1960s which helped shed light on the nature of creativity. In an experiment, 27 professionals – including engineers, mathematicians and architects – were invited to participate in an evening session. They were also asked to bring a problem with them they had been working on for months but not managed to solve yet. Participants were given a small dose of a psychedelic drug as well as some time to relax, after which they were asked to work on the problems they brought with them. And over the course of just a few hours, they produced an impressive number of interesting and valid solutions. These included new building designs, furniture designs, numerous engineering solutions and the design of a space science experiment. It was a highly innovative evening.

As Brown explains, the most important learning has little to do with the effects of drugs. What this experiment demonstrates is that our adult norms can get in the way of our creativity. But when we break out of our normal thinking patterns and inhibitions, brilliant ideas can rise to the surface.

Overcoming our self-consciousness is not easy, but great workplace cultures and playful environments can help. I'm sure you've seen office spaces that look like theme parks. And while some of them are a bit of a joke (pardon the pun), many of them are designed with the serious intention to help people transition into that inspired and carefree state where game-changing ideas can easily emerge.

IS IT POSSIBLE TO HAVE TOO MUCH FUN AT WORK?

I believe fun has an essential place in every innovative organisation. Fun can lead to greater success while making work more enjoyable for everyone.

It's not a zero-sum game. You and your team can be relaxed and playful, *and* at the same time fully committed and productive. Even while cracking jokes and laughing, you can take your job very seriously. You can 'forget' about your obligations and make unprecedented progress.

So instead of wondering how you can strike the right balance between work and fun, you might be better off asking:

- 'Are we having enough fun?'

- 'What's the right kind of fun?'

- 'How can we do things better by playing more and laughing more?'

- 'What is the best time and place to play games and use humour at work?'

In a trusting workplace culture that values both excellence and fun, you and your teammates will know where the boundaries are and how to play by the rules. You'll also feel more motivated to look after each other and contribute to the best of your abilities.

Are you concerned about how the skeptics you work with might handle all this? Here's my suggestion: invite your inner child to work. Come up with new ideas, communicate your points, and nurture your relationships in ways that feel authentic and inspiring to you. Always keep an eye on your goals, but play and laugh as much as it feels right. And if anyone questions your work ethic or performance, let your results do the talking.

INDIVIDUAL/TEAM EXERCISES

Take a stubborn problem you just can't seem to be able to move past. Can you laugh about the situation? Is there anything ridiculous about it? Explore the funny side of the issue and see how this helps you get a step closer to the solution. (You could also do this exercise as a team.)

Pick an idea you'd like to develop further, and play with it. Forget about risks and boundaries. Imagine that your idea is a child who dares to dream big. What do they want to be when they grow up? What are their 'super-powers'? What kind of magic are they destined to bring to this world? (You could also play this game as a team.)

TEAM EXERCISES

At your team meetings, spend a few minutes with playful activities. Have some laughs. Notice how the dynamics of the team change. Do you notice any shift in attention, engagement, and the quality of ideas? Do you find it easier to solve problems?

Share with each other how you think about play. When is a good time to unleash your imagination and forget what's right and wrong? How can play be helpful? What's stopping you (if anything) from running with your wildest ideas? What are your concerns? And what can help you rise above your inner critic and play full out?

35 SMART CHOICES

CHOICES

PART III

PART III

HOW CAN I MASTER
REMOTE WORKING?

At some point in your career, you've probably worked remotely – either for a few days here and there, or full time. Perhaps you were (or still are) regularly working from home, or in coworking places, cafes or libraries. But even when you're in the office, every time you collaborate with people from other locations, technically you're engaging in remote work.

Some people find remote work a pure joy while others battle with endless frustration. And most of us probably sit somewhere in the middle; we enjoy the convenience and freedom, and at the same time, we struggle with the lack of boundaries, motivation and social connection.

What you and I like and dislike about remote working may be vastly different, but most of us share one thing: after getting a taste of remote work, we eventually realised that it's quite a different experience to what we'd imagined. It presents some unexpected opportunities along with many sneaky pitfalls.

The early days of the COVID pandemic were a massive learning curve for everyone who suddenly found themselves working from home for the first time, but also held a few lessons for those who were already familiar with the practice. A lot of new knowledge and technology emerged during this period, which answered many important questions but also created much confusion.

The tips and insights in this Part will hopefully help you find your way around this maze and stay on top of your game whenever you work remotely or as part of a hybrid team. You'll discover how you can communicate and collaborate effectively, and what it takes to look after yourself and your teammates. We'll uncover hidden traps that can undermine your life quality, wellbeing and performance, and look at strategies to avoid them. And we'll explore when it's worthwhile to make the effort to travel to the office and to see your colleagues and clients in person.

Although this is a huge topic, my research and experience has led me to one simple conclusion: the key to effective remote work is to create the right conditions for your human qualities to shine.

WHEN SHOULD I MEET OTHERS FACE TO FACE?

Why do face-to-face and virtual interactions feel so different?
How can in-person and online meetings lead to different outcomes?
Why should I take the time to travel to certain meetings?
When is it a good idea to meet virtually?

Organising virtual meetings is relatively quick and easy. However, face-to-face conversations often go down a more positive path, largely because people tend to show better versions of themselves when meeting in person. So when should you make the effort to get together physically? It depends on the type of discussion you're planning, as well as your relationships with the people you're going to meet.

Have you ever tried to discuss an issue with your colleagues or clients but didn't think it was necessary to be in the same room? You decided to speak over the phone or the internet, perhaps via email, online chat or video-conferencing, but despite your best efforts you couldn't fully understand each other. The distance between you was not only physical; your opinions and perspectives also remained far apart.

We all know that meeting someone face to face can be a very different experience. When you see people in the flesh and can look into their eyes, hear their true voices and feel their physical presence, you can often sense a more tangible connection. You understand them much better, and equally, you express yourself more freely and get your message across more effectively.

There are many reasons for this. When everyone is in the same room, you get a more complete message. You can see the whole person and hear their undistorted voice. Nothing is lost due to technology issues and limitations, and as a result there are fewer misunderstandings. It's also easier to comprehend people who speak very quickly, very softly, or with an unusual accent.

Face-to-face connection actually triggers physical and neurological changes in your body. For example, it activates certain areas of the brain that don't get turned on when you participate in a virtual meeting. In addition, eye contact releases oxytocin, the so-called 'social bonding hormone', and decreases the level of cortisol (stress hormone) in your system, helping you feel calmer.

VIRTUAL CONNECTION CAN BE APPEALING

Despite the obvious advantages of in-person interactions, there are many valid reasons you might be inclined to discuss an issue via digital technology.

Arranging a face-to-face meeting can be quite a quest. You need to find a time that works for everyone, along with a suitable and available meeting space – a constant challenge in the modern workplace. Some participants might need to travel, which means additional costs and time.

You might also find it more convenient to communicate digitally when the documents you need to use are already in your system, easily accessible on your devices. Email, chat and videoconferencing platforms are also handy if you want to keep a record of your conversations.

Or maybe you just feel you're better at writing than talking. Writing allows you to carefully formulate your message and thus to present your points more logically and compellingly. Written communication also gives recipients the opportunity to reply at a time that suits them, think through their responses first, and obtain additional information if needed.

Remote communication can also be tempting when you need to discuss sensitive issues. Staying behind the keyboard can feel like a safe option, since it allows you to avoid direct confrontation.

So what should you do? Is it worth the effort to physically get together with your colleagues and clients to talk through certain issues, or is it more practical to communicate with them through digital means?

The best approach of course depends on the particular situation. In certain circumstances it's extremely beneficial, and maybe even necessary, to meet people face to face. At other times it makes more sense to discuss things online or over the phone.

SIX VIRTUES YOU'LL SEE MORE OF IN PERSON

Before jumping to conclusions, let's explore more in depth how we think and behave differently when we meet people in person, compared to when we connect with them remotely.

1. Objectivity

Team members can harbour (often unconscious) biases towards each other due to differences in experience, communication style, gender or cultural background. During videoconferences such imbalances are often amplified. People who feel their opinions are superior are more likely to interrupt, while other participants may struggle to be heard. Under such circumstances, it's naturally difficult to evaluate people's contributions or viewpoints objectively.

Something else to think about ... When someone has a different point of view from you, you'll consider each other's arguments more thoughtfully if you can meet in person. You'll also find it easier to overcome any potential assumptions about one another. And if this happens to be your first meeting, you'll be able to form more accurate first impressions of each other.

So, when somebody has vastly different perspectives, or you sense they might have preconceptions about you, or perhaps you're concerned about your own unconscious biases, meeting them face to face will help you see each other for who you really are.

2. Consideration

Have you noticed how quickly people can become detached when communicating remotely? We can see a sad manifestation of this tendency on social media. Some folks seemingly forget that the opinions they read are actually coming from thinking and feeling human beings. When responding, they say things they wouldn't say and use words they wouldn't use if they were talking to a person in front of them.

Of course, you're nothing like these keyboard warriors. However, communicating with others from a distance still influences how you judge and relate to them. You probably find that you're a bit more curious about people when you get the chance to physically catch up. And even when you seem to disagree about something, you tend to be more considerate and kind, more interested in their perspectives and experiences, and thus more successful at finding common ground.

3. Empathy

When you're chatting with a person sitting in front of you, you can pick up subtle non-verbal cues from their voice and body language that today's telecommunication systems are unable to transmit. These might be, for example, the twitch of an eyebrow, a slight rasp in the voice, a tiny change of colour of the skin, or the lift of the chest during a deep breath.

You don't need to be an expert in non-verbal communication to make sense of these kinds of signals. These cues can guide your intuition and, even if unconsciously, help you better understand the other person's thoughts and emotions.

I'm sure you know the feeling when you try to describe an abstract idea or an unusual experience, but language seems very limiting. Keep in mind, the person you're talking to might be experiencing the same frustration, struggling to articulate their thoughts. But this is less of a problem when you connect in person, since you can see into their mind a little and thus get a better grasp of what they are trying to tell you.

4. Openness

It always takes courage to talk about something you care deeply about when you feel uncertain as to how others might react. But if you open yourself up, say, during an online chat or a phone or conference call, you put yourself in a particularly vulnerable position.

Conveying emotionally charged messages can be awfully difficult using technology. Unless people are able to see and hear you perfectly clearly, they could easily misunderstand your thoughts or intentions, which could lead to conflict. Or worse, the response could be dead silence. We can therefore feel somewhat cautious and contrived in remote conversations. And staring at a screen or a camera doesn't make it any easier to expose our thoughts.

In contrast, face-to-face interactions leave less room for ambiguity. We're also able to ask questions in real time and get instant answers and feedback. These are some of the reasons we tend to act more naturally and express ourselves more honestly, and have more genuine, candid conversations in person.

5. Presence

Do you sometimes multitask during phone or conference calls while no-one can see what you're doing? Perhaps you're getting some important work done. Or you're browsing through your inbox, checking the latest news or dipping into social media. Most of us are guilty to some extent. Even if you believe you're capable of focusing on several things at once, these conversations always suffer.

You must know what it's like when you're trying to carefully explain something to your team and you just sense that they're not really paying attention. It's hurtful and frustrating, and an effective way to kill the conversation.

On the other hand, people tend to be more present when sitting down together. They might still check their phones a few times or get lost in their thoughts, but they listen more closely to you, partly because they face fewer distractions and partly because they are more conscious of displaying good manners.

6. Patience

Why is it so hard to stay focused while connecting with others through technology? Part of the problem is that verbal communication is slow, whereas the digital world puts us in a headspace where we expect things to happen very rapidly. Technology allows us to access and browse massive amounts of information in seconds. We might have dozens of windows and tabs open on our device (or multiple devices), and we can switch between them with a click.

Much of the content on the internet is tailored to a short attention span, which only perpetuates the problem. Therefore, when we engage with each other through digital media, we're inclined to disperse our attention and to think fast.

Sitting down with someone, perhaps over a coffee, puts us in a different frame of mind. We slow down a fair bit, and find the patience to explore subjects in detail and to learn from (and about) each other in greater depth.

WHEN ARE IN-PERSON INTERACTIONS MOST BENEFICIAL?

The benefits of human connection are clear. In a nutshell, we tend to see one another more *objectively*, and listen with greater *consideration* and *empathy*, when sharing the same space. We're more *open* to expressing our honest thoughts, and also more *present* and *patient* than in a virtual setting. And it's easy to see how conversations can go down a more positive path when we all bring the best versions of ourselves to the table.

On the other hand, there's also a lot going for modern communication technologies which allow you to connect with essentially anyone from behind your desk. Reaching out to others via email, online chat, phone or video call is often quicker, cheaper and more practical than getting together in person.

Whether it's worthwhile to organise a face-to-face meeting depends a lot on the nature of the discussion you wish to have, as well as the relationship between the participants.

So if you're in charge of arranging meetings, you should weigh up the pros and cons before making a decision. From what I see, in the typical workplace too many issues are discussed online that should be addressed in person. And ironically, too many in-person meetings are held that are simply unnecessary. So much time and energy wasted, and so many problems left unresolved! I'm sure you can help turn this trend around.

Now, let's look at a few situations where *objectivity*, *consideration*, *empathy*, *openness*, *presence* and *patience* are hugely important, and therefore in-person interactions will really pay off.

Building and maintaining a cohesive team

Team members tend to collaborate better virtually after they have already worked together, or at least built a connection with each other face to face. So, before you jump into collaborating remotely with people you don't know well – perhaps because the team has just formed or new members have joined – it's a good idea to bring everyone together. This can be especially beneficial when you join forces with people with vastly different cultural backgrounds and work styles; for example, when you become involved in a partnership between a large corporation and a small entrepreneurial business.

After you've had the chance to sit down for a friendly chat and perhaps also to work side by side for a while, you'll likely feel closer to your teammates, know them better and trust more in one another. You might find you don't even need to run any team-building exercises to achieve stronger cohesion. This can also be a good time to discuss communication strategies and protocols. All this will make communication and teamwork much smoother, even when the team collaborates remotely.

Teams with remote members can also benefit from regular face-to-face catch-ups. In some organisations, remote employees who live close enough regularly travel to the office for meetings. In others, members frequently get together at community events, or attend multi-day retreats once or twice a year where they can work on group projects and engage in social activities. These events are not only productive but also fun and memorable. They bring people closer and make them feel they're part of a great culture.

Discussing complex or ambiguous issues

Work would be so much simpler – and certainly less interesting – if all our ideas and expertise could be translated to documents and spreadsheets. But our minds are nothing like well-organised archives. Some of our most valuable thoughts are tangled with countless irrelevant ideas and questions, as well as an array of memories and emotions.

The problems we face in our jobs are also often complicated; we need to deal with competing priorities, constant change and moving targets. And let's admit, collaboration itself can also be hard work; sometimes our teams and clients can be emotional and unpredictable – they are human, after all.

Put simply, we often try to solve complex and ambiguous challenges with a messy, imperfect mind. Hence, we need all the help we can get to communicate clearly and effectively. We can't afford to have parts of our messages lost in translation or misunderstood because of the limitations of remote communication.

One of the trickiest situations you can face at work is when you and your teammates can't even agree on the basic parameters of the challenge ahead of you, such as:

- What exactly is the problem?

- How will you know if you've solved it?

- What resources do you have?

- What information or resources are missing, and where can you find help?

- What are the priorities, and where can you compromise?

In a situation like this, it's best if everyone gets together face to face to find common ground.

But there's a catch. Challenges like this often come up when a task can't be completed with your existing tools or processes, or when you must innovate to meet new standards and expectations. As such, productive work goes off the boil. This creates extra time pressure, so you naturally want to start working on the solution as soon as possible. To save time, you might be inclined to communicate via emails and phone calls instead of bringing everyone together. But this could be a mistake.

Studies show that trying to resolve a complex or ambiguous problem through digital media can sometimes lead to misunderstandings and conflict. Members often message each other back-and-forth and have several failed attempts before the issue gets resolved – if it gets resolved at all. Now, that's a real waste of time … So when you need to progress quickly, you have even more reason to carve out an extra hour or two to get together with your team and talk things through thoroughly.

Tapping into imagination, intuition and emotions

In this age of artificial intelligence, we can only remain valuable and competitive by doing what machines cannot do: channelling our imagination, intuition and emotions into our work. Our clients and team members alike are looking for real connections and exciting experiences. Their problems are unique, multifaceted and often personal, and we can only give them what they truly need if we're able to move beyond robotic, linear thinking.

I've spent several years in professional environments where some colleagues found me touchy-feely and soft because I refused to mute my right brain. But the business world is different today, and you can find plenty of evidence supporting why it's worth inviting people to bring their whole selves to work.

We tend to think more expansively and solve problems more successfully when we tap into our imagination, intuition and emotions. We learn more quickly and also share our knowledge more effectively. We express ourselves more powerfully, and build stronger and more caring relationships. As a workplace consultant, I've produced my best received works and developed my most fruitful collaborative relationships from this space.

However, most of us can't just drop our guard at the click of our fingers; we need to feel safe and inspired. And being surrounded by empathetic and attentive people who are in a similar frame of mind can really help. When they give instant feedback, and their responses and expressions leave no doubt in our minds about how our words are being received, we're more prepared to play full out.

So, whenever you plan a conversation where you need participants to go deep – perhaps sharing personal experiences, creating an inspiring vision for the future or listening to their sixth sense – make sure you bring them together. (You can also find a handful of other tips in Choice 13.)

Dealing with stress, disagreements and conflicts

Here's perhaps my most important advice: try to discuss issues in person when there's tension in the air. When you're dealing with stressful situations, disagreements and conflicts, for example. When you expect the collision of different opinions and conflicting interests. Or when you're giving feedback that might stir up emotions.

I don't need to explain why *objectivity, consideration, presence* and *patience* are especially important when emotions are high. (Lawyers know this very well. Mediation sessions, for example, can drag on for a very long time when conducted online, and still, they frequently fail. On the other hand, when the parties are in the same room, these sessions tend to be shorter and more often successful.)

Still, in my experience, it's during turbulent times that team leaders and members are most inclined to discuss problems remotely, usually because they want to save time or to avoid in-person confrontation. To make things worse, they often communicate in an ad-hoc manner, being reactive rather than proactive. The outcomes can be less than ideal and potentially disastrous.

We've all experienced stressful and frustrating situations that could have been handled better with smarter communication. For instance, I collabo-rated with team members under significant pressure where none of us had enough time or resources to complete all the deliverables. On other occasions we disagreed about priorities, budgeting, and what our clients really needed. Tense discussions conducted via emails, online chats or over the phone rarely led to satisfactory solutions. Despite our intentions to communicate intelligently, we were not always objective, empathic or patient. Sometimes things were said that created further tension and left a bitter taste.

Even in a well-managed organisation, misunderstandings and stressful situations can occur. To give yourself the best chance to save the day, I strongly recommend that you dedicate time and effort to creating focused, rational conversations where all members are heard – *truly* heard. These discussions might not be a walk in the park, but they will certainly help you and your team understand each other and make the most of the situation while experiencing the least amount of pain. (And when you're already in the same room, you can also break out the boxing gloves ... and have some healthy cardio exercise together. You'll all feel more upbeat afterwards, guaranteed.)

THE HUMAN FACTOR

Work also presents countless other situations where it's worthwhile to meet people in person, including coaching and mentoring sessions, sales conversations, project handovers and debriefs. As a rule of thumb, whenever you intend to share tacit knowledge – such as ideas, insights and experiences that are personal, contextual and thus difficult to put on paper – you can expect better results from face-to-face interactions. (Of course, you can run almost any kind of meeting remotely if you really have to, but you might experience more challenges. In Choice 18 we'll explore how you can bring more human qualities to virtual sessions.)

On the other hand, when you're looking to discuss clear-cut plans, facts and figures, it might be unnecessary to bring people together. You'll probably find you can effectively discuss progress updates, technical issues or routine activities, for example, through videoconferences, phone calls or emails.

Every team, project and situation is different, and the choices are not black and white. However, it's always worthwhile to stop for a moment before you send out a meeting invitation, and ask yourself, 'Could the human factor play a significant role in the conversation I'm planning to have?'

INDIVIDUAL EXERCISE

Keep a 'human factor' journal for a couple of weeks. After each important conversation – whether face to face or virtual – rate yourself as honestly as possible on these six factors: objectivity, consideration, empathy, openness, presence and patience (on a scale from 0 to 10). Then rate your conversation partner as well, based on your perception. Have a look at your notes after the two weeks. Can you see any patterns?

TEAM EXERCISES

Divide your team into two groups and give each of them the same innovation challenge. One of the groups should work together in one room, while the other collaborates remotely. At the end of the challenge, bring everyone together, present both solutions and have a debrief. How do the two solutions compare? What did you enjoy, and what did you find frustrating during this exercise? How effectively could you contribute? And how happy are you with the final result?

Have a relaxed catch-up with your team where everyone shares their personal stories about face-to-face and virtual encounters. Are there any inspiring success stories? Any deeply frustrating experiences? Any surprising ones perhaps? And what can you learn from all these?

CHOICE 17

SHOULD I WORK FROM HOME OR GO TO THE OFFICE TODAY?

What are the pros and cons of working from home?

When should I work remotely, and when should I join my team?

How can I find the right balance between working from home and in the office?

With today's technologies, most tasks can be completed from pretty much anywhere, and you probably have more freedom than ever to decide where to work. So, when you wake up in the morning, how do you make up your mind? There's a lot to consider: working from home, or in your company's workplace, each has its own challenges and rewards. My tip is that you observe how the different environments can influence your focus, motivation, energy and creativity, and you'll quickly learn how to make the right choice.

You wake up in the morning, pour yourself a coffee, look out the window and contemplate the day ahead. You don't have any meetings today that require you to be there in person. You have a lot to do, and you're not really in the mood to get dressed up or leave the house.

How do you decide whether to work from home or go to the office? Do you make up your mind on a whim, or plan ahead? Do you try to spend as much time around your team as possible, or only join them when you need to meet face to face?

Working from home can be tempting when you need a few uninterrupted hours to get things done, or you don't want to face the hassle of commuting. It's also nice to enjoy the freedom and convenience that comes with working by yourself, in your own space. But how effectively can you work at home? Before you head to your wardrobe and reach for your tracksuit or office clothes, here are a few things you might want to consider.

WHERE CAN YOU FOCUS BEST?

At home you're safe from the **usual distractions of a busy office**: loud conversations, colleagues tapping you on the shoulder with a 'quick' question, the eclectic range of ringtones, and so on. You can also find a soothing refuge from the uneasy air of (hopefully occasional) office politics and colleagues with irritating habits. (They are wonderful people of course, but it's a bit difficult to love them while they are humming R&B songs right beside you, chewing on sunflower seeds all day, or sharing the details of their visit to the doctor loudly over the phone.) So when you're tired of trying to stay sane and productive in an often stressful and distracting workplace, your home can feel like an oasis.

However, **keeping your home and work life separate** can be challenging. If you have a comfortable and well-equipped home office, and your family or housemates respect your boundaries, count yourself lucky. Unfortunately, many employees don't even have an adequate desk or chair at home, let alone a dedicated office. In fact, some people can only work at the dining table, on the couch or in their bed, and in such conditions it can be particularly difficult to concentrate all day.

Technology can also be a double-edged sword. You're keeping in touch with your teammates via phone, email and numerous online platforms and apps. But amid the **constant flow of calls, emails and notifications**, where can you find the time to immerse yourself in what you do?

Another question is whether you're able to refrain from **distracting yourself**. When working at home, it's way too easy to procrastinate. The kitchen won't miraculously clean itself, so you might as well get it over with. While you're there, why not grab a snack … And once you're back at your laptop, there are also all those places on the internet you love to visit.

Be honest with yourself. When work is a bit challenging or dull, and there's no-one around to keep you in check, are you able to stay on task? Or do you take countless 'quick breaks', only to find hours later that you've made very little progress?

WHERE WILL YOU FIND MOTIVATION AND INSPIRATION?

If you usually work in an office, working from home on the odd day can be a refreshing change. You probably enjoy being alone with your thoughts for a little while and working in a way that suits you. And having **the chance to concentrate** and tick a few items off your to-do list always helps with motivation.

At the same time, **working from home can be monotonous**, especially when you're alone. Not much is happening around you and nothing breaks up your day. Every hour feels the same. It's also more difficult to feel connected to your team when everyone is far away. You might not miss the distractions of a bustling office, but don't you **miss being around people**?

When you need some stimulation and a community vibe, it's perhaps a good idea to go to the office. Even if you don't actively collaborate with your colleagues, having some company could enliven your spirit and help you work more effectively.

Being around others gives you **a sense of accountability** and the commitment to act professionally. You certainly don't want anyone to see you wasting time with stupid things. More importantly, being visible can also trigger your intrinsic motivation. When you know that your coworkers can see what you're doing, you start to see yourself through their eyes, which helps you gain a broader perspective of your job, and consequently a stronger sense of purpose. Put simply, when you're visible, your work seems more important.

If you can work next to people whose strengths and talents complement yours, you'll likely feel more **motivated to challenge yourself** and up your game. (We looked deeper into this in Choice 11, 'Who should I sit with in the office?') In a social setting, you'll probably also find it easier to let your personal qualities shine. In this turbulent world, your imagination, trust, caring and empathy are the very attributes that will allow you to rise above major challenges and produce transformative results.

Once you've accomplished something, you'll **get a greater buzz** if you're able to share it with others, rather than celebrating in solitude – and this feeling of achievement can give you the drive to keep kicking goals.

HOW WILL YOU STAY ENERGISED?

Have you planned any virtual meetings for the day? Or maybe a bunch of them? Keep in mind that **virtual meetings are more exhausting** than face-to-face catch-ups. We all experienced this during the most intense months of the COVID pandemic when in-person meetings were simply not possible, and our calendars were filled with video calls.

Still, this is all a bit counterintuitive. You don't need to travel any distance. You can log into your meetings from the comfort of your home, in your slippers and track pants, while sipping coffee from your favourite mug. So why do you get so tired?

Technology can give you a lot of grief. But even when it works well, you may **need to concentrate intensely** to understand what people say, and to read the room. Technology only transmits a small fraction of the cues that guide face-to-face conversations, such as body language and tone of voice. It's difficult to grasp how people feel about what's being discussed or who is paying attention. The conversation doesn't flow naturally, and it's hard to tell when it's the right time for you to speak. And we've all had that 'You're on mute!' experience.

The challenges don't stop there ... You're constantly **seeing yourself on the screen,** as if you were sitting in front of a mirror, which can trigger self-criticism. What's more, everyone seems to be looking at you all the time, even when you're not speaking. Nothing is natural about this. Being on display can also make you feel self-conscious. You want to look both professional and genuine, but when you join a videoconference from your messy home office (or living room or bedroom), this can bring up insecurities: *What if my team can see the real me?*

All this is mentally and emotionally taxing. Studies find that videoconference participants start to feel fatigued after around 30 to 40 minutes. And when they attend meeting after meeting, **stress builds up** in just a couple of hours. So when you have lots of meetings scheduled on the same day, I suggest you consider travelling to the office and seeing everyone in person – if that's possible. It's quite likely that overall your day will be more enjoyable and less exhausting, even with the commute.

The reality is that when you work from home, you may be inclined to **work with high intensity** and to exhaust yourself even when you're not in meetings.

After rolling out of bed, maybe you're heading straight to your desk or sofa, or picking up your laptop and getting back into bed. You don't have to walk anywhere, and no-one is asking you to join them for coffee or lunch. All your interactions are online. So you're sitting all day, in the same spot. You're not moving your body, taking breaks or getting fresh air often enough. Your eyes don't get much chance to rest either, as you're continuously focusing on a screen.

You know too well that these habits put **a strain on your body and mind**, and limit what you can achieve. But developing healthy home-working habits takes time and effort. The question is, do you have what it takes to look after yourself and stay energised when left to your own devices?

WILL YOU NEED TO THINK OUTSIDE THE BOX, OR SIMPLY GET THINGS DONE?

Working from home can be ideal for completing straightforward, **process-driven tasks** that require deep focus but little creativity, such as researching, managing data, completing standard reports or answering simple emails. You might find that spending a day in peace and quiet (if your home office offers you this 'luxury') can also **unlock your imagination**. Personally, I prefer to explore certain strategic and design problems and map out my thoughts in solitude.

When you find your groove, you can be incredibly productive at home. However, there's a catch: when you're away from your teammates, you're more inclined to focus on your individual goals and less on your team's goals, and as a result you might **set the wrong priorities**. To work truly effectively, you need to look at the bigger picture and remind yourself what your team is aiming to achieve.

For any team to succeed, it's important to balance efficient, process-driven tasks with innovation. However, **innovating by yourself is not easy** – in order to come up with a breakthrough idea, someone (or something) needs to take you beyond the boundaries of your own thinking. This is why innovative solutions most often arise through in-person collaboration as well as impromptu conversations.

When you work remotely, **you're likely to collaborate less**. Unlike in the office where you can bounce ideas off others, ask quick questions and get help when needed, you're more inclined to figure things out by yourself. And even when you do connect with your team, it's very difficult to generate new ideas and solve complex problems in a virtual environment. Since it's harder to build rapport or to get a sense of how others feel, you're probably more careful about what you say or ask. Without your teammates' full presence, it may feel safer to keep your wildest ideas to yourself.

Unplanned interactions, which are common in the office – such as catching up with people after meetings or bumping into members from other teams in the kitchen – often spark creative ideas and new insights. Seeing what others are working on or overhearing conversations can also inspire innovative solutions. While working at home, you miss out on a lot of these serendipitous, transformative moments.

COMMUTING - WHAT GOOD COULD IT DO?

Few people enjoy commuting. Sitting in a traffic jam during rush hour, or rattling on a train packed with unhappy people who clearly want to be somewhere else – perhaps on another planet – can be disheartening and stressful. And while some people are able to send emails and read documents on public transport, most of us find it very **difficult to do anything productive** during this time.

If you travel to the office first thing in the morning, chances are you'll spend some of those precious hours on the road when your brain is at its sharpest. By the time you arrive you'll have **lost a valuable part of your day**, along with possibly a good dose of energy and motivation.

So when you have the option to work from home, saving yourself all this time and hassle seems to make sense. Understandably, you only want to travel to the office when there's a necessity or some sort of benefit.

But have you considered that the time spent commuting could actually add value to your day, rather than being a necessary evil? A walk or a short bike ride to the office could **energise you and improve your mood,** helping you to start the day on a high note. Personally, I love walking to work. After one of my holidays filled with physical activities, I found it difficult to get back into my usual routine. My body wanted to move, so I decided to walk to the office instead of using public transport. It was time well spent; I not only became happier and fitter, but also more focused and creative. During those walks, I came up with lots of great ideas and solved quite a few curly problems.

And here's another benefit of commuting: it can help you **maintain a healthy work-life balance**. When you work from home, it can be difficult to close your laptop and unplug at the end of the day. The boundaries between your professional and personal life can easily become blurred. In contrast, commuting gives structure to your day, marking the beginning and end of your working hours. After arriving home, you should find it easier to switch off and relax. Even if you sometimes need to do a bit more work, you'll know where the boundaries are, and you'll be able to end your workday without too much guilt.

WHAT IF YOU WORK FROM HOME TOO OFTEN?

If you're highly productive while working from home, you might be tempted to do this really often, and only go to the office once or twice a week. But keep in mind that this may lead to further challenges:

- **Work relationships:** If you spend a significant amount of time away from your team, you risk weakening your social ties. Developing and maintaining close connections and friendships through digital channels is possible, but certainly not easy. The lack of personal interactions could also take a toll on your social skills and emotional intelligence.

- **Visibility:** When you see your teammates less often than they see each other, it's difficult to maintain your influence. In this situation, you and your teammates need to make extra effort to keep one another in the loop and to treat each other as equals; otherwise you might find yourself on the periphery of the team. It's incredibly frustrating when you feel you're shouting in a void, or you don't receive the recognition you deserve because you're frequently out of sight.

- **Learning opportunities:** You might be missing out on opportunities to learn from others and to grow professionally. Impromptu chats and overheard conversations can teach you a lot about your job, but in a virtual environment these are nearly impossible to recreate. It's also more difficult to tap into mentoring and networking opportunities remotely.

- **Health and wellbeing:** Unless you have an ergonomically sound home office, you might be putting your physical health at risk. Bad posture and lack of movement also affect your emotions. In addition, spending a lot of time alone could take a toll on your mental health. Many home-based workers feel isolated and lonely, missing the face-to-face connection with their peers.

- **Work-life balance:** When working remotely, you may feel some pressure to put in extra hours to prove to yourself and your team that you are being productive, and you could soon end up overworked and burnt out. You may also put the expectation on yourself to be contactable 24/7. Without clear boundaries between work and personal time, both areas of your life could suffer.

WHERE TO FROM HERE?

Whether you should work from home or go to the office can sometimes be a tricky decision. But if you spend a few moments in the morning (or the previous evening) thinking through the pros and cons, you'll have a clearer idea of which is the better choice.

You may choose to make the best of both worlds, perhaps by working from home for a few hours in the morning and then in the office during the afternoon. Many people love this schedule and notice that they achieve more each day. Or you may decide to spend the day in a coworking place, cafe or library when you feel you could do with a change in your routine, or enjoy some company – aside from your cat.

Wherever you work, it's a good idea to pay attention to the joys, benefits and challenges you experience in that environment – how it affects your focus, motivation, energy and creativity, as well as your emotional and mental health. After a while, you'll intuitively know which is the right decision for you.

Working at home and in an office both have their difficulties; however, none are impossible to overcome. In the following Choices we'll look into how you can communicate and collaborate better with your team remotely, and how you can also look after your own health and wellbeing.

INDIVIDUAL EXERCISES

For a few weeks, keep track of where you work, using your calendar or diary. Also note down at the end of each day how you were feeling during the day, what your challenges were, what might have been missing, and what you've achieved. Check your notes weekly. Do you notice anything unexpected?

Reflect on the pros and cons of working from home and in the office. Also think about the hidden, not-so-obvious challenges and benefits. What's good about commuting? How can those office-based annoyances and distractions be beneficial? And what are the possible downsides of working in a quiet and comfortable home environment?

TEAM EXERCISE

Experiment with different team schedules. For one week, make sure you're all in the office each day, working side by side. The next week, spend three or four days together. The following week, get together for just one or two days, and work by yourself the rest of the time (either at home or in separate areas of your office). Then have a debrief. Which schedule works best for the individuals and for the whole team? How can you work most efficiently and effectively?

HOW CAN WE COMMUNICATE BETTER IN VIRTUAL MEETINGS?

What does it take to build personal connections via the virtual space?

What communication tools should we use during online meetings?

What are the dos and don'ts of videoconferencing?

How can we make remote meetings more successful?

Online meetings are part of our everyday reality. However, connecting and collaborating with each other via the virtual space is not easy. We need to find the right technologies and make smart choices about how we use them. And the way we engage with each other is just as important; we should listen intently, show support and empathy, and express ourselves authentically. Effective communication takes a lot of skill, but by simply trying to treat others the way we'd like to be treated, we can take huge leaps forward.

I'm writing this Choice during a marathon COVID lockdown in Melbourne. This is a challenging time, when keeping in touch with my teammates (and loved ones) via digital means is not a choice but a necessity. I not only miss seeing people, but as a nerd on this subject I'm also painfully aware how difficult it is to communicate well remotely.

When we're in the same room with someone, the conversation tends to flow differently. For example, it's much easier to explain complex issues, solve problems collaboratively and overcome personal differences. I've also noticed that after catching up with a teammate in person to discuss new ideas, I usually feel more inspired to take action. If we talk remotely, on the other hand, it's less likely that the discussion will have a lasting impact.

The reality is, sometimes our circumstances don't allow us to get together. Still, we should not give in to the notion that our communication must inevitably suffer. Remote meetings are an essential part of our work life, and while it's not easy to get them right, it's not impossible either.

Carefully selected, well-functioning devices, platforms and apps of course play an important part. However, I don't believe that cutting-edge technology is the Holy Grail of effective communication. Even if one day we can sit at our dining tables with impressive, lifelike holograms of our remote teammates, and chat as though we are all in the same room, we'll still need to rise to the challenge.

VIRTUAL COMMUNICATION IS A SNEAKY BEAST

We all express ourselves in unique ways. For instance, we use an individual vocabulary, enriched with quirky words and phrases we love. We speak with our own pace, volume and intonation, and some of us with a strong accent. Some people talk very slowly and take looooong pauses, while others always seem to be in a rush. I know lots of chatty folk who won't stop talking unless interrupted, along with those quiet types who tend to give really short answers. To further complicate matters, we have many things on our minds that we don't put into words, and which are only reflected in our tone of voice and body language.

Even when you meet someone in person, you may need to watch, listen and speak very carefully to truly understand each other. But in a virtual environment, it's even harder. You can't see the whole person, and with limited-quality picture and sound, you miss out on a lot of cues that guide face-to-face conversations. The all-too-common technical problems such as fragmented video and delayed audio do not help. As a result, online meetings are often riddled with awkward moments and misunderstandings.

During a rocky conversation when you and your teammates just can't get on the same wavelength, your feelings and behaviour are naturally affected. Maybe you lose your cool, or you quit trying to get your point across and you withdraw.

But here's the issue that could really hurt your conversations and work relationships if you're not careful: the virtual space brings out different attitudes in us compared to face-to-face meetings, and reveals a lot of our flaws. Most of the time we're not even aware of this.

In Choice 16 I explained that we often think and act more constructively when we get together in person. We are more:

- **Objective:** We think more deeply and objectively about the other person's views.

- **Considerate:** We better understand where the other person is coming from.

- **Empathetic:** We feel more connected to the other person's emotions and experience.

- **Open:** We find it easier to show vulnerability and express ourselves authentically.

- **Present:** We listen more attentively to the person we're talking to.

- **Patient:** We have greater patience to explore subjects in depth.

If any of these tendencies ring true for you, you only need to look at the other side of the coin. Hopefully it's not hard to acknowledge that you may be more *biased, judgemental, detached, reserved, distracted* and *impatient* while talking to others remotely. The same goes for your teammates. So how can you overcome these issues? It's time to rethink online meetings, and make a conscious effort to negotiate the obstacles that stand in the way of insightful, engaged conversations.

AGREE ON GOOD COMMUNICATION PRACTICES AND VIRTUES

A good first step is to have a chat with your team and develop a communication etiquette: How can you all create a safe, inclusive and non-judgemental environment to express potentially radical ideas, concerns and challenges? What do you need to do to better understand one another? How can you become more active listeners? How can you encourage and support each other? What are the most tactful ways to handle disagreements and give feedback?

Here are a few simple practices and virtues I personally strive for, not only because they make virtual meetings more enjoyable and successful, but also because, in my view, they are simply the right way to treat others and yourself.

Put yourself in other people's shoes

When a teammate shares something controversial, think twice before you draw conclusions and respond. Give them the benefit of the doubt. Try to understand their motives, and ask questions if you're unsure where they're coming from. Think about how they might be feeling, and respond truthfully but respectfully.

Be mindful and kind

Your colleagues might be battling with some insecurities, as you possibly do too. During video meetings, many people are somewhat self-conscious. They feel they are on display and the whole team is looking at them. They want to look both professional and genuine, but it can be hard to know where the boundaries are. And when they're joining a videoconference from their messy homes, they may be overcome by shame or self-doubt … In short, it's normal for a person to feel vulnerable in front of a camera – just keep this in mind when connecting with others remotely.

Make sure everyone is heard

In virtual meetings, it can be hard to know when it's the right time to speak and for how long. Some people find it easy to interject and tend to talk a lot. Others speak less often and more succinctly, perhaps because they're a bit nervous, or they're careful not to take up too much space. Therefore, some members may end up dominating the discussion while others struggle to make their point. In fact, potential inequities and biases in a team are often amplified when meeting online. To get around this, make sure that even the quietest members have a fair chance to speak. It can help to ask specific questions and to invite everyone to answer in turn.

Provide instant feedback

During video meetings, it can be difficult to gauge what your teammates are thinking about what you've just said. Have you ever shared an exciting idea, an interesting story or a joke in an online meeting, and had no clue how it landed? You only saw blank faces staring back at you and heard crickets. This is an incredibly awkward but all-too-common situation we all want to avoid. So, I suggest you and your teammates make it a habit to give instant feedback. When someone says something courageous and heartfelt, make sure you respond right away. Let them know if you agree or feel inspired. If it's not the right time to interrupt, you could use the 'reaction' feature of your meeting platform, type in the chat window, share emojis, or make large gestures like thumbs up or a wide smile.

Express your emotions clearly

When meeting remotely, you also need to be more vocal about your feelings compared to when you get together face to face. A person in the same room with you can probably easily tell if you're pumped, relaxed, confused or stressed without you needing to say a word. But your virtual team might not be able to pick up on any of this unless you explicitly tell them. Voicing your feelings may feel a bit odd at first, but this should make it much easier for you and your teammates to get on the same wavelength and understand each other.

Focus with all your attention

Please don't multitask while listening to others, even when no-one can see what you're doing. I'm sure you can sense when someone you're talking to is not paying full attention. Well, other people can sense it too, and this could discourage them from sharing their thoughts openly. Moreover, you're unlikely to have a productive discussion when you're not fully present – so block out all distractions, minimise any windows and silence devices not in use, and focus intently on the person speaking.

Channel your curiosity

When you're listening to someone at the other end of the line, you might start to feel a bit restless after a while. Your brain can process information much faster than a person can speak, so it's not surprising if you find it difficult to be still. But instead of doing something irrelevant to keep your mind occupied, why not use your curiosity in a productive way? You could get more out of the discussion or presentation by making notes or doodling your ideas, for example. Perhaps even better, try to focus on the subtle details of what you're seeing and hearing. You'll grasp much more than what's on the surface.

Slow down a little

Allow plenty of time for conversations beyond what's necessary to cover the agenda. Be okay with going on tangents at times. Explore topics that spontaneously come up. Without a strong sense of urgency, you'll be able to explore subjects more deeply, uncover hidden issues and opportunities, and learn more from each other.

Make time for breaks

Virtual meetings tend to be exhausting, both mentally and emotionally. It's important that you leave enough time to recover between meetings, and also during very long sessions. Ideally, you should spend this time away from the screen, giving your eyes and brain a rest. This will give you the chance to recharge your batteries and bring your best self back to the 'virtual table'.

I know most of these suggestions are common sense, but don't we all forget them occasionally? Sometimes it's good to remind ourselves what it takes to build rapport and connect with others. It starts with the simple intention of becoming better communicators and listeners.

FIND THE RIGHT COMMUNICATION TOOLS – AND USE THEM WISELY

When it comes to communication software and apps, everyone has their preferences and blacklists. Different tools can make it easier or harder for you to express yourself, understand others and learn. (What about you? Which are your favourites, and why?)

It's also worth chatting with your colleagues about their individual communication and learning styles – you might be surprised how diverse your team is in this regard. If possible, take everyone's preferences into account when choosing tools and platforms for different types of meetings. This will help the conversation flow more smoothly, and make it easier for everyone to contribute.

Here are a few tips.

Choose the right media for presenting your ideas

There are many ways to present your ideas during a virtual meeting, just like when you get together in person. Besides talking, you can write down key points on a shared screen, draw graphs, figures and mind maps, and share documents, photos and videos, for example. By choosing your media thoughtfully, you should be able to get your message across more easily and make a stronger impact.

Images, drawings and short videos can be especially powerful, since they allow you to explain complex ideas and tell stories without having to say a thousand words. Visuals also capture attention, which is particularly helpful during online meetings when people tend to have short attention spans. When it comes to technology you have plenty of options, including virtual whiteboards, screen sharing platforms and countless other collaboration apps. Just make sure you pick software programs or apps that let you express yourself powerfully and authentically.

Use video during team calls

Many people prefer to only use audio when joining an online session from home. However, this is like having a conversation in the dark. You're trying to get your points across and find answers to your questions, but no-one can see your face. And when other members speak, they can't really tell if you're paying attention, let alone what you're thinking. Wouldn't it make more sense to 'turn on the light'? You will find it easier to explain your ideas, and you'll feel a stronger connection when you can all see one another. The conversation will flow more smoothly, and you'll interrupt each other less. Being visible will also keep you from multitasking or tuning out.

I had several frustrating experiences in the past when the people I connected with preferred not to use video. They said they didn't want to waste time setting things up and dealing with potential technical issues. The result? We struggled to build rapport and to understand each other. We kept accidentally talking over each other. Despite our efforts, we didn't manage to solve anything – and even worse, our work relationships suffered. So, what exactly was a waste of time?

Think twice about using a virtual background

People have different views on this. A background protects your privacy, and a creatively selected image can also provide an interesting talking point. However, I believe that a virtual background can sometimes stand in the way of personal connection and collaboration. No-one should feel the need to hide where they are. If you agree, just let your teammates know that they don't have to put on a 'professional facade'. It's okay if their place is a bit messy, their child interrupts or their cat poses in front of the camera – they still do a wonderful job.

Set the scene for a flowing conversation

During informal discussions and brainstorming sessions, you want everyone to speak spontaneously, dropping their guard. For these meetings, choose communication tools and platforms that allow you to show personality, express feelings and bring in humour. Check how everyone feels about the different options. You might find that platforms with serious styles and clunky functionality make some people feel cautious and guarded, while user-friendly apps with playful, informal vibes help them relax and open up.

Also pay attention to the view mode of the platform you're using. Some of them offer the feature to see yourself and your teammates on the screen as if you were sitting in the same room. Interestingly, after switching to this setting, many people find it easier to participate in an open discussion and speak naturally.

Again, make sure everyone is heard

Some digital collaboration platforms are designed to create a level playing field for everyone. You could, for example, set up activities where everyone has 10 minutes to answer a question in writing, or to vote on their favourite ideas. It's possible to keep all responses anonymous, if you wish. Such features can be particularly useful in environments where hierarchies or biases are present. While in a great team psychological safety and inclusion are strong, some organisations still have a way to go. Giving all participants an equal opportunity to contribute – with the help of technology – should help steer the culture in the right direction.

Approach sensitive issues and conflicts thoughtfully

When it comes to difficult conversations like addressing performance issues or conflicts, you need a tailored approach. Creating a safe and non-judgemental environment is especially important. At certain times, you and your teammates might find it easier to talk openly and to share your feelings over the phone, rather than via video. Phone calls can feel more private, because there are fewer distractions, and you don't need to put yourself at the centre of attention. However, at other times it may make more sense to talk through differences within the team using video.

Discussing problems in writing can also help in certain situations, because it gives you the opportunity to sort out your thinking and give a level-headed response. You don't want anger or frustration to guide your words. But at the end of the day, it's best to settle on common ground while looking into the other person's eyes – even through a camera.

BECOMING BETTER HUMANS

When all you need to do is discuss straightforward, unambiguous information with your colleagues, you certainly have an easier job. You may not even need a meeting, and can successfully work through issues in writing. But you and your teammates are not robots, and as smart, creative and sensitive human beings, you have greater roles to play than just the cold exchange of data. To thrive as a team, you need to understand each other on a deeper level.

This is harder to achieve in a virtual environment, and using appropriate, functional tools is only the starting point. You need to make smart choices about how you use technology, and just as importantly, you need to set the intention to become better communicators and listeners.

If you're able to express yourselves more richly, make more careful judgements, and look after one another as if you were all in the same room, you and your team will handle challenges better and reach greater heights. You might even become better humans … And naturally, when you do see each other in person, you'll continue reaping the benefits.

INDIVIDUAL EXERCISES

Once your team has agreed on a communication etiquette, write down the key points on a piece of paper and put it on your desk as a reminder. Do your best to live up to it. After your next online meeting, ask yourself: how did the meeting go, and what was your experience like?

Think about the different tools and technologies you could use to present your ideas to your team. Try out your favourites and see what kind of feedback you get. Did you manage to get your point across? Was it easier than just speaking?

TEAM EXERCISES

Experiment with different meeting practices and technologies, and see how the vibe and flow of conversations change. For example, you could run a meeting with everyone using a virtual background, and another one with no-one using it. You can also experiment with turning the video on or off, using various videoconferencing platforms, and so on.

Have a conversation with your team about the various challenges and discomforts you each experience during virtual meetings. Are there any common threads? What could you do differently to make these meetings easier and more enjoyable for everyone?
For the second part of this exercise, pick a platform that allows participants to answer questions anonymously. Again, ask your teammates to describe the challenges they experience during online sessions, and to share their ideas about how you could work better as a team. Are there any new insights? Was anonymity helpful in any way?

HOW CAN WE COLLABORATE MORE EFFECTIVELY IN A HYBRID TEAM?

How can remote and office-based colleagues successfully work together?

How should we run meetings in a hybrid team?

How can we ensure that everyone is an equal member of the team,
regardless of their location?

Some of your teammates are in the office while others are working remotely. How can you collaborate effectively? Here's the key: make a conscious effort to treat each other as equal members of the team. Everyone should be fully included, heard and valued, regardless of their location. Create a level playing field where office-based and remote members alike can bring their best game.

Imagine you're catching up for lunch with a group of friends. You can't wait to see everyone, hear what they've been up to and chat about your favourite topics. But there's a small issue. One of your friends, Thomas, has a hearing problem – he can only hear people well when they sit right next to him or speak very loudly. Thomas is in his element when meeting only one or two mates, but he struggles to follow the conversation in a larger group. During the lunch, he asks people a few times to speak up and repeat what's been said, but he doesn't want to be a nuisance.

Thomas has many fascinating ideas and stories to tell. Unfortunately, he finds it challenging to join conversations. He doesn't want to accidentally repeat what's already been said, or to say something out of context – that would make him look silly, as if feeling like a second-class citizen already wasn't bad enough. By the time he gathers what everyone has been talking about, the conversation has moved on. So Thomas mostly remains quiet. He's smiling, trying to look positive, but he'd rather be somewhere else.

I've been at many gatherings in the past where one or two guests found it difficult to fully participate, because of certain disadvantages. At those times, I thought I was doing enough by paying special attention to them every so often. However, only when I had similar experiences myself did I start to understand what it's like to be on the outer.

I have no hearing problems, thankfully. But in recent years, I attended several team meetings where I was at a clear disadvantage: I logged in remotely while almost everybody else was in the same room. Although I knew that my teammates appreciated and cared about me, and were trying to involve me in the discussion, the distance between us was palpable. I was 'Thomas' in those meetings, feeling small, disconnected and helpless.

TWO VASTLY DIFFERENT EXPERIENCES

The situation where some people are physically present in a meeting room while others join virtually is probably not foreign to you. These so-called hybrid or blended meetings are becoming increasingly common, with more and more people working regularly from home, but not all at the same time. In many workplaces, it's a rare moment when a whole team is in the office together, or when every single member works remotely.

When you attend a hybrid meeting virtually, you have a vastly different experience compared to those who are in the office together. Which experience are you more familiar with?

When you're in the office, there are no obvious major hurdles. After setting up videoconferencing equipment (and ensuring it actually works), you can carry on business as usual and talk as if the whole team was sitting around the table. Technology allows you to interact with remote members relatively smoothly as long as you can see their faces on the screen and hear their voices clearly enough.

On the other hand, when you connect virtually, participating is hard work. Chances are you can't see or hear everyone and you miss parts of the conversation. It can also be difficult to find the right time to speak and to capture your team's attention. Even when you have a lot to contribute, and your teammates respect your knowledge and experience, you may still struggle to have an equal share in the discussion. And having to jump hurdles to be heard is naturally frustrating and exhausting.

What makes this situation especially confronting is the fact that there's no-one really to blame. We all know that it's easier to connect face to face. What's more, we're actually hardwired to pay more attention to people we see in the flesh. We also tend to have higher opinions of those who are physically close to us, and value their efforts and knowledge more. Being aware of our own unconscious biases unfortunately doesn't solve this problem – our thinking and behaviour are still affected. However, when you don't receive the attention and appreciation you deserve from your team, knowing that it's just human nature won't make your life any easier.

When hybrid meetings are not set up and managed well, everyone is impacted. Remote participants often lose enthusiasm and decide to step back when they realise that they are at a disadvantage, and as a result, the team misses out on their valuable input. To make things worse, the frustrations that arise from unequal opportunities and experiences (a phenomenon called 'presence disparity') can also escalate into personal conflicts.

DIFFERENT WAYS TO PROMOTE EQUALITY

So how can you create equal experiences for everyone? Well, this is a tricky problem. You can't give remote members the perfect illusion that they are in the office, surrounded by their teammates. However, office-based members have the option to act as if they were by themselves. Trello and then Atlassian have run with this idea and developed a strategy which is now widely known: when the time comes to meet, team members in the office actually disperse. They say goodbye to each other momentarily, find a quiet spot, and join the meeting via their own laptops or devices. This gives everyone an equal opportunity to be involved and to contribute to the conversation.

Is this a good idea? Well, many teams swear by it, because this strategy supports transparent communication and an inclusive workplace culture. In fact, some teams rarely run in-person meetings anymore. Others hate this idea with a passion since it deprives them of the irrefutable benefits of face-to-face collaboration. And some organisations opt for a third option; instead of virtual meetings, they prefer long-form written communication, such as emails and discussion threads, to explore issues and solve problems.

I suggest you try out various strategies a few times before committing to one. You might find that you have a clear favourite, or that different approaches suit different situations. There are a lot of pros and cons to consider … What's best for the individuals, and for the team as a whole? Which strategy supports productivity and innovation? And what's the smartest way to nurture your workplace culture and relationships?

GIVE EVERYBODY A FAIR CHANCE

I would also question whether it's worthwhile to even try to provide similar experiences for everyone. In my view, you can invite equal participation and engage each person by focusing on inclusion and fairness. You want to make sure that each person receives the same level of attention – regardless of their location – and feels heard and understood. All ideas and views should be considered with equal weight, and all contribution should be evaluated objectively.

Here's the bottom line. If you're part of a hybrid team – even when only one person attends the meeting virtually – you should adopt the mindset of a remote member. You need to follow similar communication practices as if you were attending a fully remote meeting. (We drilled down into this in Choice 18.) For example, it's important that you make space in the conversation for everyone, provide instant feedback, express your emotions clearly, and allow enough time to discuss issues without having to rush. Naturally, you should also focus all your attention on the person speaking, and make a point of treating people the way you want to be treated.

In the lead up to a meeting, I recommend that you plan things carefully and stay highly organised. When possible, distribute a detailed agenda (and other pre-meeting materials) in advance to make it easier for the team to get on the same page. Select communication tools and media that will help engage everybody in the conversation. And finally, set up your meeting space in a way that each participant can see and hear everyone else clearly, throughout the whole meeting. Let's explore how you can achieve this.

CREATE SPACE FOR SEAMLESS VIDEOCONFERENCING

It's time to put an end to those tiresome videoconferences where communication is a struggle for almost everyone. You know what it's like … People in the meeting room are sitting around a long table. They can't see each other well, and the whole set-up suggests hierarchy. Only a single camera and microphone are in use, so participants at the other end of the line only get snippets of what's happening in the room. You can do so much better!

Naturally, you need to make sure that the meeting space works for those physically present. There's a lot to consider, including the look and feel of the interior and the type of furnishings. You need to decide about a suitable seating arrangement as well. U-shaped, semicircular and theatre-style layouts, for example, each support different types of meetings, presentations and workshops. You may choose to sit around one large table, or in small groups at several small tables.

You should also carefully consider the location of whiteboards and any other surfaces and tools your team might want to use for capturing ideas and sharing information. People in the room will need to be able to see these easily, without twisting in their seats. All this might require some experimentation and planning, but getting it right is critical. There's no point making all that effort to engage remote participants if the experience of office-based members is compromised.

The next essential step is to set up videoconferencing equipment to support the natural flow of conversation. Place screens, cameras and microphones in a way that every single member – whether physically present or joining remotely – can clearly see and hear each other. Make sure that people in the office stay on camera even when they move around the room.

It's best to use separate screens for showing remote participants and for sharing content, rather than switching between the two views back and forth. This way, everyone will be able to see each other throughout the session, and at the same time, follow the discussion without interruption – just like in a face-to-face meeting.

Whiteboards and other writable surfaces will also need to be on camera. Or you might have the option to use a digital (or interactive) whiteboard – a physical device you can write or draw on directly, and which allows you to add notes and images from your own devices as well. Remote members are also able to see the content of the whiteboard on their screens and to contribute with their ideas.

Setting up a space for seamless videoconferencing is, without doubt, a logistical and technical challenge. You may need to explore a few different arrangements and use more pieces of equipment than you currently do. But you'll find that with the right technology and set-up, the dynamics of your meetings will transform. Rather than trying to overcome the distance barrier, people will be able to focus their efforts on helping the team succeed.

INNER CIRCLES AND OUTER CIRCLES

Apart from creating communication challenges, hybrid working can also test your relationships and workplace culture. Naturally, people in the office find it easier to build trusting relationships. They can work side by side, hang out together, and share stories and ideas with each other that no-one else can hear. And they probably find it easier to understand and appreciate one another, because this is (guess what!) human nature.

In contrast, when you frequently work away from your team, you have a good chance of eventually finding yourself in the 'outer circle'. As you rarely see your teammates in person, it's much harder to influence what they think of you. When you talk to them, you sense that they know things you don't. Bringing your ideas to life can be particularly challenging, because you may not get a fair chance to prove your point or address potential objections. And when you'd like to share some of your unique knowledge, it's difficult to find the time. If you could just attend those lunchtime catch-ups and Friday drinks, things would be so much easier!

When you have a disagreement with someone – which, by the way, is completely normal even in a well-functioning team – resolving it remotely is not easy. Your relationships with other teammates could also suffer if you don't get the chance to talk to them in person. Have you ever had an argument with a family member or a colleague you rarely saw in person? Chances are that people close to that person all took the same side, since they could only hear one, incomplete version of the story.

In short, remote members have a more difficult job contributing to the team and initiating change. On top of this, their skills and the value they bring are often underestimated compared to their office-based colleagues, because they are out of sight. So it's not surprising that remote members frequently miss out on recognition and promotion, which has been observed in hybrid teams worldwide. As you can imagine, 'it feels like a kick in the guts' – to quote a hard-working but unfortunate friend of mine who is a textbook example of 'far away and forgotten'.

IT'S TIME TO REDEFINE THE MEANING OF REMOTE

So, what can you do to create a truly inclusive and cohesive team? Running effective meetings is only the starting point. If you can't bring the whole team – every single person – together on a regular basis, you need to operate with the principles of a remote team, every single day. (We'll delve deeper into this in the next Choice.) Let me reiterate, because it's so important: if one person is remote, the whole team is fundamentally a remote team.

It's essential that you communicate skillfully and look after your relationships with extra care. Your workplace culture is a precious commodity, which can easily be hurt in an imbalanced environment. You don't want any of your teammates to feel like Thomas, and you certainly don't want to discourage anyone from sharing their magic.

INDIVIDUAL EXERCISES

Catch up with a teammate you rarely talk to one on one – either via video, or if possible, face to face. Have a relaxed chat. Do you see them any differently after this conversation? Do you understand them better? Can you now see a side of them you haven't seen before?

For one week, keep a journal of your conversations with your teammates. Write down who you're talking to, and whether it's a work-related or a social chat. Look at your journal at the end of the week and see if you notice any patterns.

Record one of your hybrid meetings and watch it back. Focus on the people attending remotely. Are they participating fully? Do they take equal part in the conversation? Do they receive a fair share of attention?

TEAM EXERCISES

Run a quick survey in your team. Do people feel they have a fair chance to influence decisions? Do they feel heard and considered? And do they feel valued, appreciated and connected to the team? See if there's a divide between the answers of office-based and remote members.

Pick a few days when everyone will work from home. Run meetings and communicate with the usual frequency. At the end of this exercise, ask people who usually work in the office what they have learned about remote collaboration.

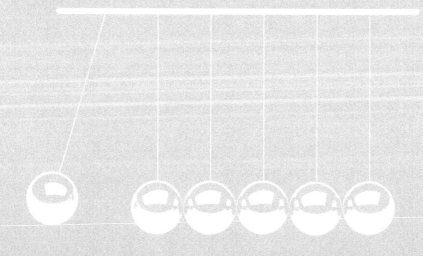

CHOICE 20

HOW CAN WE COLLABORATE BETTER REMOTELY?

How can we create a strong workplace culture remotely?

How can we communicate more effectively in a distributed team?

How can we maintain strong relationships from a distance?

Remote and face-to-face collaboration require different skills and strategies. Without the right approach, remote work can become an isolating experience; but when you get the hang of it, you can conquer challenges together as if you were in the same room. To successfully work together from a distance, you and your teammates need to organise yourselves carefully, and proactively plan for those kinds of interactions that would naturally occur in an office.

My favourite science-fiction book, *The Martian Chronicles* by Ray Bradbury, was published in 1950. One of the stories in this book, 'The Long Years', tells the touching tale of a doctor who is accidentally left behind with his family on an abandoned Mars. Tragically, his wife and three children soon die of illness, and the desperate doctor creates lifelike android replicas of his loved ones to combat his loneliness. He does his best to live a 'normal family life', while waiting and hoping that someone will rescue him. Two decades later a rocket arrives … but it's not exactly a happy ending.

Some sixty years after *The Martian Chronicles* was first published, Andy Weir's novel *The Martian* hit the shelves, and soon after, it was adapted for the big screen. If you've seen the movie with Matt Damon's stellar performance, you know that it's an upbeat story about ingenuity, resilience and teamwork. Matt Damon's character, a botanist, is left behind on Mars, alone and injured. Determined to be rescued, he manages to establish a connection with Earth. As you'd expect, earth-bound politics complicate things, but after overcoming a series of adversities, he is successfully brought home.

These two stories are vastly different, but just like any great piece of science fiction, they both tell a lot of truth about our lives in the here and now. The tragic tale of the doctor reminds us how desperately we need human connection. The feel-good story of the botanist shows that it's possible to collaborate effectively over any distance. We also learn that with the help of strong relationships we can conquer massive obstacles. And both narratives make the point that technology can bring us closer to each other – physically and emotionally – if we use it wisely.

DO YOU FEEL LIKE YOU'RE STUCK ON MARS?

Working remotely can sometimes feel like you're alone on a distant planet.

I'm not talking about you working from home once in a while to have a bit of quiet time or the flexibility to take care of some personal issues. I'm talking about you being away from some or all of your teammates most of the time, which is a vastly different experience.

To succeed in remote work, you need to master specific skills. You also need to make an extra effort to collaborate effectively and to maintain close connections with your teammates. Without preparation and discipline, things can go down in flames. Communication may break down, relationships may suffer, and teamwork may fall apart. But if you get it right, remote work can bring wonderful opportunities and an amazing experience.

I'm about to share a few tips and strategies to master the art of remote collaboration. These should make your life much easier if you work away from your team on a regular basis. But you'll find these equally relevant if any of your teammates work remotely, if you work in a hybrid team where you rarely see everyone together, or if you're collaborating with another team that's based in a different location. Remember, even if just one member is remote, the whole team should operate as a remote team.

Okay, it's time to take off.

1. COORDINATE WORK CAREFULLY

Remote collaboration is a monster challenge, and to get on top of it you need a lot of structure. You need to be more organised, and to implement more detailed systems and processes compared to what traditional office-based work requires. You may not get a kick out of meticulous planning and coordination, but with the right preparation you can make remote collaboration highly rewarding, rather than a disaster.

Set clear goals and targets

Make sure there's no ambiguity around what you're aiming to achieve as a team, and who is doing what. In *The Martian*, the objective is straightforward – bring the protagonist home safely – and every single person contributing to the mission has well-defined roles. Just imagine the chaos otherwise.

Even when everyone works in the same space, teamwork is most effective if members understand how the pieces of the puzzle come together. But in a distributed team it's especially important to operate in a coordinated way. What problems are each of you solving? What deliverables are you working on? What are the agreed milestones and deadlines? And who has the answers to specific questions?

Naturally, things don't always go to plan, but when something unexpected happens, changing an existing strategy is usually easier than coming up with a new one from scratch. Agreed goals and targets also allow you to evaluate your teammates' performance objectively – and equally, to receive a fair evaluation from others. As we touched on earlier, it's hard to objectively judge the performance of people you don't see very often, unless their KPIs are very clear.

Find a good rhythm for communication

When you all work side by side, you can sense if a teammate prefers to be left alone or is happy to be approached. Starting impromptu conversations and meetings is easy. Communication in the team picks up a natural rhythm and information flows smoothly. Achieving the same level of connectedness from a distance, however, is a real challenge. You want to interact often enough, but without creating unnecessary distractions or wasting time.

For your remote team to work like a well-oiled machine, you need to create structure around how you keep in touch – including when you provide updates, discuss certain issues and make decisions together. When should the whole team get together? When should you be available to take calls or answer messages? And when is a good time for everyone to focus on their own tasks?

Experience shows that it's more effective to communicate in bursts than in an ad hoc fashion. But it's up to you to decide what rhythm works best for your team.

Some teams lean towards synchronous communication; in other words, catching up often, being available for each other most of the day, and discussing pretty much any topic in real time. Others opt for asynchronous communication, which means they allow members to participate in conversations in their own time. Asynchronous teams have short and infrequent meetings, and aim to work through most issues in writing, via emails, chats and shared documents.

Both approaches have their benefits and drawbacks, so I suggest you discuss with your teammates where to draw the line. Take into consideration the nature of your work and your culture when deciding about the frequency of your meetings. It's also worth having a chat about individual work styles and communication styles, so you can come up with a schedule that suits everyone.

Choose your communication tools

Okay, now that we've looked at the timing of communication, the next question is, which channels and platforms will you use for different purposes?

Again, all options have their pros and cons. For example, email allows you to write carefully considered messages and to easily keep records of what has been discussed, but it might not be the best media for expressing your intentions and emotions. Video is great for building personal connections and exchanging quick feedback, but on the downside, many people feel self-conscious and uncomfortable in front of a camera. Making a phone call is quick and easy, and you may find that it provides a safe space for talking through sensitive issues. At the same time, relying on voice alone to get your message across can be quite limiting.

And then there are countless online communication and collaboration platforms available, with a variety of features and qualities, each shaping the flow of conversation in its own way.

Any communication platform can support flowing and productive discussions, and equally, give way to confusion, misunderstanding or tension. However, you'll probably find that different types of conversations flow better on different platforms. (I personally prefer to explore ideas with my teammates via video calls, share new discoveries through chat, have social catch-ups over the phone, and resolve simple misunderstandings in writing.) So I suggest you experiment a little to work out where certain types of discussions should take place to get the best results. (You can also find some tips in Choice 18, which looks deeper into virtual meetings.)

Disconnect when the time is right

While working away from your team, out of sight, you might feel pressured to be always 'on'. In fact, many remote workers fall into the trap of making themselves available all the time, even outside of work hours, because they want to prove to their teammates that they are being productive and helpful.

This is of course counterproductive. Just like when you work in an office, sometimes you need to block out all distractions and disconnect completely to get things done. You also need time to switch off and rest. After you've discussed with your teammates when you should be contactable and connected – an agreement which you'll no doubt respect – make sure you respect your own boundaries too.

If you think it's necessary, discuss with your team how you can be reached in case of emergency, and what actually constitutes an emergency. Then, when the time comes to disconnect, silence your phone, change your online status to 'away', switch off notifications, and take a break from emails and messages. Make the most of your quiet time – whether you want to concentrate, contemplate or simply relax.

2. SHARE INFORMATION AND PROVIDE FEEDBACK

Even in workplaces where people see each other in person every day, communication issues are common. But when your means of connection is reduced to the digital space, leaving things to chance is a doomed mission. To keep everyone in the loop, you need to be deliberate about sharing your thoughts and knowledge with your teammates. This takes time and focus, but the payoffs are enormous.

Share what you're working on

Don't wait until a piece of work is complete to show it to your teammates. Sharing your work in progress will make the collaboration much more effective.

I know, it's easier said than done. I don't always feel comfortable showing my messy drafts to anyone. There are so many loose ends, and with lots of ideas still only in my head it's nearly impossible to explain what the final outcome will look like. But I've learned that this is an essential part of teamwork.

The more you share, the better you understand each other's thought processes. By seeing everyone's half-finished work, you can exchange ideas, help each other out and inspire one another. This is also how you make sure the project is coming together nicely – there are no holes, no double-ups and no redundant efforts.

When you work remotely, your colleagues can't just pop over to your desk and peek over your shoulder, so you need to bring your work to them. For example, you could share images and documents online, or talk about your progress in video calls. These conversations don't need to be formal – the point is to keep each other in the loop and move together as a team. This routine can also be very motivating, making you feel visible and accountable, even though you're far away.

Provide frequent feedback and recognition

Some of your teammates might be more independent, confident and motivated than others. However, everyone needs regular feedback to stay on course and engaged, and remote workers need it even more often than office-based members.

Interestingly, as studies show, the majority of people prefer to receive constructive feedback over recognition. I can certainly relate. While a lack of praise can be a bit upsetting, it's rarely as painful as sensing your colleagues' or manager's dissatisfaction with your work but having no clue as to what the issue might be. (Although if you leave somebody on Mars, you can probably guess where you went wrong.) Of course, it's not exactly fun to hear about your mistakes and shortcomings, but the point is that you learn and become better at what you do.

Keep in mind that giving constructive feedback can be just as challenging as receiving it, especially in a digital environment. And like many people, you may have a tendency to sugar-coat criticism, or to avoid it whenever possible. So how can you make these conversations easier and more straightforward? The answer is reassuringly simple: offer feedback as often as possible. Build it into your routine.

Frequent feedback tends to be more accurate, and thus more useful. It allows people to make minor course corrections early on, rather than having to go into damage control later. Such conversations also build trust and connection within the team, and help everyone work in sync.

Naturally, you want to share positive feedback just as generously. Say 'thank you' often, and help each other to see how everyone's efforts translate to tangible results. You all want to be motivated by making a difference rather than an unhealthy desire to prove your worth.

Schedule online learning sessions

Have you realised just how much smarts you pick up from your colleagues when you share the same space? Studies show that in the physical workplace, people tend to learn more about their jobs through impromptu chats and overheard conversations than through formal training.

In a remote team you could miss out on the chance to pick up some priceless insights. In my experience, at the end of virtual team meetings everyone tends to be in a rush to get back to their tasks. There is always something urgent to do, and if you keep waiting for the perfect time to exchange knowledge, you'll find that it never happens.

You need to be proactive. Consider scheduling informal learning sessions with your team. If you live close to each other, it's worth getting together in person, but you can easily run such sessions online too. I attend virtual knowledge sharing events around once a month, with participants from all corners of the globe, and I find them invaluable.

Here's a tip: to get the most out of a session, pick a discussion topic in advance, raise a couple of questions you'd like answered, and share some reference materials about the subject – so that people can prepare for the conversation. If someone happens to be a subject expert, they can run a short presentation, but always allow a generous amount of time for a free-flowing conversation.

Share all news and updates

In the office, you probably don't think twice before sharing interesting news with your closest colleagues … Some unexpected feedback you've received from a client. A new project opportunity in the air. An uncanny introduction to a business prospect you've been hoping to meet for a long time. A podcast you've stumbled upon that's worth listening to. You finally got Matt back from Mars.

These kinds of updates are not actually that important – in isolation. However, by sharing them you're letting people know that you're thinking of them and that you care, which in itself is very important.

So, make sure that no-one in your team feels left out or forgotten. Connect with your teammates frequently, and share all news and updates with them, no matter how small. Don't just discuss issues and decisions that they must know for their jobs. If it's worth talking about with a colleague over a coffee, it's also worth sharing with those far away.

3. BUILD AND NURTURE SOCIAL BONDS

We are social beings, wired to belong. In Ray Bradbury's tale 'The Long Years', the lonely doctor installs speakers throughout a deserted city to fill it with the sounds of daily life – airplanes, cars, people talking – so that it feels like a lively and buzzing place. This story was written more than 70 years ago, by a man with a limitless imagination. How relevant is this idea today?

Well, in recent years, once it became clear that many people who had to work from home missed the noises of their offices, several apps were developed to fill this void. These customisable apps – including 'Sound Of Colleagues', 'Calm Office' and 'I Miss The Office' – allow you to mix different sounds such as a coffee machine, keyboards, muffled conversations and printers. Rain on the window and the office dog are parts of my favourite mix. Munching, humming and ping-pong are definitely not for me, thank you.

Times are changing rapidly, but our connection to others remains a core part of our human experience. When we're in the office and some of our coworkers are getting under our skin, it's perhaps hard to imagine that we'd ever feel very lonely without them around – but ironically, we do. What we miss the most when working remotely, according to studies, is people: social activities, impromptu catch-ups, and the sense of being a part of a community.

It's not easy to maintain personal ties through digital channels. Without frequent social interactions, relationships can fade, which inevitably affects workplace culture and performance. To nurture trusting and supportive relationships, you and your teammates need to make plans for social activities and experiences, filling the hole created by the physical distance.

Allow time for social interaction

In the office, conversations don't always revolve around work. You bump into your colleagues at the coffee machine, hang out in the break room, travel to meetings together – and you chat about whatever's on your mind. Your favourite TV series, holiday plans, current affairs, sport – you name it. And naturally, with frequent social interactions, your personal ties become stronger.

When you work remotely, you can't leave things to serendipity. You won't accidentally bump into your workmate in the kitchen. You need to set aside time, and make plans for nurturing your personal connections. It could feel a bit odd at first to recreate 'spontaneous' catch-ups in the virtual space, but after a bit of experimentation I'm sure you'll get the hang of it.

Your options are limitless. Call a teammate each morning to check how they are doing and what's happening in their lives. Dedicate the first few minutes of your team meetings to social conversations. Run virtual lunches or after-work happy hours.

Staring at your teammates in the name of social connection can be quite awkward, so you'll probably need to create some structure to make your catch-ups engaging. For example, you could play social games, or organise brainstorming sessions to tackle non-work-related challenges.

And why not think outside the box? Many remote teams hold wacky, themed events like pyjama days, talent shows, yoga sessions, 'meet my pet' days, cooking classes and painting sessions. Some even attend virtual reality events together. Do any of these sound corny to you? Same here, but the people involved love them – and that's what matters. Just go with whatever seems fun.

While it's nice to have a great time, you don't want to ignore the personal struggles and frustrations your colleagues might be experiencing. So it's a good idea to balance fun activities with serious conversations where you can lend each other an ear and offer emotional support.

To help everyone get into the right mood, it's worth running virtual social activities on platforms that are different from those you use for work. And even though nurturing social connections is important business, to ensure they serve their purpose you want to make these activities optional. If they're attractive enough, people will want to join in.

Get together in person

Meet your remote teammates in person once in a while, if possible. I'm sure you know what it feels like when you catch up with a good friend you haven't seen for a long time – the friendship suddenly feels stronger and more real. In this regard, work relationships are very similar.

Meeting in person gives you the opportunity to get to know each other better, which should help you collaborate more successfully. Frequent face-to-face interactions should also increase commitment and support within your team, as suggested by studies.

Simple social catch-ups like having lunch or attending events together can work magic. It's also worth getting together when you need to discuss certain personal and work-related issues, including disagreements and performance challenges. You'll have a better chance to repair and strengthen your relationships by talking things through face to face.

Every now and then, you may also want to get together with one or two teammates for a full day to work side by side and enjoy a break from the usual solitude. You could set yourself up in a coworking space, a cafe or someone's home, for instance. Even if you work on different projects, this is a great opportunity to learn from one another and build stronger connections.

Connect to your team via a 'wormhole'

No, this time I'm not talking about bringing Matt back from Mars. A 'wormhole' is an always-on, real-time video connection between two locations. It acts more like an open window rather than a meeting platform. (A never-ending virtual meeting would be a nightmare. Thankfully, the wormhole is much more user friendly.)

You can talk to people at the other end whenever you have a question or you're up for a casual chat, but most of the time the video is running in the background. You see each other working, and coming and going – not much is happening, and yet your connection is becoming stronger. Your teammates might be thousands of kilometres away from you, but it feels like they're next door. You're very much aware of one another, and you see each other as integral parts of the same team.

Wormholes are usually set up between two offices, and tend to run all day. But there's no reason you couldn't connect to your teammates from home. You'll need a well-positioned camera and an extra screen – ideally a large one, creating the illusion that your teammates are just a few steps away. And when you need privacy, you can easily switch everything off.

NOT AN EPIC MISSION

Remote collaboration can be challenging – but it doesn't need to be an epic mission. As I'm writing this, humans are yet to land on Mars, but NASA's latest rover, Perseverance, is already exploring the terrain. And if we can communicate across the Solar System, we must be able to work as a team when we're merely streets, cities or continents apart.

You and your teammates need to develop your own remote working strategies, ensuring that they align with your culture, work styles, communication styles, and the nature of your work. Collaborate with intelligence and discipline, look after yourselves and your relationships, and you won't look back.

INDIVIDUAL EXERCISES

Reflect on your relationship with your team. Do you feel part of a community? Are your efforts recognised and valued? Can you see clearly how your work contributes to the greater whole? Are you able to resolve differences and conflict? What do you need more of from your teammates? And what might your teammates need more of from you?

Call one of your teammates just to check how they're doing. What's going well and what are their challenges? Be fully present. Do they need some help, or just someone to lend an ear?

TEAM EXERCISES

Assess how organised you are. Does everyone know what the other team members are doing? Do you have a detailed communication plan? Have you created opportunities to learn from each other? Do you have any strategies for maintaining a strong culture remotely?

Come up with new ideas for fun online social activities. Put the most interesting ideas to the test, and if they go well, build them into your routines.

HOW CAN I LOOK AFTER MYSELF BETTER WHILE WORKING FROM HOME?

How can I maintain my health and wellbeing when working remotely?

How can I stay motivated and energised without the stimulations of the office?

How can I maintain healthy work-life balance when my home is my workplace?

Working from home regularly offers the promise of great freedom and a wonderful lifestyle. But what does the reality look like? Home-based work is riddled with sneaky traps, affecting your health, wellbeing and the quality of your life. It's definitely in your power to create a positive experience for yourself; however, you need to draw some boundaries and use your freedom wisely.

I spent my early career working in corporate offices, mostly full time. In one of my jobs, my bosses allowed me to work remotely once a fortnight, which was a treat. On these special days, not having to commute, I was able to get enough sleep and also have a leisurely breakfast with my partner. I started and finished work at the usual hours, but time seemed to pass very quickly. I was filling in spreadsheets and writing reports in my comfy and bright living room, with no interruptions or worries. No watchful eyes. No office politics. My favourite tunes were playing. I was super productive and in flow. And by around 5 o'clock, with the satisfaction of a job well done, I was ready to go out to exercise, meet friends or enjoy the city life.

On my usual days in the office, I often fantasised about the 'bliss' of being able to work from home most of the time. I thought my days would be similar to those occasional Fridays when I felt a bit like I was on holiday. What did I know!

One day my wish came true and my home became my everyday office. And guess what? I fell into many of the classic traps of remote work. Heaps of extra free time? Work-life balance? Healthy routines? The blissful air of freedom? *Ha!* ... In the beginning I only made my life more difficult, and it took a fair bit of time and effort to figure out how to look after myself while working from home. I've come a long way since the early days, but there's still room for improvement.

During the COVID pandemic, millions of us got a taste of working from home day after day. And from the stories I've heard, it's clear that many of us went through a similar journey. At first you may have felt that this was a dream come true (despite the grim circumstances). But after a few weeks, you started to notice some serious challenges that tested your health and sanity. Maybe you were even beating yourself up over your struggles. Then you tried to find a way forward, achieving only moderate success.

Don't blame yourself. Remote work has lots of sneaky pitfalls. The good news is that with the right approach you should be able to avoid pretty much all of them. Let me share with you a few tips I've learned through my experience and research that could help you to be healthier and happier while working from home. Whether you work remotely every day, or once or twice a week, you'll probably find these useful.

DO YOU HAVE ACHES AND PAINS?

After leaving the office behind, one of the first problems you may notice is your body crying out for help. Many people experience increased aches and pains in their neck, back, shoulders or wrists when starting to work from home regularly. In fact, during the 2020 lockdowns, chiropractors noticed a surge in patients experiencing various musculoskeletal issues.

This is not really a surprise if you consider that a lot of people don't have a suitable desk and chair at home, let alone an ergonomic home office. Even if you have other options, you might feel tempted to sit at your dining table, on a soft couch or in your bed while typing away on your laptop. (I admit I certainly do at times.) Since nothing is distracting you, and you don't have anywhere to go, you just sit there hunched over for hours on end.

As if all the muscle and joint pains weren't enough, extended bad posture can also cause headaches and sleeping problems. It can even take a toll on your mental performance, energy and mood, and contribute to stress and depression. The list goes on … I know, ergonomics may not be the most exciting topic, but there's a reason why getting it right is so incredibly important when setting up your workspace.

It's easy to find detailed advice on setting up your workstation properly, so let me just point out the essentials. First and foremost, you need a good-quality, highly adjustable chair. Do your research. Many products are labelled 'ergonomic', but not all of them will suit you (or in fact anyone). A great chair may not be cheap, but it will transform your health and work life.

If your feet can't comfortably rest flat on the floor, get a footrest too. You'll also need a monitor – in addition to your laptop display – along with an external keyboard and a mouse or trackpad. With the correct set-up, you should be able to maintain a relaxed, neutral posture – with your ears, shoulders and hips aligned, neck straight, knees slightly lower than your hips, and forearms horizontal.

It's also worth investing in a sit-stand or height-adjustable desk. Standing for short periods of time has many exciting health and cognitive benefits. (We'll unpack these in Choice 23, 'How can I use my body to hack my brain?') And when sitting, you'll be more comfortable if you can adjust the desk to your height, especially if you're particularly tall or short.

You may prefer not to work at your desk all day long, and that's great – moving between different spots not only reduces the impact of sedentary work but can also increase your focus and brain power, as you're well aware by now. But wherever you sit, do your best to minimise the strain on your body, and shift your posture frequently.

ARE YOU JUST NOT FEELING IT?

Do you find it difficult to get enthusiastic about your job at home? You're not alone. Many people feel disoriented and disconnected from their purpose when working remotely. It's difficult to see your progress or the results of your efforts. You're away from your team, and digital communication simply can't give you the same sense of connection as face-to-face catch-ups.

At the same time, everything around you reminds you that you're at home – your comfy couch, your pantry filled with your favourite snacks, your lively family or housemates, those noisy neighbours, and your pet who loves attention. So you may need some tricks to spark your motivation and shift your mind into work mode.

Set up your environment with a great deal of attention. Good ergonomics are only the starting point. If possible, carve out an area in your home that's dedicated only to work. Make the commitment: whenever you are in there, you do nothing else but focus on the task at hand. This space is your office.

Depending on your personality and the nature of your job, you might be happy to set yourself up in an open space – say, in a section of your living room. Or you may prefer your own room with a door where you can work in peace and quiet. Either way, with a dedicated, comfortable and functional home office, you'll likely enjoy your work more and feel more connected to your team. You should also be able to get things done more effectively, as suggested by extensive research.

Some experts advise against working in the same space where you relax, play or sleep. Well, I see their point, but personally I love reading, writing and solving problems in different parts of my home, including my bedroom, lounge and even the kitchen. Having to do all my work in a single spot would be torture for me, and I'd certainly be less motivated and switched on.

I encourage you to explore what it's like to work in different areas of your home. Use different spaces for specific purposes if you wish. For example, you could get comfortable in a cosy, grounding corner when you need to think deeply about a problem. And if you have a spot with lovely views and lots of sunlight, this might be a great place to hang out when it's time to give wings to your imagination.

While we're at it … remember that your home office deserves as much TLC as the rest of your home. Lots of people have plain and soulless home offices they can't wait to escape, which of course defeats the purpose. So, make sure your environment is welcoming and uplifting, wherever you work. Create a space – or several spaces – that reflect who you are and what you strive to achieve.

DO YOU FEEL UNINSPIRED AND STUCK?

Let's not beat around the bush: working from home can sometimes be quite monotonous. Sure, it's nice to be away from the noise and distractions of the busy office, but when everything is at a standstill, that won't help you find your flow either.

When working remotely, you don't have to commute or walk to meetings. You don't have any teammates around inviting you to join them for a coffee across the street. Nothing prompts you to stretch your legs. As a result, you hardly move – you keep sitting or standing still while you work, while you socialise and while you relax. You might change your focus, but you keep busy with essentially similar, screen-based activities all day long, in the same unchanging environment. The days can blur together, and sometimes several days may pass without you even walking out the front door.

Sound familiar? If so, are you surprised that you feel drained and you struggle to think outside the box? It's difficult to find energy and inspiration when you feel like a prisoner and the walls are closing in. To find exciting and creative ideas, you need stimulation and change.

So go ahead and shake things up a little. Starting with the obvious, play around with the way you work, and change your environment often.

I also suggest you move your body frequently. Experts recommend that you take micro-breaks every 15 to 30 minutes to stretch. If you've been looking down at a screen, look up for a few seconds. If you've been sitting, stand up and take a few steps. Maybe grab a glass of water from the kitchen or walk to a window and see what the weather is up to.

Also take some 3- to 5-minute breaks throughout the day, and go for short walks or do simple exercises. We all do this in the office without a thought – walking to meetings, dropping by a colleague's desk, or running downstairs for a cuppa. Now you need to consciously build physical activity into your routine. For instance, it's a good idea to allow some time between online meetings for short breaks, mimicking the rhythm of office life. This is such a simple trick, but most of us don't think of it when scheduling back-to-back meetings.

Finally, make sure you also get some exercise, ideally every day. You can always work out indoors, but going for a walk or a run, or heading to the gym, are excellent reasons to leave the house. I know people who always go for walks in the morning to start the day on a high. You might prefer a different routine. But once you get into the habit of going outside and staying active, your mind and your world will open up again.

IS YOUR MENTAL HEALTH AT STAKE?

Here's the tragic irony of home-based work: it promises freedom, health and a wonderful lifestyle – yet, many of us end up with mild or moderate mental health issues such as depression and anxiety. Sleep problems are also common, along with increased stress and fatigue. Isn't it a real bummer when you anticipate a happier life but things go downhill instead, and even those areas of your life that used to go well start to suffer?

As we touched on earlier, working by yourself is often a lonely experience. You can call your teammates anytime, and you may see them on screen every day, but something is missing. After endless online chats and virtual meetings, you only feel exhausted. That deep sense of belonging you sometimes feel in the office is gone.

On top of this, without excellent communication strategies, information flow can be far from perfect, and so you may miss out on news and updates. It can also be difficult to know how you're performing – at least in the eyes of others – and how your efforts contribute to the team's goals. Without regular feedback, you may eventually lose confidence and start questioning your abilities and self-worth.

Do you feel the urge to constantly prove to yourself and your team that you're actually being productive? Or are you overcome by that nagging feeling that you're hopelessly behind? How you deal with these worries and insecurities is critical. Many remote workers battling with such issues put in extra hours on a daily basis, trying to get ahead. They tend to take fewer and shorter breaks, as well as less sick leave. Being in a constant state of rush, they also often eat poorly. But sadly, these kinds of sacrifices rarely do any good. Overworking only makes life more difficult, rather than helping to regain a sense of control.

The list of self-destructive habits doesn't stop here. Some people choose to work well into the night, when everything is quiet, even if they need to wake up early the following morning. They may even load up with caffeine late in the day to stay alert. This habit can really mess with your body clock, and thus damage your physical and mental health.

When you work from home, you might find that you have more free time than in the past. Or perhaps you have less ... But whatever leisure time you have, the question is, do you use it wisely? The reality is that remote workers often kill time with passive activities like watching TV or videos, or getting lost in social media. Such pastimes can be entertaining for a while but rarely create a lasting sense of satisfaction. On the other hand, active leisure such as socialising or going outdoors are more likely to boost your happiness. But when you're based at home, it takes extra effort to go out and meet friends, and unfortunately many people choose the easy option.

Now, after all this grim news, I'd like to give you a gentle reminder: make your mental health a top priority. Value your personal time. Respect the needs of your body and mind. Take enough breaks and also make time to eat well. Get plenty of fresh air. Connect with people. Spend quality time with your family and friends, and also by yourself ... Do whatever helps you recharge your batteries and makes you feel whole.

DOES THE IDEA OF WORK-LIFE BALANCE SOUND LIKE A FAIRY TALE?

I'm writing this on New Year's Day. Currently I'm working from home full time, and my work rhythm looks very different from the days when I was based in an office. I often work outside traditional hours, and this lifestyle suits me well. But it's certainly not for everyone ...

In a *Harvard Business Review* article titled 'Building Work-Life Boundaries in the WFH Era', author Nancy P. Rothbard identifies two types of personalities: 'segmentors' and 'integrators'. Segmentors strive to maintain clear lines between their professional and personal lives, while integrators are comfortable with blurred boundaries. I know I'm an integrator, but I can still find it challenging to achieve work-life balance when my home is also my office. For segmentors, this must be even more difficult.

When you work from home, you may notice that work starts to take over. In fact, many remote workers struggle to maintain a healthy work-life balance.

Without a commute, it's easy to roll out of bed, grab your laptop and start working straight away. And when you feel you need to catch up on work (which may well be your default state of being), you may be inclined to work late and on weekends. If you're an integrator, you probably find it easier to cope. But regardless of your personality, you should be careful.

What are the risks?

Home-based workers often work long hours. In different studies, remote employees were found to put in three to six extra hours a week, on average. Adding salt to the wound, this additional time is often wasted on unproductive work. Parkinson's Law plays out in full: 'Work expands so as to fill the time available for its completion.' And when your home is your workplace and your personal time becomes your work time, it can be very difficult to switch off at the end of the day. You're always on, and your personal life takes second place – which is a recipe for burnout.

So how can you achieve a healthy work-life balance? By establishing new boundaries.

Protect your personal time

If you're a segmentor, I suggest you set clear work hours, create a regular schedule and stick to it. If you're an integrator, you may want to mix things up a bit, work flexible hours, and take time out for yourself and your family in the middle of the day. Either way, make sure you have a life outside of work. Nurture and enjoy your relationships. Play with your pets. Pursue your personal goals. When you feel great about your life, or at least optimistic, it's much easier to keep work in its place.

Adopt new routines and rituals

Consider creating routines and rituals that help you transition into and out of work mode. Now that you don't need to commute, find other ways to add structure to your days. What can you do to start your day strong? Go for a walk? Journal? Meditate? Prepare a healthy smoothie? Have a chat with a loved one? … You can create any routine you wish, as long as it helps you get into the right frame of mind. If you're a segmentor, you'll probably also find it helpful to dress for work.

Another great tip is to mark the end of your workday somehow, after which you know you can switch off and relax. I know people who simply walk out of their home office, and at that point, work is over for the day. But when your whole home is your 'office', you need other tricks. Finish the day with something you look forward to – perhaps a nice snack or drink, calling a friend, enjoying awesome music or heading outside. It can also be very satisfying to write a 'done list'. Your chosen ritual should help you celebrate what you've achieved, rather than remind you of the tasks still ahead of you.

Rethink where you work

If you're a segmentor, using the same space for both work and leisure could really mess with your mind and make it difficult for you to unplug. So, set clear lines between your work area and the parts of your home reserved for family life and relaxation. You could even mark these boundaries with plants, screens, artworks or other beautiful design items.

If you're an integrator, you're unlikely to need such clear spatial boundaries. Still, you might find this tip useful: whenever you're faced with a task that keeps you on your toes or weighs you down, do that in your dedicated workspace. If you can confine any agitating activities to a single spot, and physically walk away from the 'battlefield' at the end of the day, you'll find it easier to leave your worries behind.

USE YOUR FREEDOM WISELY

Remote work offers a real opportunity to create a great lifestyle and find more joy in what you do. There's a lot you can do to develop a healthy relationship with work and thus prevent stress, mental health issues and burnout. You don't need to become a different person – just think differently about your needs. Prioritise your wellbeing and you'll enjoy life more, work more effectively, and find it easier to handle the challenges thrown at you.

And remember, on days when you feel isolated and unmotivated despite your best efforts, you still have the option to see others in person. You can visit the office or a coworking place, or catch up and work together with other people who can help you reignite your spark.

INDIVIDUAL EXERCISES

Spend a few days working in the same place in your home. Then spend another few days working in several different areas of your home, moving every couple of hours. Which routine suits you best? Which one helps you focus better, think more creatively and feel more energised?

For one week, keep records of the time you spend working, as well as the time you spend with your loved ones and hobbies. At the end of the week, add up your hours. What do you notice? Do you work more or less than you thought? And do you make good use of your free time?

Spend a couple of hours putting some love into your home office. Give it some character. Decorate it with photos, artwork or other items that lift your spirit. Put distracting objects out of sight. How different does it feel to work in a nice space? And what about your focus and productivity?

For one day, refrain from passive leisure activities, like watching videos, playing online games or engaging in social media. Spend your free time actively; perhaps talk to your friends, go for walks or be creative in the kitchen. See if you notice any shifts in your energy and mood.

TEAM EXERCISE

Exchange ideas with other home-based teammates about your self-care routines. What are your morning routines? How do you stay focused and motivated? What do you do to maintain a good work-life balance? What's working for you, and what's not working so well?

35 SMART CHOICES

PART IV

PART IV

HOW CAN I GET INTO THE RIGHT FRAME OF MIND?

You hear a piece of music, and suddenly you're flooded with memories and emotions. You grab a beautiful notebook and pen, and your hand just starts to write – you're not even sure where the words are coming from. You decide to make a cup of tea, and as soon as you step away from your desk, the solution you've been trying to find all morning pops into your head. You spend your free time in meaningful and enjoyable ways, and you also see a shift in your relationship with work.

Humans are wired in intriguing ways – the connections between our senses, thoughts and feelings sometimes seem to defy logic. So when you need a boost of motivation, a spark of inspiration, or just a clear and peaceful mind, you have to be really savvy about where to find that 'switch'.

You might use the best technology, access the latest information, and follow state-of-the-art processes (which of course are great for productive work), but these won't necessarily help you come up with creative ideas and solve curly problems. And when you're feeling stuck either mentally or emotionally, you're unlikely to reach a breakthrough sitting at a desk in front of a screen.

In this Part we'll explore how you can get into the right headspace to produce outstanding results. Many of these tips are somewhat counterintuitive and look nothing like hard work; yet, they can bring powerful shifts.

You'll probably need to try out different tricks before you find your groove. But once you learn to shift your emotional and mental states at will, you'll be able to progress in quantum leaps while having an amazing time.

CHOICE 22

HOW CAN I GET MOTIVATED?

What should I do when I just don't feel the passion?

What can I do to feel more excited about work?

What tricks can I use to spark my motivation?

Motivation is a powerful force, yet it's highly elusive. On some days you can feel unstoppable, while on others you may not even want to get out of bed. So, what can you do when you're really not in the mood to be productive? You don't need to wait for the magic to strike. You can build motivation in yourself through simple steps, by reconnecting with exciting aspects of your work as well as your personal life.

Your heart is beating faster, and you're full of energy. You feel you could move mountains, and no-one can stop you. The future looks promising, and your head is buzzing with ideas. You feel connected to the people you're serving, and you're eager to create change. You know that your goals matter, and there's no doubt in your mind that you're heading in the right direction.

This is what motivation feels like to many of us. And why is it so important? Because it prompts you to focus on your goals, tackle challenges and do your best work. With no motivation at all, on the other hand, you have little chance of getting anything done, let alone succeeding. We've all been there, struggling through days when each minute felt like hard labour, and we grabbed every opportunity to procrastinate.

But even when you love what you do, motivation can come and go. You may feel unstoppable one moment, perhaps after chatting with an inspiring person, setting an exciting goal or hitting a milestone – and then something happens that crushes your mood. You hear some disappointing news, dismissive comments or unfair decisions … Even though you felt like a hero just minutes ago, now there's only emptiness inside.

The feelings you're looking for can also arise unexpectedly, and equally, they can vanish without an obvious reason. So what can you do to create and maintain motivation rather than just waiting for it to show up?

You need to remember that we're talking about a state of mind, not about an esoteric force. Motivation, in essence, is a cocktail of empowering thoughts and feelings, and it's in your power to tap into these. By generating the thoughts and feelings you need, you can essentially reverse-engineer motivation in almost any situation.

Some of the key ingredients of motivation are:

- a sense of connection

- a sense of meaning and purpose

- a sense of progress

- a sense of autonomy and mastery.

You'll be happy to hear that you can use any strategies you wish to tap into these states of mind. When your work happens to be less than exciting, you can find sources of inspiration from your personal life, and channel your inner fire into professional activities.

Okay, let's look at the ingredients more closely.

FIND A SENSE OF CONNECTION: NURTURE TRUSTING, CARING RELATIONSHIPS

Think about what motivates you about your job. If being part of a team of amazing people is high on your list, you're not alone. In fact, having a great connection with teammates is one of the strongest motivators in the workplace.

When you know you're going to collaborate with people who mean a lot to you, you naturally look forward to work. A trusting and supportive team can inspire you to think big and to believe in yourself, which is hugely important in an age when imposter syndrome is rampant, especially among highly qualified and capable professionals.

Spend time with your colleagues

Spend enough time with your teammates to maintain strong bonds, in good times and bad. Be there for them even when they feel a bit lost or disengaged, and they're not exactly fun to be around. They too will be there for you, lifting your energy and spirit on those days when you just don't feel the passion. So, when you're in need of a motivation boost, all you need to do is call someone or get together in person, and remind yourself that you belong.

Connect with people outside of work

You could also catch up with someone outside of your organisation if you feel a bit isolated. Whether you're connecting with a professional ally or a personal friend, as long as you have a great relationship with them, your motivation will grow. You'll feel that you're part of a broader community.

FIND A SENSE OF MEANING AND PURPOSE: PURSUE IMPORTANT GOALS

Focus on goals that mean something to you. You don't have to try to conquer the universe. If a goal positively challenges you, builds on your skills and strengths, or makes a difference in other people's lives, you'll likely find it meaningful – even if it's very small. Most of us find the simple act of helping others hugely gratifying.

Of course, even the most exciting jobs involve some mundane tasks that appear pointless in the grand scheme of things. Now, here's the good news: according to research, if you can pursue meaningful activities for just 20% of your working week, that feeling will sustain you throughout the whole week. You'll maintain a positive relationship with your work, and will be less likely to burn out.

Any type of job can offer meaningful activities, but you need to be able to notice them rather than constantly chasing a fairy tale in which every single moment oozes purpose.

There are also a few tricks you can use to boost your sense of purpose.

Make yourself more visible

You may have noticed that you feel more motivated and work harder when you're seen by others. Part of the reason is that you want to impress those watching you, but there's certainly more to this. As psychologists explain, when you feel other people's eyes on you, you're more conscious of their perspectives, and thus the importance of your job is magnified.

You don't actually need to be observed to feel visible. Show your work to your teammates as you progress, keep them in the loop, and you'll sense their motivating presence even during the times when you're by yourself. You will know that your work matters.

Have an inspiring workspace

Your physical environment can also help you connect with your purpose. The right space can send you empowering messages; for instance, why you care about your team and clients, and how your efforts translate to tangible results.

In a workspace that reflects the purpose of your work and the qualities you strive for, you'll have a greater drive to grow as a person and to succeed. On the other hand, if your surroundings say 'why bother' or 'your efforts don't matter', that negative vibe will inevitably rub off on you. If your space looks a bit confused, it might confuse you too.

So choose carefully where you spend your time, especially when you feel a bit flat. Put some love into your workspace, if you get the chance. Perhaps plaster the walls with thank you letters from happy clients, along with photos and images reflecting your vision and your contributions. Use your environment to celebrate the difference you're making and to keep your purpose in sight.

Embrace your passions

Connecting with your personal passions can also boost your motivation at work. Many workplaces have hobby clubs, book clubs and other curated events where members chat about subjects they love. One of my past clients who is an avid sailor has covered one of his office walls with photos of yachts to make the space more inspiring.

I love travelling and nature, and I'm a huge fan of live music events. Even when I think about my dream destinations, or the possibility of seeing my favourite artists perform live, I feel pumped. I want to leave no stone unturned to make these dreams a reality. I want to succeed at work and earn that holiday. And I want to do good, especially because that's what my heroes do too. However, I find that simple moments can also be very powerful. Seeing the sheer beauty of nature – the sunset reflected in a clear pond – can lift my desire to make this world a better place.

What kind of experiences are most meaningful to *you* outside of work? Look for opportunities to connect with these passions in the workplace – perhaps bring in some amazing photographs, initiate exciting conversations or listen to music you love. With increased energy and awakened enthusiasm, you'll feel more eager to launch into work and bring your 'A' game.

CREATE A SENSE OF PROGRESS: KEEP THINGS IN MOTION, CELEBRATE ACHIEVEMENTS

Motivation gives you the energy and focus to improve and change things. But the reverse is also true: progress and change can fuel motivation. When you see yourself getting closer to achieving a meaningful goal, you don't want to stop working. Even little steps can give you a sense of progress, as long as you're clear and excited about where you're heading.

The challenge is, when you're immersed in head-down work, it can be hard to see the fruits of your efforts. So it's a good idea to make every bit of progress tangible and visible. Write your tasks on a list and cross them out as you complete them. Track key metrics of your projects on the wall, or at least digitally. As I'm writing this book, I'm updating my tracking sheet after every session, and seeing those little cells turning from red to green, one after the other, is a real buzz.

Reward yourself for hitting any milestones. Celebrate any achievements with your team as well, and remind each other how everyone's efforts contribute to the greater vision.

Look for 'small' breakthroughs

Sometimes very small steps can feel like major achievements ... like the other day while I was walking to my gym, pondering a creative challenge which had been nagging me for weeks, and suddenly the perfect solution popped into my head. Even if I hadn't done anything else productive on that day, I would have felt that I had taken a major leap forward. But as soon as I got back to work, I started developing the idea straight away. I was so excited that I couldn't wait.

How can you achieve quantum leaps in your job? Coming up with a simple idea can often change everything, so make sure you create opportunities for such breakthroughs. Brainstorm solutions to stubborn issues with your team. Meet new people. Engage in stimulating conversations. And sometimes the best thing you can do is have some quiet time to just ponder, allowing game-changing ideas to rise to the surface.

You probably also have other kinds of breakthroughs within easy reach. Think of those items on your to-do list that keep haunting you. They aren't huge tasks but are rather unappealing, and so you keep putting them off. I suggest you grit your teeth and tackle a batch of them in one focused session. Chances are, you'll enjoy being on a roll so much that you'll want to keep going, even after completing what you've planned. Either way, you'll feel much lighter at the end, and miles ahead of where you started.

Create some healthy discomfort

Your work environment can also spur you into action. While your workspace should be inspiring, you don't want it to be too comfortable. In a relaxing space you're more likely to become complacent – as suggested by studies – and to take things a bit slower. Slight discomfort, on the other hand, can give you a sense of urgency to get things done. When you feel a little bit irritated in a particular place, you really want to keep moving without wasting a minute.

Innovation workshops and hackathons are often held in simple, stripped-down spaces, with foldable chairs and timber boxes to sit on. And as it turns out, these no-frills environments actually help participants to engage in high-energy, fast-paced work. So, no couches, bean bags or sushi chefs at your next hackathon. (A bit of discomfort can also enrich your life in many other ways. We'll dive deeper into these in the coming Choices.)

How can you create some healthy discomfort in your workplace? Hold standing or walking meetings. Work with your hands, using tactile tools. Change things around in your office. If you and your teammates have your own desks, swap around once in a while to shake everyone out of their routine.

Just get up and move

How else can you generate a sense of movement when you feel stuck? Simple. Stand up and move – go for a walk or exercise. As energy starts to move through your body, your thinking will shift and ideas will find you faster. Even the change of surroundings should help you see things differently. Your world will seem larger and more dynamic, and you'll feel more empowered to take action.

ACHIEVE A SENSE OF AUTONOMY AND MASTERY: LEARN, GROW, AND MAKE THE MOST OF YOUR FREEDOM

Autonomy and mastery are two different dimensions of your work experience, but they go hand in hand. When you have autonomy, you know that you're in control and have meaningful choices. And when you reach mastery, you're able to make the most of your options through your excellent skills and valuable knowledge.

There might be times when you feel you don't have a lot of freedom at work. Perhaps it's decided by others which projects you should work on, what processes you should follow, which meetings you should attend, and so on. Still, you most certainly have plenty of great choices, some of which you might not be conscious of or see much value in. In fact, the very reason I decided to write this book is to show you these choices, and I trust that you're now starting to see more and more opportunities to gain control over your work.

And how can you achieve mastery? Keep learning and growing. Deepen your existing skills, acquire new ones and put them into practice. Use your unique knowledge and play to your strengths whenever you get the chance. Your confidence will grow, and you'll find your work more satisfying.

Autonomy and mastery is a potent mix. When you see opportunities to create positive change and possess the knowledge and skills to excel, you have what it takes to become unstoppable. And you certainly don't need to go next door to borrow a cup of motivation.

Master your own life

Appreciate the freedom in your personal life and make the most of it, and your relationship with your work will transform. Maintain a healthy balance between work and other areas of your life. Spend your free time wisely, nurture your passions, and enjoy the company of those close to you. If you feel trapped or powerless, consider engaging in meditation, mindfulness or personal development practices.

Invest in yourself, keep learning and growing as a person, and you'll find that your motivation also grows. Develop your skills and explore new interests. Elevate your health, fitness and relationships. Set ambitious goals and make them happen.

I know of teams where members periodically set exciting personal goals for themselves – such as becoming fluent in a foreign language, learning to play an instrument or competing in a new sport – and encourage each other to succeed. As you can imagine, this experience is not only empowering but also does wonders for the team's culture and makes work more enjoyable.

JUST LIKE TWO PLUS TWO

Motivation is hard to put a finger on. It's not a matter of logic or will, and you can't just switch it on when you need it. If you leave things to chance, you probably find that it arises unexpectedly, and is easily destroyed.

But you can build up your motivation, bit by bit, through invoking specific feelings and emotions that are easier to tap into. Even if your relationship with your job is somewhat complicated, it's in your power to find the building blocks you need, perhaps by drawing on experiences in your personal life.

When you feel low, it may be hard to picture yourself getting fired up. But every step of this experience is rewarding, and once you get the hang of it, you won't want to stop. You just need to take that first step.

INDIVIDUAL EXERCISES

Develop your own step-by-step plan for days when you feel unmotivated. What do you need to do to shake yourself up? Call a friend? Revisit your goals? Look more closely at your progress? Do some exercise? Learn something new? … Make sure your plan is appealing, filled with activities you enjoy.

For a couple of weeks, keep a diary of how you spend your free time. Write down when you engage with your passions, when you spend quality time in the company of friends and family, and when you just fritter away your hours. During the same period, also keep track of how motivated you feel at work. Do you notice any patterns?

TEAM EXERCISES

Share your thoughts about what you consider as achievements. Coming up with a game-changing idea? Completing a deliverable? Fixing a glitch in the system? Signing a new client? Enlisting a new team member? Learning to pronounce their name? Getting through the day without an emotional breakdown? Landing a spacecraft on Mars? … All ideas are valid – large or small, serious or lighthearted.

Brainstorm with your team how you could celebrate meaningful milestones. What about creating your own oddball awards ceremony? Sharing the news with the larger team? Having a social get-together? Playing fun games? Going out for lunch? Attending an event together? … Come up with exciting plans that you will all look forward to.

Have a conversation with your teammates about what meaningful work means to you. What makes you feel connected to your purpose? When do you feel that you're making a difference?

HOW CAN I USE MY BODY
TO HACK MY BRAIN?

When should I sit, stand or walk to have the best experience at work?

How can my posture and the way I move help me feel and perform better?

How can I turn work into a full-body experience?

The state of your mind is inseparable from your body. In fact, engaging your body is perhaps the easiest way to boost your mood and brain power, unleash your imagination, and take collaboration to the next level. How can you do this? Simple. Pay attention to your posture. Stand up frequently, move your body when you can, and go for walks. Perhaps even swing or bounce ... Work will feel less like work, but you'll be more ready to produce serious results.

If you could peek into my kitchen, on some days you'd witness an unusual juggling act. You would see me hastily chopping vegetables and stirring the chicken soup, and in the seconds in between, making notes on a piece of paper on the only clean spot on the bench. And you'd certainly notice how much I'm loving it all.

So why would I write so feverishly when I'm already busy preparing dinner? You could easily assume that I'm jotting down my next shopping list or an exotic new recipe I'd come up with on the spot ... But the truth is that in these odd moments I'm actually doing something very important. In fact, I might just be producing some of my best work.

Don't get me wrong, I can be highly productive at my desk. I can undertake research, develop spreadsheets, generate charts, draft technical drawings or answer simple emails all day long. With such left-brain tasks, the more time I spend on my backside the further I progress. At the same time, sitting still doesn't do much good for my creative side, and I often find it difficult to think outside the box if I can't move around.

In contrast, when I'm cooking up a storm in the kitchen my mind is often flooded with ideas. Sometimes I make more headway with tricky problems during those 30 or so minutes playing domestic goddess than in a whole afternoon glued to a chair.

Of course, what fuels my creativity is not the food I'm preparing, but the simple act of standing up and moving my body. (I also like to be inventive with my cooking, but that's an entirely different story. And I certainly won't be giving up my day job for that.)

YOUR GATEWAY TO BRILLIANCE

The human body is not just a machine to feed the brain and to take instructions from it. As we touched on earlier, there's a strong connection between the state of your body and the state of your mind, and as your physiology shifts, so does your thinking. So whenever you actively engage your body, you not only nurture your health and wellbeing but you may also give your brilliance a massive boost.

I'm sure you've experienced many epiphanies in your life while roaming the streets or meandering through a park ... and perhaps also while doing mundane household chores like hanging out the laundry or whipping up dinner. Perhaps you've also noticed that conversations tend to be more upbeat, and people are usually more open minded and switched on, when everyone is physically engaged – maybe standing or walking together – rather than sitting motionless like potted plants.

In fact, engaging your body is an incredibly effective and simple way of tapping into your creative genius, connecting with people and solving complex, unique challenges. Even small shifts can make a difference, but the more consciously you use your body, the more benefits you'll notice. Let's look at a few tricks and tips.

IMPROVE YOUR POSTURE

Holding a good posture requires effort, even in an ergonomically sound set-up. But in an era when your mobile phone and laptop are your 'best friends' and you can work anywhere, it's especially easy to slide into a slouch.

Poor posture puts your body under stress while compromising your breathing, blood flow and nerve function. When you're hunched over, it doesn't take long before your focus and energy starts to fade, and you find yourself in a bleak mood. But as soon as you sit upright with your chest open and your head centred over your spine, you can immediately feel the difference. You not only become more comfortable, but also more **confident, positive and energised**. So it's definitely worth cultivating this habit.

Even when you tend to sit in a healthy position, it's still a good idea to regularly shift your posture throughout the day. You may switch between different types of seating, use a highly ergonomic office chair that allows you to lean back, alternate between sitting and standing, or take frequent breaks to stand up and stretch. Your body will certainly appreciate this, and so will your creative mind. By changing your posture, you can quickly **refresh your thinking**, break out of mental loops and stimulate your brain to explore new avenues.

You may also use different postures as a trigger to **access specific emotions and mental states**. For example, when you'd like to send a friendly personal message to someone, you might want to compose it while sitting on a soft couch. When it's time for creative play, perhaps get comfy on a floor cushion. And when you need to gather your focus to work with systems and procedures, you're probably better off sitting on a traditional office chair.

STAND UP

When you sit, your brain activity can start to slow down in as little as 30 minutes. Your mind may become a bit foggy and more vulnerable to distractions. But once you're on your feet, you'll likely notice you can **focus better, think sharper and make better decisions**. You should also find it easier to learn and remember. And while standing up, you may be able to complete certain tasks more quickly, as suggested by studies.

Standing can also **improve teamwork**. During standing meetings, participants tend to be more active, present and enthusiastic, and less protective of their ideas. As a result, they share their thoughts more freely and work better together.

When you'd like to have a quick, 10- or 15-minute discussion with your team, having a standing meeting is a good idea. You'll probably find that the conversation will be more focused and efficient compared to when you're all seated. And when you're planning a longer collaboration session, pick a space where participants can easily stand up whenever they wish, and where they can't get too comfortable.

To achieve the best results, you need to know when it's a good time to be upright, and when you should rest your behind on a chair. Standing is not only more physically tiring, but also requires more mental effort than sitting. When you need to tackle a particularly challenging task, it might be a better option to stay seated – this way you can focus with **undivided attention**.

Also be aware that standing for extended periods of time could harm your health, wellbeing and performance – just like sitting. Alternating between sitting and standing is often the **healthiest option**, and as an added bonus, it gives you the benefits of physical movement. (Some experts recommend that you sit for 20 minutes, stand for 8, and then spend a couple of minutes moving – walking or stretching – before starting the cycle again. Others suggest that you switch between the two positions about every 30 minutes. It's of course best if you find what works for you and stick to a rhythm that feels right.)

MOVE YOUR BODY

When you get moving, you naturally breathe more deeply and your circulation improves. Your grey matter receives more oxygen and glucose (the primary brain fuel), along with a cocktail of feel-good hormones. As a result, you immediately **feel more upbeat and energised**, and stress starts to melt away.

Put simply, you're showered with rewards for physical activity. Your brain has likely evolved this way because in the lives of your hunter-gatherer ancestors, positive experiences – including finding food – were closely linked to movement. Just think about this … they wouldn't have had a long or exciting life had they preferred resting on their backsides all day long.

Moving your body also helps you **think outside the box** and overcome creative blocks. While dicing onions and slicing carrots might not be your favourite method of jump-starting your creativity, I'm sure you know what it's like when you walk away from your desk and you're suddenly struck by a brilliant idea. The problem that was hanging over your head, and which perhaps seemed unsolvable, is no longer a problem.

The benefits of movement don't stop there. By staying in motion and keeping your energy high, you **become more open** to other people's ideas and perspectives, as well as to new learnings – which is how you become a better professional, innovator and team player.

You can even use your body to develop an **empowered relationship with the challenge** you're facing. Consider turning the problem-solving process into a full-body experience. For example, you may map out the issue and the possible solutions on a wall, interact with a physical model, or act out different scenarios through role-play. These techniques not only support innovative thinking but can also help you understand the context better and build your enthusiasm for the challenge. And when tackling a problem is not just a cerebral but also a physical exercise, you'll come to see yourself as part of the solution, which is incredibly motivating. (I shared a few practical tips and tricks back in Choice 9, 'How should we run meetings to ensure problems are actually solved?')

But what can you do when your work doesn't lend itself to physical activity? Easy. Stand up often. Take frequent breaks and move around a little. Have a stretch, go for a quick walk or do some light exercise. Perhaps tidy your desk, or go to the kitchen and throw together a healthy snack … I know somebody who plays the drums between his work sessions. And I've heard of a team that plays indoor cricket in a vacant area of the office. (Just don't do these right next to your colleagues who're trying to concentrate … or near a glass wall.)

TAKE A WALK

The time you spend walking could be the most valuable part of your day, even though you're not working in the traditional sense. And when it comes to health and wellbeing, walking offers all the benefits discussed so far – and more.

The simple motion of putting one foot in front of the other can **skyrocket your creativity** and help you reach new insights. In an in-depth study, people who walked for a brief period of time produced 60% more creative, unique ideas compared to those who were sitting. In one particular experiment, every single person who went for a stroll outside came up with a high-quality, original answer to a creative challenge, while half of the subjects sitting indoors failed to do so. (This matches my own experience; whenever I take a creative problem for a walk, I know for sure that ideas will come to me.)

And the cherry on top: walking has lasting effects. Your creative juices should keep flowing for a short while even after you return to your desk.

Now, here's something to keep in mind: while walking helps you see things from a fresh perspective and come up with plenty of unique ideas, it may hold you back when you need to find the single best solution to a problem. So when you need to narrow down your options, using 'convergent thinking', it might be a smarter choice to stay at your desk until you make good progress with your task.

But whatever kind of work you do, it's worth taking some time each day to go for walks. It's hard to find an easier way to **elevate your energy and mood**; allocating just half an hour a day can make a great difference, as shown by research. If you go for a 30-minute stroll in the morning, for instance, you'll likely feel the energy boost throughout the day. And if you choose to have a brief 5-minute walk every hour or so instead, you'll not only feel more invigorated but also happier compared to those days when you sit without a break. Interestingly, frequent short walks can also reduce food cravings.

Meandering outdoors in an inspiring landscape is a lovely way to lift your spirit and jump-start your creativity. Green spaces and bodies of water, in particular, can have a wonderful impact on your psychology. But walking indoors, even on a treadmill, is still very beneficial. Your surroundings might not be the most exciting, but your body still pumps all that oxygen- and glucose-rich blood to your brain, and releases the chemicals that help you feel great.

Walk with your teammates

Walking with your team can make it quite easy to get on the same wave-length and **develop a collaborative spirit**. You're all side by side, facing the same direction, perhaps even stepping to the same rhythm – and as such, you're more inclined to focus on finding common ground and solving problems together, rather than what the others might be thinking of you. You'll probably also notice that you can listen better, put aside any possible barriers, and have a more frank and candid conversation compared to when you sit across from each other – say, in a meeting room or a cafe.

Walking meetings are as simple as they sound: you walk and talk. How-ever, there are a few common-sense rules to keep in mind. Make sure that the discussion you're planning is suited to walking, and doesn't require any physical tools or digital resources. Keep the group small – ideally up to four people – and limit the length of the meeting to about 30 minutes. Check if the weather is suitable and pick a relatively quiet route. Notify your team-mates in advance, so that they know what to expect and can change shoes if needed … Enjoy the walk, and note down the most important points and decisions either during or immediately after the meeting.

You can also run virtual walking meetings if you wish, where you and your teammates all wander by yourselves while connecting through a voice call. It's a very different experience from getting together in person, or sitting at your desk and staring at the digital images of your teammates. So I suggest you give it a go and see how it can bring a new dimension to your teamwork.

SWING, BOUNCE OR JUST LIE DOWN

Office swings, trampolines and hammocks – are they ludicrous fads or tools for joy and brilliance? Well, it depends on how you use them.

If you happen to work in one of those 'cool' offices that most mortals only know from the media, you may have a few swinging chairs at your disposal.

At first glance they can look a bit gimmicky, but if you can actually swing in them (and avoid slamming yourself into the edge of a table or putting a colleague in hospital), luck is on your side. Rhythmic swinging can alter your state and help you **engage a part of your intelligence** that rarely reaches the surface. I have countless memories of deep, insightful conversations involving swinging – mostly from my childhood, but some from recent years. So, if you have the option to swing, either by yourself or with your colleagues, enjoy the opportunity and see what magic might emerge.

The same goes for trampolines. As I'm writing this, office trampolines are extremely rare, but I really hope they will eventually become common features of the creative workplace. Bouncing is fun, energising, and if you do it the right way, it's also great for your health. In addition, it can be a powerful **bonding experience**. I once spent a couple of hours with a professional contact (and friend) jumping on a large trampoline, and it turned out to be one of the best business conversations I've ever had. Yes, I'm aware that the idea of bouncing up and down in an office may sound like a joke, but in truth, this could be a pathway to achieving serious success.

Okay, so far we've looked at various high-energy activities, so let's close this topic with something different. Even lying down can enhance your performance. Scientists theorise that when you're horizontal, your brain activity alters in a similar way to when you fall into REM sleep (which is where most dreams occur), and this shift could **stimulate creative thinking**. Even though science is yet to confirm this, nothing is stopping you from lying down when you're ready to unleash your imagination and seeing where your mind takes you. You'll soon find out if this simple trick works for you. And if it does, perhaps look for a reclining chair, a daybed or a hammock when you need a good idea. (And perhaps set a timer on your phone or watch, just in case …)

A FULL-BODY EXPERIENCE

Changing posture. Standing up and turning work into a full-body experience. Going for walks – alone and in teams. Swinging, bouncing or lying down, in search of inspiration and good ideas … This is not how most of us picture effective work, but these simple tricks can unlock the door to your brilliance.

These are in fact some of my favourite 'mind hacks', and whenever I feel a bit flat, sluggish or stuck, I instinctively change how I sit, or I stand up and start moving. Sometimes I have a stretch or go for a walk. At other times – when I work from home – I jump on my mini-rebounder or head to the kitchen with a notepad. And I always reap the rewards. In fact, I routinely compose articles and tricky emails, develop creative design concepts and solve strategic challenges in my head while moving my body.

Through posture, movement and physical activity, you too can alter your emotional and mental states in an instant, tap into your creative genius and find your groove. Your options are abundant. The question is, are you ready to move?

INDIVIDUAL EXERCISES

Create a list of activities you can do when you feel you need to move your body. You could include options like visiting a colleague at the other end of the office, grabbing a cuppa from the furthest kitchen in the building, mapping out your thoughts on a whiteboard, taking the stairs or walking around the block. (Let your imagination run wild. What about covering a colleague's workstation in sticky notes while they are away for lunch, or roaming the office telling people you've lost your favourite paperclip?) Keep this list handy and act on it as often as you need to.

For one week, go for a five-minute walk every hour during your workday, when you get the chance. Notice how this habit changes your productivity, creativity and mood.

TEAM EXERCISES

Experiment with walking meetings. Choose different locations, have different group sizes and discuss different subjects. Explore when walking meetings are appropriate and helpful to your team, and how they can lead to better ideas and decisions. Also have a chat about how you can run them successfully, ensuring that everyone is involved and the conversation flows smoothly.

Brainstorm with your teammates how you could turn your collaboration sessions into full-body experiences. Could you sometimes work with physical items, build models or enact different scenarios as part of the innovation process? See how working together in a physically engaging way can improve your ideas, experiences, and relationships with the challenge.

CHOICE 24

WHAT KINDS OF TOOLS AND TECHNOLOGIES SHOULD I USE?

When should I use digital technologies, and when should I work with my hands?

What are the advantages and limitations of different tools?

How can digital and tactile tools shape my thinking and drive my results?

How can old-school tools help us create a better future?

Our work tools influence how we think and feel, innovate and collaborate. They also have different advantages and limitations, and thus affect what we can achieve. The most productive teams know this very well, and skillfully combine digital technologies with old-school physical tools. To follow their lead, we need to have a hard look at our potential biases towards digital technologies, and learn to choose our tools wisely. Remember, using intelligent tools is not always the most intelligent choice.

The world has been looking to technology companies for a long time to learn about individual and team productivity. They are the developers and front-runners of agile practices such as Scrum, Kanban and Lean, which focus on developing effective solutions and producing deliverables through fast-paced, flexible processes.

Their workplaces are not just among the coolest, but are also designed to help people perform to their best at each stage of a project. Some of these offices have impressive meeting rooms, concentration spaces and recreation areas, built to a sizeable budget. Others are more low cost and stripped down, with a do-it-yourself feel. But regardless of their styles, these workplaces promote great cultures and smart ways of working.

Interestingly, the typical tech office doesn't scream technology. When you look around, you see team spaces and project rooms (or 'war rooms') plastered with sketches, diagrams, handwritten notes and printouts. No walls, whiteboards, doors or windows are left empty. Every conceivable surface is utilised to capture and share ideas and track information using good 'old-fashioned' physical tools.

Of course, tech teams also spend a lot of time in the virtual space, collaborating through digital tools. They have been early adopters of flexible working, and after the start of the COVID pandemic, many of them opted for a 'remote-first approach', with people working from home most of the time. But if you check out the most popular online collaboration apps, you'll notice that many of these are designed to mimic the look and feel of analogue tools such as whiteboards, sticky notes and storyboards.

Isn't it interesting that technology experts are often such prolific users of low-tech tools? If you think about it, this makes perfect sense. To do their jobs successfully, they need to have a good grasp of the capabilities and the limitations of various tools and technologies, as well as the nuances of the user experience. Specifically, they need to understand how people think, feel and act, and what they can achieve, when interacting with different devices and applications. And given that they have all this knowledge, they'd be crazy not to use it in their own practices. They know that combining digital and physical tools intelligently helps them produce the best possible results.

ARE WE PERHAPS A BIT OBSESSED WITH DIGITAL TOOLS?

In the meantime, the rest of the world is lost in its obsession with digital innovation and collaboration technologies. Admittedly, they are often fun and exciting – exactly because they've been designed by geeks who know what makes us tick – and offer an ever-growing range of cool features.

Now, you might actually hate some of the software and apps you must use for work. But even then, all you have to do is click, and it's all right there in front of you. You can access, edit, save and share information with relatively little effort. It's all so much more convenient than standing up, finding some good old stationery and a suitable space, and starting to scribble, sketch or build something with your hands.

For all these reasons, many of us routinely turn to our devices, in almost every situation, without asking ourselves, 'Is this really the best way to do my work?' What we perhaps don't realise is that intelligent and creative digital tools don't necessarily help us think creatively and work intelligently. They *do things for us* rather than *bring out the best in us*, and what they can do is inherently limited.

In fact, by opting for digital tools too often, we work less productively and produce lower quality ideas, compared to when we keep them at arm's length. Scientists have found that despite the exceptional innovations in information technologies over the past few decades, productivity in the developed world has increased very little. This phenomenon is called the 'productivity paradox'.

So instead of seeing digital solutions as the Holy Grail of productivity, I suggest we look to the people who understand technology really well and learn some geek smarts.

LET'S GET TO KNOW THE 'OLD SCHOOL'

Okay, it's time to explore when and how those often-ignored physical tools can help you achieve greater results at work. (I'm sure you have a fairly clear idea of how digital technologies can make you more efficient, so I hope you don't mind if I focus more on the analogue side of the story, in this Choice.)

How you read, learn and remember

Your brain functions differently when you read from a screen compared to when you read from paper. For example, you probably read slower, and also less accurately and comprehensively, when information is presented digitally – as suggested by research. (This is why, when you need to proofread a document, you often find more mistakes if you use a printed copy.) It's also more exhausting to read from a screen, and as a result, more difficult to recall what you've learned later on.

And what about taking notes? Studies show that people who take notes using pen and paper tend to remember information better, compared to those typing on a laptop or tablet. You can probably type much faster than you can write freehand, which means that by using a keyboard it's easy to capture what you hear almost word for word without thinking deeply about the content. On the other hand, when you scribble notes on paper (or a digital notebook), you need to first absorb the information and distil what's most important, which is an essential part of the learning process.

I love taking hand notes at meetings and trainings, even though this can look a bit old-fashioned. Very often, I put these notes away and never read them again – not because they are useless, but because I tend to memorise all the key points while writing.

How you grasp a subject

Depending on your individual learning style, you might prefer to read books and articles, listen to audio recordings or watch videos, for instance, to delve into a subject. Conversations with colleagues and experts can also give you invaluable knowledge. However, if you're a tactile or kinaesthetic learner, you learn best through hands-on and interactive experiences; in other words, by doing and feeling things. That's also how I'm wired, and I truly enjoy building 3D models or experimenting in a lab, for example. These are the moments when everything I've previously read or heard about a subject falls into place.

In a research study, one group of children engaged in a presentation about physics using a computer screen, while another group participated in a 3D, real-life demonstration of the same subject. All of the children studied essentially the same content. But astoundingly, the second group learned almost five times more than the first group, and also had more fun.

Even though we all have different learning styles, we're all tactile learners to some extent. Sadly, adult education rarely favours hands-on, experiential learning, but with a bit of creativity you should be able to find ways to make essentially any subject tangible.

How you focus

The digital world is riddled with distractions – emails, chat messages, pop-up notifications and so on. When your device is right in front of you, it's also tempting to click around and check your favourite sites. And when you hit a wall or start getting bored, it's just too easy to switch to another task or take an unnecessary break and indulge in online entertainment. Put simply, your devices prompt you to multitask and procrastinate – unlike any physical work tools, which can really draw you in and help you find your flow.

Even during face-to-face meetings and collaboration sessions, you're less focused and present with a screen in front of you. Many people think they can save time by getting some work done – for example, answering messages or checking facts – while others are talking. But even when you're doing your best to listen, a simple glance at your screen can take your mind elsewhere. Many organisations find that teamwork sessions are more productive when laptops, tablets and phones are left outside the room.

A Danish university has also proved this point after one of the lecturers became so frustrated at seeing his distracted students missing out on deep learnings that he banned all mobile devices in discussion sessions. Without their screens, students were more engaged and present, and thus learned more. Since they couldn't use Google to find out more about their subject, they interacted and developed as a group – and they also enjoyed this experience.

How you feel

Most of us are guilty of spending more time in front of our screens than necessary, and this has a massive impact on our wellbeing. The health issues associated with sedentary lifestyle and poor posture are only the starting point. Digital overload manifests in a variety of symptoms, including stress, anxiety and fatigue. You may also suffer from headaches, eye problems and sleep issues.

The majority of people frequently hold their breath or have shallow breathing while working in front of a screen. (I'm definitely one of them.) This issue – also called 'screen apnoea' – is not just an indication of how tense we often are when using digital technologies, but also a problem in itself, draining our energy and harming our physical and mental health.

In contrast, using physical tools can help you relax and become grounded. You have fewer distractions. You're focusing on one thing at a time, so you have space to think. You're allowing your body to move. You're feeling the materials you're working with and can see your creation come to life … And you're in the present moment, without a burning desire to jump onto social media, scroll through your friends' holiday photos and humble brags, and feel sorry for living a 'normal' life.

Taking a break from technology and getting your hands dirty, literally, can also be heaps of fun.

How you create and innovate

When you're developing a fresh idea using software, your mind is attuned to working within the limitations of the technology, perhaps relying only on the features available to you. You're also inclined to make all the details perfect straight away and finish what you're working on as soon as possible, rushing the creative process.

Game-changing plans often start with a 'napkin sketch'. Doodling or jotting down a sprouting idea is like thinking out loud – there are no rules or barriers. The idea can develop in any direction, and no-one expects you to get it right or to finish it on the spot. Those scribbles and sketches entice you to play with them, to change them and to ask for input.

In a well-equipped innovation space, apart from pen and paper, you see a variety of craft tools and modelling materials such as crayons, sharpies, paints and brushes, as well as wires, strings, toothpicks, cardboard, fabrics, balloons, adhesive tape, rubber bands, Play-Doh, LEGO pieces … you name it. The range of objects you can use is virtually limitless. Even kitchen cupboards and bathroom cabinets are packed with items that can get your imagination going.

Once a nice selection of real-life, tactile materials are in front of you, you can't help but start to play. You probably notice that your hands begin to do their own thing, creating curious little images and objects you may not even have names for, without you thinking too hard about what you're doing. Different tools and materials draw out different parts of your creativity and take you on different journeys.

3D modelling materials also allow you to quickly build and test your ideas. For example, one of the prototypes of the first Apple mouse was built using the cover of a butter dish (which formed the top of the mouse) and the ball from a roll-on deodorant (which became the mouse ball).

How you express yourself

You've probably noticed that you use different words when typing on a computer, writing on a piece of paper or speaking to another person, even when you try to say the same thing. Certain types of media prompt you to conform to expectations while others give you creative inspiration and invite you to jot down your thoughts as they come to you.

Ajahn Brahm, a beloved Buddhist teacher and author, has an enlightening story about how he wrote one of his books which, aptly, is filled with enlightening stories. He initially engaged someone else to compose the manuscript for him, but it was of such a poor standard that he decided to write it himself. He was writing by hand, and it was much easier than he thought. He got into the zone and the words just flowed. He was feeling happy. And the manuscript turned out to be of excellent quality; it hardly needed any editing.

Many creative artists swear by pen and paper while others prefer typewriters. The messages that emerge from using these instruments are often more inspired and authentic than those produced on a computer. One of my favourite artists Eddie Vedder once said, 'I'm not a computer writer. For some reason, there's no romance in it.'

How you understand others

Finding rapport with colleagues and clients always makes collaboration smoother. When you're on a similar wavelength, you appreciate each other more, better understand each other's points of view, and find it easier to make decisions together.

Mimicking the body language of a person is an effective technique to build rapport. (I once participated in an exercise where this technique was pushed to the extreme. I accurately copied every tiny detail of a fellow participant's body posture, and became so attuned to her state of mind that I could correctly guess what she was thinking, without her speaking a word. It was mind-blowing to realise that this was actually possible.)

At work, there are of course limits to how far you can go; mimicking a teammate's or a client's every move could make the situation incredibly awkward. But here is an idea. You know by now that the tools and technologies you use in your job guide your thinking. This means you can develop a better connection with anyone simply by copying their work styles. There's nothing awkward about that – rather the contrary. When I first tried this in my consulting practice, I was blown away by the feedback. The first design concept I developed using a client's favourite tools turned out to be exactly what they needed. It didn't need any revisions. Since then, when I seek better alignment with the people I work with, I check out the tools they use, and if practical, use similar ones myself.

How you get your head around and solve problems

To solve a complex challenge, you need to get your head around a lot of information. However, your short-term memory can only retain a handful of information at any given time. So, if you study the problem without using any visual aids, perhaps just by reading, thinking or talking about it, you'll struggle to keep everything in your head all at once.

On the other hand, your spatial memory has a significantly greater capacity. Thus when you create a physical representation of each important element of the challenge and map things out on a large surface, it's much easier to grasp the whole picture. Physical objects such as sticky notes, index cards or paper drawings are also easy to reconfigure. It's as if they are calling you to shift them around until all the pieces fall into place.

I use this technique in my own practice all the time, and it never fails me. Whenever I come across a complex challenge, I write down the key points on colourful pieces of paper and stick them on a wall. Then I keep moving things around until the problem and the solution become crystal clear.

Many collaboration platforms incorporate virtual whiteboards and pin-boards, complete with virtual sticky notes and index cards. These features are certainly useful when you need to collaborate remotely, but aren't equal to their real-life counterparts. To make the best use of your spatial memory, your thoughts and ideas must be able to find their way to the space around you, well beyond the boundaries of your screen. (We delved deeper into this in Choice 9, 'How should we run meetings to ensure problems are actually solved?')

How you communicate and collaborate with your team

Whiteboards, pinboards, walls, and even doors and windows can provide a democratic canvas for collaboration where everyone can add their piece to the puzzle. When you see the challenge you're working on as an evolving story, with all of its elements in plain sight, it's easy to develop it as a team. And in a space where everyone's ideas and thought processes are mapped out, you can expect some interesting discussions.

Hand-drawn images, in particular, can evolve in fascinating ways. By expressing yourself through drawings and sketches, you can also bridge potential cultural and language barriers that could otherwise hinder communication in a diverse team. Digital environments can rarely support this level of inclusion. When everyone can contribute freely, teamwork becomes highly dynamic and engaging.

By capturing all key information and decisions on the walls, you also leave little room for ambiguity. This ensures that everyone's on the same page, knowing exactly where the project is at and what needs to be done.

How you engage with your clients

The secret to producing outstanding customised products and services is to tease out a client's ideas early on and receive candid feedback as the solution develops.

A refined, finished-looking drawing or plan can sometimes look intimidating to clients, especially in the early stages of the creative process. If it's presented digitally, clients could find it difficult or impossible to edit. And if you give them a printed version, they might feel uncomfortable about 'ruining' it. A polished presentation may also give them the impression that the concept is your 'baby' and they are not welcome to contribute.

In contrast, when clients see a hand sketch, they feel more involved in the conversation and more comfortable to suggest changes. It's evident that the concept you're showing them is not carved in stone. They can also take those rough drawings or plans and add their own ideas without making things awkward. It's not their clumsy scribble or sketch over your flashy rendering. It's a shared creation; a work in progress.

When you give them some craft tools or modelling materials, clients might also be able to express abstract thoughts and half-baked ideas that are difficult to draw or to put into words. And when your clients see their input incorporated into the final solution, they will naturally be happier with the results.

How you hone your most important skills

To solve today's challenges and succeed at work, you need to exercise self-awareness, critical thinking, imagination and empathy. In this world brimming with artificial intelligence, such human skills are more valuable than ever.

Modern technologies can make work easier and more efficient in many ways, but every time you rely on some kind of software to think for you, you lose an opportunity to think for yourself. And if you depend on technology too much, some of your most important skills may start to erode.

Digital technologies can remember things and make decisions for you. They can suggest what you should read or watch, and who you should connect with. They're also able to tell you how other people are feeling, and even give you feedback on how *you* are feeling. Just think of those popular devices and apps that are designed to tell you what your body and mind need in a given moment; for example, when you should push hard with your exercise, when you should take a break and when it's time to meditate.

In this 'intelligent' environment, you need to be especially mindful about honing your skills. It's important that you frequently exercise your imagination and memory muscles, connect with people deeply and make decisions consciously. This means that sometimes it's a good idea to say no to the help that artificial intelligence can offer, allowing your own wisdom and intuition to guide you.

CHOOSE YOUR TOOLS INTELLIGENTLY

I'm not suggesting that we go back to the dark ages. The world is moving fast, and intelligent tools and technologies have key roles in our lives. However, they are not the means to all ends. Rather than reaching for a device each time we face a problem, we need to select the tools that best suit the task and the situation.

When you use the right tools at the right time, individual and team performances soar, innovation and collaboration thrive, and work becomes highly engaging. What could be a better measure of intelligence?

INDIVIDUAL EXERCISES

At least once each day for a couple of weeks, stop for a moment and pick a tool you don't normally use for the task ahead of you. What do you notice? Are you perhaps more focused than usual? Are you thinking more creatively? Are you enjoying what you do? After your experiments, decide which tools are worth adding to your personal 'toolbox'. (Keep in mind that new ways of working can sometimes feel a bit unnatural, but this can quickly change as you build a routine.)

Find a teammate who prefers different tools to you for tackling specific tasks. Put yourself in their skin and complete a few tasks with their favourite tools. Are you happy with the results? Are they different from what you would normally produce? Did this exercise help you better understand how your teammate thinks and creates? (Perhaps also show them the results of your work and ask what they think of it.)

TEAM EXERCISES

Divide your team into two groups and give each group the same challenge or problem to solve. One of the groups can only use digital tools to capture and develop their ideas, while the other can only use physical tools. Once the time is up, compare the two solutions and then discuss the creative processes. Also encourage everyone to share their individual experiences. What can you learn?

Have a chat about your relationships with different tools and technologies. Talk about your favourite and least favourite instruments, devices and software. What are your go-to tools for different tasks? Do you use these because you believe they are most suited to the task, or out of routine? What's working well, and where should you look for smarter options?

SHOULD I LISTEN TO MUSIC AT WORK?

How can I use music as a productivity tool?
How can different types of music or sounds support different work activities?
What should I listen to?
When should I work in silence?

Music has incredible power. It can transport you through places and times, and shift your emotions in an instant. But have you ever considered using music to enhance your performance? It's far more than a source of entertainment. Carefully selected tunes can sharpen your thinking, support your focus and boost your creativity. Moreover, they can help you get into the right state to excel – whether you need courage, confidence, optimism or a sense of connection with your team. The benefits are endless; but of course, there are also times when silence is golden.

Listening to music is not just an auditory experience; it can transform your whole being.

A great friend of mine once told me after a gym session that hearing a particular techno/dance song enabled him to lift around 40% more weight than he otherwise could. And a lot of people find that they can run faster and with less effort while listening to their carefully curated playlist.

Many public speakers routinely listen to music before they get on stage, because this helps them get into the right state for engaging the audience and presenting most effectively. Barack Obama also had his favourite songs to tune into while getting ready for his presidential debates, which put him in the right frame of mind.

Music can even alter your senses, which I find most intriguing. In one study, for example, people listening to music with a positive vibe found that chocolate tasted sweeter and more enjoyable, in comparison to those who were listening to negative music.

And you'd certainly be familiar with how music can transport you to places and sway your emotions in an instant. As soon as you hear certain songs, your mind goes on a journey. It might be a hit you danced to as a teenager. The tune that was playing during your first kiss. A ballad from the first concert you went to. Or even your wedding song … But also think about movies, commercials and even reality shows. The chosen soundtracks – even the ridiculous 'tension music' played while an unfortunate cooking show contestant serves a slightly overcooked piece of chicken to the judges – are essential parts of the storytelling.

I'm sure you know exactly what to listen to when you want to cheer up, let off steam, connect with a loved one or be carried back into the past. But have you ever wondered how listening to the right sort of music can make you more productive and successful in business?

Many professionals already draw on the power of music to perform better. Some software developers work more efficiently, and produce better quality work, when listening to the right tunes. And surgeons have been seen to perform operations more accurately when listening to well-selected tracks.

THE SPELL OF MUSIC

Music affects how you feel, how you think and what you do. And I'm not only talking about those moments when you simply can't stop yourself from dancing.

The right types of music can:

- energise and motivate you to get things done

- sharpen your thinking

- make you feel happier, more confident and more optimistic

- fire up your creativity

- help you recall information from memory

- make it easier for you to stay in the zone by taming your monkey brain

- mask or block out distracting sounds around you

- make boring, repetitive tasks more enjoyable

- help you complete certain tasks faster and more accurately

- enable you to get into other people's shoes and embrace their experiences

- relieve stress, and help you to switch off and relax

- help you get in touch with the part of yourself you want to be in the moment – whether a wise man, an adventurer, a fighter, or a productivity queen or king.

A FEW CLEVER HACKS

Let's zoom into some particularly interesting uses of music …

With a little practice, you can train your brain to associate specific songs with specific ways of thinking. For instance, when you listen to a certain song repeatedly while engaging in critical thinking, that song eventually becomes a trigger. Then, when you need to think critically again, all you have to do is put on that song and you'll find yourself in the right headspace in an instant.

Well-selected songs can help you see the world the way you want to see it. When you listen to happy tunes, you're more likely to perceive the world as a happy place, filled with joyous people. In contrast, when you listen to sad tunes, everything appears a bit more sad. The question is, which lens should you look through at any given time to be able to do your best work? On occasion, it might help if you can really tune into people's pains and frustrations. And at other times, you'll achieve more if you feel that you live in a wonderful world.

Would you like to bring specific qualities to your work? Why not learn how to do this from a true genius? Albert Einstein was not only a gifted violin player; he also saw music as a pathway to creating knowledge. He's known for reaching for his violin whenever he got stuck on a difficult mathematical problem, which usually helped him find a solution. His favourite composers included Mozart, who had the unique talent of expressing deep emotions even with just a few notes, and Bach, who was able to create beautiful, layered harmonies. Einstein himself strived to create scientific theories that are both pure and harmonious, and the music of Mozart and Bach gave him inspiration and guidance to reach such beautiful insights. (Interestingly, an architecture professor I knew often listened to Mozart when designing buildings, and his designs also embodied a lot of qualities that are characteristic of Mozart's pieces.)

WHAT TO LISTEN TO WHILE YOU WORK

When you listen to music in your free time, your choices are limitless. However, when it comes to finding the right background tunes for work sessions, you need to consider your choices more carefully. You want to find songs that stimulate your mind but don't consume too much of your attention.

Of course, music is a personal choice. Everyone is different. But if you're open to experimenting with your playlists, science can give you some direction on what might work for you in different situations. According to research, the **genre**, the **lyrics**, the **tempo** and the **key or mood** of the music, as well as your **familiarity** with the tunes, can all have an impact on how you perform.

Genre

Positive, high-energy classical pieces have great potential to enhance your creativity, as long as you enjoy them. Baroque music, in particular, is also found to be excellent for improving productivity and focus.

Electronic tracks can stimulate your mind and keep you switched on, and because of their repetitive nature they tend to be unobtrusive. Many people listen to video game tracks to get into the zone, which may seem like a strange idea but actually makes perfect sense. Just think about it – game music is specifically composed to assist players perform complex and challenging tasks without creating a distraction. (For example, the SimCity soundtracks are highly popular for aiding concentration.)

When you need to get your head around a difficult problem, ambient music (think Brian Eno) can be a good option, since it's easy to ignore and still does a great job at blocking out background noises. At the same time, you want to avoid songs with uneven rhythms and complex structures, such as rock music, which can be very distracting. But when you need to get on with a dull job and all you need is stimulation and entertainment, the story is very different, and catchy, sing-along pop and rock tunes might give you just what you need.

Lyrics

Music with lyrics can make it easier for you to immerse yourself in repetitive, mundane tasks, by giving your brain a large amount of stimulation. On the other hand, you'll probably find that instrumental music is a better choice for complex tasks that require a lot of brain power.

Lyrics can be in fact quite distracting when you need to concentrate. It's a bit like trying to focus with people talking around you. Listening to songs with lyrics can make it especially difficult to read or write, because the language centre of your brain is trying to run two processes simultaneously. Mixing languages is the worst. I find that listening to music in my mother tongue (Hungarian) while trying to read or write in English leads to the ultimate brain fry.

Tempo

Can you imagine that music with the right tempo may increase your intelligence? One study found that students who listened to upbeat music performed better on IQ tests compared to those who listened to slow music. On the other hand, music with around 60 beats per minute could help you significantly reduce stress.

Key or mood

Studies show that background music written in a major key better supports productivity than music written in a minor key. This could be explained by the fact that music in a major key tends to sound more cheerful. Either way, if the music you're listening to lifts your mood and makes you feel empowered, you can't really go wrong.

Familiarity

Playing familiar tunes in the background is probably a better choice when you need to concentrate intensely, because music that's new to you could more easily distract you or hijack your attention. However, be mindful when selecting music that plays an important part in your personal history and means a lot to you. Tunes from your past could bring up all sorts of memories – inspiring thoughts and feelings, or sometimes disempowering ones.

CHOOSE WHAT WORKS FOR YOU AND YOUR TEAM

Not sure what to listen to? Go and have a play. It's a lot of fun to explore how music can enhance your mood and performance.

You'll probably find that different types of tunes better suit different activities. Some might ground you and help you focus on detail-oriented, analytical tasks, while others could open up your imagination and entice you to think expansively. Some music might give you the courage to take risks, and create a sense of urgency – which can be especially handy if you're a seasoned procrastinator. Other grooves could prompt you to slow down a little and be cautious – a great state to be in when checking for errors and making certain critical decisions.

When played before or during team activities, the right music could also enhance collaboration, energising members and getting everyone on the same wavelength. It could help establish a warm and friendly atmosphere and invite everyone – even the quietest members – to open up and speak their minds.

Whatever your preferences are, always remember your priorities. Music should not distract you – or anyone else around you – from doing your best work. If you and your coworkers can't agree on what to play on the sound system, or whether to have any music at all, it's best to keep the workspace quiet and perhaps put on your headphones. (As much as I loved my internship experience in the Netherlands in the late '90s, hearing *Give me a reason to love you* what felt like a hundred times each day certainly tested my resilience and possibly caused some of my nightmares later in life.)

MUSIC, AMBIENT SOUNDS OR SILENCE?

Chances are that the way you respond to music will sometimes defy logic and science. For example, some high-energy alternative rock songs often put me in a dreamy state in which my creativity soars. On one occasion, a friend of mine suggested that I listen to an album that got him revved up, and it literally put me to sleep. So don't question yourself; just pick whatever puts you in the right headspace.

Sometimes you might find that silence is your best friend – especially when you need a clear headspace or your work requires 100% of your attention. For example, like most people, you likely find it easier to learn something new or to get your head around complex information in a quiet space. (Depending on your environment, it might still be a good idea to keep the headphones on, which can help block out distractions even when no music is playing.)

In many modern workplaces white noise or pink noise is played in the speakers to mask distracting sounds, including people talking. Playing nature sounds – such as streams babbling, birds chirping, rain falling or trees rustling in the wind – is another popular option. Nature sounds are also shown to enhance brain function and concentration, and to improve mood and wellbeing.

In recent years, listening to 'office sounds' became quite popular, which can help home-based workers feel a bit less isolated. Several apps are available that allow you to create your own mix; you can choose from options like printer noises, air-con humming, keyboard clicking and chatty colleagues.

MIXING THINGS UP?

I find that my habits around music have an actual rhythm. I prefer to work in silence for a few hours in the morning, then turn on the tunes in the afternoon, and then enjoy some more silence again later.

However, we are all different. Perhaps you want to work in a quiet space all the time. Or if you're like Bronwyn, my author buddy and friend, you simply can't stand working in a silent room.

Either way, you have the choice to combine your love of music (or silence) with the joy of productive and rewarding work. I believe this is an amazing choice to have!

INDIVIDUAL EXERCISES

Experiment with listening to different types of music during different work activities. Take notes on what task you're working on, what's challenging about it, what skills you're using, what music you're listening to, how the music makes you feel, and how you rate your productivity. Use these notes to work out your ideal playlists for different types of work.

Try using music to get into the right headspace before important meetings and presentations. Think about who you need to be and how you need to feel to succeed. Pick tunes that resonate with you. What do you notice? Is music helping? Have you found the right songs, or do you need to check out some others?

Spend one day listening to no music at all while you work. The next day, listen to music every time your work allows. And on the third day, mix things up – listen to music for a little while, and then take a break from it and enjoy the silence, as your mood dictates. What works best for you?

TEAM EXERCISE

Listen to some cheerful, upbeat hits with your team before a meeting or collaboration session. If you're using a soundproof space or an area of your office where you don't disturb others, turn up the volume. Have a quick debrief after the session. How did it go? What effect did the music have on the mood and dynamics of your session? Were you and your teammates more energised and engaged than usual?

CHOICE 26

HOW CAN I INVITE CREATIVE INSPIRATION?

How can I tap into my creative flow and unleash my imagination?

How do I need to think and feel to create something special?

What does it take to create masterpieces quickly?

Creative work can sometimes be very slow and require painstaking effort. But what if you could create masterpieces really quickly while having a wonderful time? Many artists are familiar with the experience of tapping into their creative flow and running with the ideas that come to them. By learning a few tricks from these successful artists, we too can make it easier for ourselves to unleash imagination and create something incredible.

Whenever I come across a piece of art that moves me – whether it be literature, music, architecture or a movie – I like to find out about the creative process behind it. Some of the masterpieces I love took ages to create, which is understandable; developing a powerful concept and refining all the details can be very time consuming. But sometimes the creative process can take quantum leaps.

The captivating movie *Locke*, with Tom Hardy's stellar performance, was filmed over just eight nights. Author John Boyne wrote *The Boy in the Striped Pyjamas*, a beautiful and heart-wrenching novel, in two and a half days. And John Lennon composed *Imagine* – one of the most timeless and influential songs in modern history – in one brief session.

What I find most interesting is that many artistic works turn out to be transformative for the very reason that they were produced quickly, in a deep state of creative flow. Artists often describe this experience as magical and spiritual. In this unique state, you feel as if the ideas, words or music are coming from somewhere outside of yourself, and all you need to do is capture the gift that's presented to you.

Your energy shifts, and perhaps also your persona: if you're normally a shy and cautious person, you might become a confident and unstoppable force for a period of time. In this state, giving birth to a masterpiece can feel surprisingly easy. You're fully immersed in your work, and you lose your sense of time. Bodily needs like eating or sleeping take a backseat ... And when you come back down, maybe hours, days or weeks later, you can't remember much of what's been happening. But you look at what you've created and you're amazed – it certainly shows the best of you. Maybe you even struggle to believe that all this has been within you.

Indeed, works produced in this deep creative state tend to have wonderful qualities. You don't overanalyse things, and as a result, your expression is pure and authentic. And without you second-guessing yourself or trying to adhere to rules and expectations, your imagination is free to take you to some truly exciting places.

(Does this all sound a bit too enthusiastic? If today happens to be one of those tedious and tiring days for you, I imagine it does. But this is how artists often talk about their most inspired moments and achievements. When you're in that place, you see things through a different lens.)

LET'S BORROW SOME TRICKS FROM THE MASTERS

Wouldn't it be great if we could somehow find the recipe for creating great things really quickly, while having an amazing time?

Well, I don't think that science will ever crack the code, as there's something inexplicable about the ways inspiration strikes. Most people I've heard talking about their creative process agree that you can't plan for moments of magic. As Bruce Springsteen puts it, 'creativity does not work like the seasons do'.

Yet, there must be more you can do than just waiting and hoping for the best. When you're as curious about behind-the-scene secrets as I am, you notice that many of the most respected artists have a few tricks up their sleeves. They seem to intuitively know how to invite creative inspiration and what to do when it strikes.

Personally, I've never found it easy to surrender to inspiration, perhaps due to my tendencies of overthinking things and frequently doubting my creative abilities. Therefore, I'm always keen to try out any tricks that may help liberate my imagination ... Yes, I often use an analytical approach to quiet my analytical mind, the irony of which doesn't escape me. But thankfully, a lot of the tricks I've learned through my research actually seem to work – when I apply them, those special moments occur more often. My ideas flow more freely and rapidly, and I find it easier to express them authentically. So let me share these tips with you.

Plant some seeds

Big ideas usually take time to incubate – sometimes days, months or years – and once they are ready to spring to the surface, you can feel them coming. Artists often decide to write a new book or make a new album when their minds are bursting with creative thoughts. They know this is the time.

Here's how Eddie Vedder describes his experience:

> 'It really feels like your brain is a hotel, and all these songs, they are kind of tenants ... And at some point, you know ... They've been there for so long, and they are really not paying rent, and they are kind of trashing the place.'

However, in your profession, you want your ideas not only to be beautiful but also to solve specific problems. And you'll find it easier to get there if you plant some seeds first. Be clear about the problem you're trying to solve, and perhaps look at some background information. Your unconscious mind is an impressive problem solver; once it's given an 'assignment', it can steer your attention in the right direction and start joining the dots even without you noticing.

Push the boundaries of your expertise

With experience and practice, you'll naturally become better at your job. You'll be able to work faster and make better decisions. Even in highly creative domains, it pays to pick up the basics. Before Picasso co-founded the cubist movement, he excelled in various classical painting techniques.

On the other hand, being a novice in a field can also give you a creative advantage, since you're less likely to be set in your ways. (This is well illustrated by a study which found that less seasoned musicians produced more impressive improvisations.) So keep pushing the boundaries of your expertise but always build on what you're good at. This will allow you to have the best of both worlds. You'll be confident with the foundations, but your mind will be open to infinite possibilities.

Look for a spark

Creative thoughts arise when two existing thoughts are combined in a unique way. Innovation teams often use brainstorming cards showing an eclectic range of different concepts when looking for fresh new ideas. But pretty much anything can spark epiphanies or set off a whole avalanche of ideas: a conversation, a book, a movie, a picture on the wall, a travel experience, something you see on the street ...

You can never tell where the next spark will come from – but you know it needs to be something you haven't thought of before, at least not in the context of the problem you're working on. To find fresh ideas, look for 'newness' in your life. Talk to new people, learn new skills and explore new places. Perhaps find a new thinking space. With so much stimuli, your mind will shower you with original ideas, and while not all of them will be useful, chance are that at least a few of them will be brilliant.

Switch off

There's time for consuming new information, and then there's time for switching off. Don't feel the need to fill every minute of your day learning or doing something 'useful'. Your brain needs space to think and to process what you've learned. Have some quiet moments every day, unplugged. Allow your mind to wander. Even when you find yourself a bit bored, don't rush to find stimulation. As we touched on earlier, daydreaming and boredom are important gateways to creativity.

You may also need longer breaks now and then. I notice that every few months, especially after periods of intense mental work, I feel I need to fast from information for a while. So for a couple of weeks, I try to spend less time than usual reading, researching and studying, and more time thinking, playing and just watching the world go by. This really makes a difference. When I pay attention to my needs and allow my mind to take a breather, some of my best ideas emerge.

Stay open to the unknown

When inspiration strikes, you have no way of knowing where it will take you. If you try to keep it at bay, it will soon evaporate – so just surrender and enjoy the ride. Switch on your curiosity and let go of your expectations of what the outcome 'should' be.

Artists from all domains affirm that following their feelings and instincts, rather than their intellect, elevates their work. However, for knowledge-based professionals like you and me, this can be a vulnerable place. Playing without inhibitions will inevitably lead to mistakes.

My advice is, make friends with 'mistakes'. Small slips can make your work more relatable and endearing. Some seemingly irrational ideas may turn out to be game changers. And when you own your creation, including your mistakes, you also show your fears and your inner critic who's the boss, and that you won't allow them to hold you back.

You can always fix major errors and smooth out the wrinkles later. But while you're riding a creative wave, you want to maintain momentum. You could even set yourself a tight time limit for completing your work, so that you don't get the chance to fiddle with the details or second-guess yourself.

Have the best 'companions'

In a close-knit team where you're all on the same wavelength, ideas flow freely. You understand each other with few words and gestures, bounce off one another effortlessly and bring out everyone's best thinking.

Talking about partnerships … have you ever thought of your work tools as your soulful companions? Many artists do, and in fact credit a part of their success to the instruments they use. Some of them use trusted pens or typewriters to help bring out the words. (One artist I know of – someone who knows how to write lines that change lives – actually used to take a typewriter on flights.)

And here's a fascinating story. Bruce Springsteen once received a guitar as a gift from a fan after a show. He didn't play it immediately, but since it was a beautifully made instrument, he set it up in his living room. Then one day, when Springsteen felt something coming, he picked up this guitar and started playing. It sounded beautiful. And to his surprise, an entire album's worth of songs poured from it, one after another, over the course of a week. Writing was quick and easy – Springsteen talks about this as a lovely, magical experience.

Be ready, anywhere and anytime

Eddie Vedder is known for his talent to think up lyrics on the spur of the moment. Once, during a band rehearsal, he was accidentally locked out of the building. It was raining. He pounded on the door at first, but as he started listening to the tune the rest of the band was playing inside, he decided to pull out a scrap of paper and a pen from his pocket and jot down the words that came to him. And the lyrics for that song were born.

Don't be surprised if inspiration hits when you expect it least – when you're not trying hard to create or solve things and perhaps not even thinking of work. This is the nature of inspiration: it's more likely to find you once you stop chasing it. You might be out and about, running errands, cooking dinner, having a shower, relaxing or trying to sleep.

If you're serious about creativity, you've got to be spontaneous and prepared to capture those fleeting ideas when they show up out of the blue. Springsteen keeps his guitar in his bedroom while working on an album. I keep a waterproof notepad and pencil in my shower … What about you – what do you need to have handy?

Choose your beliefs

Creative flow is often described as a spiritual experience. Some artists recount a deep sense of connection with the Universe. They feel that their thoughts and moves are guided by their souls. Others sense that an ethereal force is tapping into them or storming through them, and all they need to do is channel the gift. This invisible force seems to have a will – it chooses when to turn up, what to give you and where it wants to take you.

If you haven't experienced anything like this, or have different beliefs about what is real and what isn't, it's easy to dismiss the magical nature of inspiration as utter nonsense. However, in her beautiful book *Big Magic*, Elizabeth Gilbert makes a great point. We all live with delusions, so we might as well choose one that's empowering.

What beliefs are curbing your creativity? That you only have yourself to rely on? That you have no creative talent? Or that creating something valuable must be exhausting? … And what beliefs could help draw out the best in you? Personally, I choose to believe that when I get out of my own way, the best ideas will know how to find me.

Stick to it

Working on a creative project can be exciting and gratifying, but also unnerving at times. Being invested in an unfinished piece of work can trigger feelings of insecurity and self-doubt. You don't know exactly where things are heading or when you'll be able to make any progress at all. You might be wondering … *Did I take the right approach? Will I ever get there? Do I have what it takes to succeed?*

You may be on a roller-coaster ride, but even when you're at a low point, you shouldn't drop what you're doing. Take breaks when you need to, but never give up. With persistence, you'll always make some progress, either quickly or slowly. You'll learn and grow, and you'll get better and better at tapping into your creative flow.

ARE YOU READY?

Succeeding in professional work is an art in itself – and there's an artist in all of us. We create solutions and experiences that haven't existed before, drawing on our knowledge and imagination. Turning fleeting thoughts into something tangible and valuable is deeply satisfying. Admittedly, creating a masterpiece can sometimes take a long time and a lot of hard work. However, it's also possible to create amazing things surprisingly quickly and with little effort.

When you tap into your creative flow, work becomes easier and more enthralling. Ideas fly higher and you progress much faster.

Inspired moments cannot be planned, but there's a lot you can do to experience them more often and more fully. You can make some preparations, ensure you're ready to catch them, and just run with them when they do show up. In between these moments, you may need to put in some hard yards, but always remember – magic is waiting for you. Are you ready?

INDIVIDUAL EXERCISES

For a couple of weeks, do something new each day. Meet new people. Visit or work in new places. Use work tools you haven't used before. Listen to a new podcast. Try out a new recipe … As newness becomes a part of your life, do you find it easier to come up with new ideas?

Find a beautiful notebook, and a nice-quality pen or pencil to write down your ideas. Make sure they are a pleasure to touch and work with, and suit your personality. Do you notice any shift in your mood when working with them? Do they help you come up with new ideas?

TEAM EXERCISES

Prepare for your next brainstorming session. A week before the session, inform everyone about the challenge, including what questions will need to be answered. Also prepare a few different 'stimuli packs' (including words and visuals) to spark different ideas, and send one of these packs to each member. After the session, share your thoughts. How did the brainstorming go? Did your team produce more or better ideas than expected?

Have a chat with your team about the nature of creativity. What are your beliefs about inspiration and magic? How do you perceive your own creativity? What are your experiences like when you're hit by inspiration? Which work practices invite epiphanies, and which ones might block them?

35 SMART CHOICES

CHOICES

PART V

PART V

WHAT KINDS OF SPACES HELP ME THRIVE?

Inspiring and nurturing places play huge roles in our lives. This is why we strive to live in beautiful homes with stunning views, and to travel to exciting destinations. Just look at your bucket list … Among all the amazing experiences you wish to have in your life, there must be at least a few that wouldn't be the same without the magic of the place itself.

Places can inspire you to ask new questions and to reassess your values and priorities. They can give wings to your imagination and help you find new answers. They can make you feel energised and fully alive, curious and contemplative, or relaxed and at peace.

By choosing your workspace consciously, you can also elevate your performance and transform your experience at work. In this Part we'll explore what kinds of spaces can boost your creativity, help you feel well and happy, and make you feel that you belong.

You'll also find out how your workspace can sharpen your focus and make it easier for you to get your head around your work. The trick might be to know when is the right time to tidy up your workspace, and when you should stop worrying about the mess.

Having said that, finding the right environment is not the means to all ends. While the right space can give you immense support, working in less-than-ideal conditions should not stop you from creating great results. But you need to be clear about where to draw the line and what you can do when your work environment is just too challenging – so we're going to look into this too.

CHOICE 27

WHERE SHOULD I GO WHEN I NEED A CREATIVE BOOST?

What are some of the best places for blue-sky thinking?

In what kinds of environments are my best ideas born?

How can I find great thinking spaces wherever I work?

We all have our favourite spaces to think – perhaps in a friendly cafe, on a beautiful beach or at the top of a hill with spectacular views. But what can you do when you're tied up and can't travel for inspiration? Your neighbourhood probably offers plenty of places that can elevate your creativity. And when you understand exactly what kind of stimulation or support you need, you should also be able to find your 'creative space' right where you are – in your office and at home.

Every time I travel these days, I bring an empty notebook with me. I've noticed that when I'm visiting different places, whether for business or leisure, I frequently experience epiphanies. I usually come home from my trips with my notebook filled with interesting insights about my work and life, as well as new goals and new plans.

But just like most people I know, even when I'm settled in my daily routines, many of my best ideas hit me when I'm not actually working. Sometimes my imagination takes off while I'm walking to the market, relaxing in a park, working out at the gym, catching up with friends or sitting in a cafe watching people. And of course, lots of original thoughts bubble to the surface in the shower every day. Yes, that little room seems to be one of the most common birthplaces of game-changing ideas.

There's a lot of science explaining why we often experience creative break-throughs in nature, during exercise, in buzzing social spaces or in the privacy of our bathrooms, for example. This knowledge is certainly useful when you can leave behind your usual workplace, your team and your to-do list in search of inspiration. It's nice to be able to visit your favourite thinking place whenever you need to free your mind and jump-start your imagination.

But not everyone has this kind of luxury in an average workday.

If you find it challenging to nurture your creative side without taking a long break and having a change of scenery, have a closer look at your options. You may discover great new spaces to think, just around the corner.

But first, let's go on a quick journey ...

SOME OF THE MOST STIMULATING PLACES ARE FAR FROM OUR EVERYDAY REALITY

Let me tell you about a couple of 'faraway' spaces that are probably outside your reach on most days, but when you're actually there your thinking transforms.

I know many people who do amazing work on **planes**. Being disconnected from the day-to-day pressures of your job, and from phone and email, can really free up your mind. (Although you may have access to Wi-Fi on a plane, hopefully no-one expects you to answer emails and calls while you're in the air.) In addition, there's something powerful about being at a high altitude. You may have wide open views and be able to see a large part of the world beneath you. But even when you don't sit near a window, every part of you can sense that you're high above. This is a great place to be for expansive thinking, developing a vision and reflecting on your true influence – looking at things from a big picture point of view.

Here's another example – the story of my dream workplace. A few years ago I attended a four-day speaker training event at a beautiful seaside resort in Indonesia. At the beginning of the event, participants received challenging homework: each of us needed to develop a complete TED-style talk, which we'd present on the fourth day. To make the most of the situation, I decided to spend my afternoons sitting in **a refreshing pool**, equipped with a waterproof notepad, working on my presentation. I had a wonderful time of course, but I was also very effective. My mind was flooded with great ideas and I progressed surprisingly quickly. I ended up very happy with the results, but most importantly, the audience loved my presentation.

WHY NOT LOOK AROUND OUTSIDE YOUR OFFICE?

Some of the most stimulating environments are public places.

On days when I need a boost of creativity, I sometimes visit a nearby **art gallery** to spend a couple of hours exploring ideas. Or I might choose to sit **under a magnificent tree**, watching ducks and seagulls while allowing my mind to roam free. And what a difference from sitting at my desk! Such lively places always reward me with great new ideas and insights.

Vast open spaces can also inspire blue-sky thinking, such as large halls and city squares, as well as beaches, river banks and sprawling green parks. When you're surrounded by large empty spaces, you can feel that you have room to think. There's plenty of scope for ideas and the world is like a blank canvas.

You may enjoy experimenting with your thoughts in spaces that feel a bit like a **stage or a movie set** – where you can see others and they can see you from a distance. Many public places incorporate stepped seating, which can create this kind of experience. I saw a lot of them in New York City especially – in bustling squares, along popular walkways, and at the edges of parks and playgrounds. These seats were packed with folk who seemed to enjoy watching the city life from an elevated viewpoint … This is a peculiar scenario where you may feel you are an audience member, or the star of the stage, compelled to play. But either way, you're in the middle of an unfolding story.

In contrast, many people find themselves in their element when they can **blend into the crowd** – say, on a busy shopping strip with buskers and performers, or in a lively cafe. While hiding in plain sight, you can allow your imagination to roam free. Apart from having warm social vibes, many cafes and open public places also offer just the **right amount of noise** for expansive thinking. Yes, that's right – a moderate amount of background noise can actually boost creativity, as research suggests.

You may find that visiting **places you haven't been before** – or where you don't go very often – can also liberate your mind. They don't even need to be nice or inspiring places; they just need to feel new to you. I remember a period when I was stuck in a rut working from home every day. One day I had to go to an eye clinic for a check-up. And while I was sitting in that drab and unpleasant waiting room – one of the last places you'd want to be – I was suddenly flooded with a refreshing sense of freedom. I was in this place for the first time, and it made me realise that my world was much larger than it had previously felt.

Even your own neighbourhood can offer new experiences and thus help you see the world through fresh eyes. You might be struck by moments of inspiration while checking out the alleyways around your office, exploring the narrowest paths in a park, or getting off your train or bus at a random stop.

IS YOUR WORKPLACE 'DESIGNED FOR CREATIVITY'?

Are you lucky enough to work in an office designed to promote creative thinking?

Let me clarify what I mean. The stereotypical 'creative workspace' has many distinct features.

The space offers plenty of opportunities for social activities and collaboration. It features themed meeting rooms, an impressive games room and a state-of-the-art cafeteria (which can double as a collaboration or coworking space). Some areas are reminiscent of public bars or cafes, sports facilities or entertainment centres. The walls are decorated with quirky graphics and artworks. The interior has bright, cheerful colours and a playful or artistic vibe.

Many of the rooms are equipped with the latest communication and collaboration technologies, flexible furniture, and large writeable surfaces. You can easily change things around and put your personal stamp on the space. The furnishings don't feel too precious. You feel that the space is there for you, not the other way around.

Other areas are designed for contemplation and relaxation, with a peaceful, homey feel and perhaps an air of spirituality. The interior is characterised by lots of natural materials, living plants, soft tactile fabrics, earthy colours and soft lighting. In these spaces, you can allow your mind to wander while browsing the bookshelves in the room, or unwind on a reclining chair or in an impressive swinging chair.

The bad news is there's no recipe for creativity

Creativity is a complex phenomenon. Ideas need to be born, incubated, selected, developed and tested, and every phase calls for different ways of thinking.

The creative journey may also be unique to the organisation, the team, the individual, as well as the problem that needs solving. Coming up with ideas for a disruptive product or service, and then a catchy name for it, for example, requires a very different process from ingeniously fixing a software glitch.

Certain strategies and conditions may serve you well in one situation and let you down in another. And at times, the best approach to a creative challenge might be the exact opposite of what worked for you previously. Let me give you a few examples:

- Bouncing ideas back and forth with others can spark new, more refined ideas, but sometimes profound revelations only emerge when you're left alone with your thoughts.

- While feeling energetic may help you think more expansively, unwinding in a tranquil environment could take you into that dreamy state where creative ideas naturally occur.

- In a comfortable, distraction-free environment you can more easily immerse yourself in the problem you're trying to solve. However, some discomfort or noise and movement around you could hijack your conscious mind (which is responsible for self-criticism), and thus make way for unique thoughts to emerge from your subconscious.

- Having access to a range of resources – including work tools and technology – can help you explore many different possibilities. Dealing with constraints, though, can prompt you to think outside the box.

Put simply, there's no such thing as a 'creative space'. Just because an office has plenty of exciting and stimulating features, you can't be certain that good ideas will find you there. In fact, creative experts and artists believe that you have little control over when an inventive thought will hit you. You might find that in some places and situations you are more receptive to original ideas than in others, but there are never any guarantees.

So here's the good news

Whichever way you're wired, you're more likely to realise your potential if you can nimbly alternate between different modes of working and thinking. And a workspace 'designed for creativity' can help you do just that. In an office with a large variety of settings, you have a good chance to find a spot, at any phase of the creative process, that allows you to get into the right headspace.

Just pick a space you feel drawn to, and if it doesn't work for you, move on.

Don't be too concerned if your work style defies logic. What's most important is that you choose where you work consciously while also listening to your instincts. You might end up using a space rather differently from what was intended by the designers and change managers – but that's nothing to worry about, as long as you work with awareness and respect. Remember, your mind is unique, as is the way you tap into your creative genius.

HOW TO FIND YOUR THINKING SPACE ANYWHERE

So, what can you do if your workspace is not particularly modern or diverse, and you don't have many exciting options? This is a good time to think outside the box. Literally. Go on a journey in your mind and visit your favourite thinking places outside the building you work in.

When you're out and about, where do you have your best ideas? On a plane perhaps, or other high places with sweeping views? In soothing and grounding environments? In parks and gardens? In vast open spaces? In artistic settings? In noisy cafes? Or anywhere that feels new to you?

Do you get a buzz from watching people and being watched? Do you prefer bustling environments where you can blend into the crowd? Or do you get your best ideas when you're alone?

In your office – or home office – you probably can't jump into a pool or sit under a tree, unless you're lucky enough to work in one of the coolest offices on the planet. However, you probably have some of these options:

- Work in a busy and stimulating area or in a low-key, quiet spot.

- Use a large bright room with high ceilings or a small, cosy nook.

- Find a room enlivened with green plants or exotic artwork, or create one.

- Use an elevated place from which you can look down onto the street or to a lower floor.

- Use stepped seating – one of the favourite features of the hip workplace.

- Find spaces with open, pleasant views.

- Pick a spot you don't use very often, or make some changes to your usual work area.

- Put on your headphones and play your choice of ambient sounds or music.

Such simple choices can really make a difference. I know people who often struggled to find their creative flow, but only until they realised that they needed to be in busy, social environments to find good ideas. One of my friends noticed a significant spike in his creativity once he started working in spaces with wide open views. I find that my imagination tends to open up when I work high up from the ground. And often something as simple as moving from one spot to the other within the same room can switch something in my mind, allowing ideas to trickle through.

Three easy steps

Whether you're based in a really cool, state-of-the-art workplace, in a traditional office or at home, you have quite a few choices. You should be able to find places that can evoke your creative spirit and allow your best ideas to come to you.

The steps are simple:

1. Think back to the places, even from your travels and personal life, where you were hit by great ideas and insights.

2. Reflect on what was special about these spaces. What inspiring features and qualities did they have?

3. Find (or create) places with similar qualities in your current environment.

Once you discover the many different spaces that can help you clear the cobwebs and unleash your imagination, those light-bulb moments will be waiting for you.

INDIVIDUAL EXERCISES

For a few weeks, take notes whenever a good idea pops into your head (perhaps on a notepad or your mobile phone). Don't just write down the idea, but also the place where it came to you, and how you felt in that place. Then review your notes and see if you can learn something new about the types of environments that help you think creatively.

Experiment with working on creative tasks – or thinking about problems and solutions – in different environments. Explore spaces both outside and inside your workplace, including areas that don't have a particularly exciting design. What do you observe? Do good ideas sometimes come to you in unexpected places?

Think about a place you love that always helps you get into the right frame of mind for creative thinking. What is special about this place? How could you describe its vibe? What exactly does it give you that's so valuable? And could you perhaps also find these qualities in other places – for example, in your workplace or its neighbourhood?

TEAM EXERCISE

Share your stories and strategies with each other for overcoming mental blocks. Where do you go when you need a creative boost? What kinds of places give you the inspiration and clarity you need to solve problems? And have you ever had any unusual experiences that rewarded you with epiphanies?

CHOICE 28

WHAT KINDS OF PLACES HELP ME FEEL WELL AND HAPPY?

How can I find or create spaces that help me feel whole?

What sorts of environments feel like home to me?

How can I transform my relationship with my workspace?

Few people list their offices as one of their favourite places. Most of us are drawn to beautiful natural environments, and to social settings like cosy cafes and lively streets. But here's the twist … Once you understand why you love certain environments more than others, you'll look at your surroundings differently. You'll start to notice great qualities in places you've never really appreciated before. And you'll find it easier to choose or create spaces that help you get into the right frame of mind for the task at hand – and where you feel happy and whole.

Most of my childhood memories take me to outdoor places. I spent countless warm sunny days with my parents and my sister in the hills near Budapest, the city where I grew up. When I was still little, we just drove to the parks, picked a pretty clearing among the pine woods, laid down a picnic blanket and made ourselves at home for the day. We were playing games, going for short walks and marvelling at little four- and six-legged creatures. Once I got a bit older, we went on longer walks – sometimes meandering along creeks or climbing up to rocky hilltops. And we always spent our holidays near forests, lakes and rivers.

When I think back to these places, I can recall amazing little details, and I'm filled with warm fuzzy feelings. On the other hand, I only have faded memories of the buildings we visited or stayed in. Even the home I lived in during the first few years of my life is a blur in my mind.

As you can tell, I've always been an outdoor person, so you may wonder why on earth I decided to study architecture and focus my career on the built environment. Well, in my youth, I not only noticed that certain places had a spell on me, but I couldn't help wondering what exactly made them so special. *Why do I love exploring wetlands with flooded trees so much? Why do I gravitate to places where rivers meet? And why am I drawn to the sunniest spot in my home when I need to think or study, even though it's not designed for that purpose?* … I had this vision that if I cracked the code, I would be able to bring the magic indoors and help create nicer, more people-friendly buildings.

I can't claim to have found all the answers; places have some mysterious qualities that are not meant to be deciphered. But over the years I've discovered plenty of interesting insights on the places we love, and we can all use this knowledge to create better work and life experiences for ourselves.

WHERE HAVE WE ALL COME FROM?

Before jumping too far ahead, let's quickly look at how our relationship with our surroundings has been shaped by our distant and not-so-distant history.

Our core psychological needs have been formed by millions of years of evolution as a species, which is why we feel more at home in spaces that remind us of nature. Nature carries many intricate qualities – it's relaxing and exciting, nurturing and challenging, predictable and unpredictable – and we long to see similar traits in our modern environments.

In the prehistoric era, the lives of our ancestors were hanging in a delicate balance of venturing into the wild and staying protected from predators and the weather. We are therefore drawn to places that give us a sense of security while inspiring us to embark on exciting new adventures.

And let's not forget about our personal history. As children, when we're scared or tired, we look for cosy and familiar spaces where we feel safe and loved. But once we've recharged, we go to play, learn and grow with an insatiable appetite, and explore new environments with wide eyes … We then grow up, with our own ideas of what it means to be an adult, but our basic needs and desires change relatively little.

So when it comes to finding your happy places, it's worth listening to your instincts.

Places that meet your deepest needs help you feel whole and fully alive. This is a wonderful state – you are centred and courageous, in touch with your own truth. You breathe freely and act authentically, focusing on what matters most. You feel connected to your purpose and the people around you, and work flows with ease. But it's not just about what you can achieve. Every minute is precious, whether you're free to pursue your favourite pastimes or you need to work. So why not spend your time in places that bring you joy?

NEITHER TOO EASY NOR TOO CHALLENGING

When you look at the evolution of human needs, I'm sure you see some patterns. We all thrive on experiences that are neither too easy nor too challenging, in environments where we feel safe yet inspired to create change.

Relaxing and stimulating

Experiencing a broad range of emotional states is part of a rich and fulfilling life. At times you just want to relax. At other moments, you enjoy the adrenaline rush as you face your fears and leap head first into a major challenge. And most of the time, you want to be somewhere in between – neither too relaxed nor too revved up. In fact, in the context of intellectual work, you're more likely to perform at your best when you're moderately excited and energised.

Natural environments are relaxing and stimulating, often at the same time. When you're meandering among lush trees or watching the waves crash on a rocky shore, you feel the life and energy around you, and you also sense that you're in a place you belong.

It's easier to find your centre when you're connected to nature, and you can also experience this indoors. Surround yourself with natural colours and materials like wood, stone and bamboo. Look for natural light. If you're lucky, your workspace offers views of greenery, but nature photos and indoor plants also make a difference.

Good interior designers have a variety of techniques up their sleeves to achieve a natural vibe and make a space calming or energising. Though you might not understand the nitty-gritty of design, you can certainly feel the difference, and when you're looking to work or relax, you can hopefully find a spot that feels just right.

Safe and exciting

You need a sense of safety to be able to focus on what you do and enjoy life. In a workplace or in a restaurant, for example, you probably prefer to sit against a wall or a screen, with your back protected, while being able to see what's happening around you. Having traffic and other activities behind you can be rather unsettling, since – according to your unconscious – you're unprepared for danger.

At the same time, you crave some risk and excitement. That's why it's so much fun watching a storm through a window or posing for a photo under a hanging rock. You know you'll be okay, but you can still feel the immense power of the elements.

Built environments can also provide thrilling experiences. Think of cantilevered rooms or balconies, floor-to-ceiling windows in high-rise buildings, or large decorative objects suspended from a ceiling. Have you ever stood under a car or an airplane floating above you in a building? Not an everyday sensation.

Predictable and surprising

In familiar environments it's always easier to do routine tasks that don't require much creativity. You know what to expect and where to find the resources you need. But when everything is same old, same old, you'll quickly become bored, feeling like you're stuck in a rut. You need some surprises and mystery in your environment to feel inspired.

When you can't see the whole space around you, you feel compelled to keep exploring. Japanese gardens are wonderful examples; as you walk around, new scenery opens up with every few steps. Some workplaces are designed with similar principles, taking you on a journey along a series of hidden spaces and nooks. Even after you've explored the place, that sense of mystery never completely goes away.

Buildings with blurred boundaries between indoors and outdoors also have intriguing vibes. That's why it's so enjoyable to sit on a covered deck or in a cafe that opens out onto the street. But workspaces have many other, easy opportunities to offer surprise – through flexible furnishing, quirky design, or unusual and frequently changing artwork.

You too can contribute. Perhaps bring some interesting objects to work that don't traditionally belong in an office. Are you allowed to decorate and then redecorate some of the spaces in your office? If so, go ahead, unleash your inner artist and surprise yourself and your colleagues.

Created and curated

Imagine that every time you walk into a particular room, you have to move all the furniture, open the blinds, change the thermostat, set up technology, adjust the whiteboard, and fiddle with the chair and the desk just to get started on whatever you were planning to do. It's a good thing that you have control, but when you need to go to so much trouble, you probably won't be bothered to get everything right.

On the other hand, you naturally desire some level of interaction and control. If everything is designed and pre-adjusted to your needs, you may feel more comfortable – but when you know you can't change a thing, that's rather disempowering. You can only feel truly at home in places that not only support your needs but also give you the opportunity to make them your own.

Thankfully, workplaces are becoming increasingly diversified and flexible. When you're looking for a suitable space for any activity, I suggest you pick a spot that feels inviting and has the most important features you need, but also allows you to make the changes that matter to you.

NEITHER TOO STRAIGHT NOR TOO CURVY

While extreme places can make great destinations, harmonious and balanced environments help us feel at home. We appreciate settings that are interesting and filled with life but are not overwhelming. And most of us love offbeat, unexpected features and events, though only in moderation.

Still and in motion

Busy places can sometimes be a lot of fun. Music festivals. Hackathons. Watching the traffic of Ho Chi Minh City, or blending into the crowd on a busy street in Tokyo. But dealing with non-stop noise and movement around you is exhausting, and you eventually start to crave some peace and quiet … After all that sensory overload, finding refuge in a perfectly still environment can feel like bliss, at least for a while. You can finally relax and hear your own thoughts. However, at some point the lack of motion can also get to you, and you'll soon become desperate to see some life around you.

Too much movement or zero movement – neither is natural. In nature, change is constant but rarely intense. The quality of the light shifts throughout the day. Clouds roll across the sky. Birds chirp and fly around. Leaves rustle, trees sway and the breeze carries the scent of flowers.

While buildings are largely static, it's possible to bring movement and change to the indoors. Naturally, from a room with windows you can witness how the outside world is changing. But technology can also help. For example, some workplaces are designed to provide varying temperatures and airflow rates throughout the day without making you feel uncomfortable. Dynamic lighting systems can mimic the shifting hues of natural light. Digital displays can show you any moving scenery you wish to see, whether real or imagined. And you might have nature sounds playing in the background, or a water feature babbling nearby.

Simple and rich

I haven't yet come across a dull place in nature. Forests, wetlands and reefs are all diverse and vibrant environments filled with life. But even simple-looking landscapes like deserts, snowy peaks and vast plains have fascinating details. Natural environments offer rich experiences, engaging all of your senses through a variety of colours, forms and shapes, sounds, fragrances and textures.

There were times in the past when many designers and organisational leaders believed that decorative objects and details in a workspace only created distractions. Stark, minimalist office spaces were rampant, built on the assumption that they helped people to focus better. This idea has been refuted by a large body of research, and science now confirms what most of us already knew, that barren places make us unhappy, unproductive and disengaged.

But the question still stands: how much decoration and 'stuff' is healthy and helpful? And how much mess and clutter is too much? Everyone has an opinion, but what you really need depends on your personality, what you do and how you feel in the moment.

When you're choosing or creating a space to work or to rest, make sure it's neither boring nor too busy. If you feel a room needs to be dressed up, go ahead. Decorate it with artworks, plants or any other objects you fancy. And if you find that a bit of mess helps you relax and find your flow, just own that mess. (We'll dig deeper into this idea in the next Choice.)

Nice and scruffy

Let me state the obvious: it's nice to be surrounded by beautiful pieces of furniture, materials and objects. In many office spaces, however, all you see are work-related items everywhere you look: desks covered with paper files and electronic devices, walls filled with plans, tracking sheets, memos … you name it. No wonder that in these environments work feels like work, and life appears to be happening elsewhere. Just think about how many 'nice things' you have at home and how many you have at work. Do you see a divide? If so, you know what to do.

At the same time, you'll probably find a place more engaging if not everything is neat and perfect. In a highly polished environment, whatever you do or change can only upset the order. You may feel there's nothing for you to add, and therefore you're redundant. In contrast, spaces that are somewhat scruffy and unfinished invite you to be part of the picture, giving you permission to experiment, create a mess and make mistakes. In imperfect spaces, you are welcome to be you.

Real and unreal

We're all drawn to places that feel real to us. It's difficult to put your finger on what authenticity means exactly, but when you do experience it, you recognise it. In my definition, an authentic environment is created with the sole purpose of bringing out the best in people. This is why, in my favourite places, I don't see 'clever', fashionable or cheap design solutions. I don't smell commercial interest or the designer's ego in the air. Such environments are not necessarily expensive; they simply feel honest and natural.

Having said that, I think we all enjoy moments that feel unreal – seeing or hearing things that make us chuckle. Humour and play can put things in perspective and turn on our creative taps. Thankfully, there are countless opportunities to bring these qualities into a space – for instance, through artworks, murals, written words, interactive displays (fun walls) or bold design solutions.

One of my favourite examples is a print of Banksy's artwork *Show Me the Monet*, which I've seen hanging on the wall of a coworking space in Melbourne. The image shows Monet's famous painting *Bridge over a Pond of Water Lilies*, complete with a couple of added shopping trolleys and a traffic cone dumped in the pond. As another example, when you enter Superhero's Amsterdam office, you can't miss the large wall mural depicting a llama with an ice cream cone on its snout, surrounded by floating rubber gloves, while receiving a scratch on the head. Could it get any more unreal?

THE SECRET INGREDIENT: FOSTERING HEALTHY RELATIONSHIPS

Okay, so we've touched on how our favourite places look and feel, and how they serve some of our core human needs. However, we haven't yet looked at something very important: our relationships. To feel whole, we need to have a sense of connection to others, and also to ourselves – who we truly are and what's important to us. And certain places can offer exactly that.

Supporting both privacy and connection

I find it interesting to see where people like to sit in public places. Through my travels, I noticed that in different parts of the world residents act differently. In some cities, people looking to wind down often sit quietly, side by side at the edges of busy roads, watching cars and pedestrians pass by. In others, they love hanging out in parks and at riverbanks, having drinks and picnics. And in some cities, folks up for a good time routinely get together at cafes and sit out on the sidewalks under large canopies.

Yet, one thing is common. Everywhere you go, people gravitate to places where they can have a private conversation – or the chance to be alone with their thoughts – and at the same time, see what's happening around them and feel that they are part of a larger community. This makes perfect sense. Privacy is one of our most fundamental needs, along with the opportunity to socialise and stay connected with each other.

In nature, you can sit under a tree and be alone while feeling part of the whole. When it comes to the built environment, one of my personal favourite places is the covered balcony of the Port Elliot Beach House in South Australia. This special little spot offers open views across the street to grassy parklands and the Southern Ocean, without making you feel exposed. People-centric workplaces also offer many of these kinds of spaces; for example, soundproof rooms with glass walls, as well as private nooks and meeting booths positioned next to walkways. As workplaces are evolving, such semi-private settings are becoming increasingly popular.

Reflecting who you are and who you want to become

Every space has some sort of a personality. Some of them are serious, conservative and uppity, while others are friendly, playful and warm. And certain spaces have more layered personalities. For example, a coworking space I used to work in comes across as intelligent, confident and refined. In contrast, another workspace I know has the vibe of a hyperactive and carefree adventurer.

Environments that resonate with who you are help you feel comfortable and welcome. When you see some of your own traits in the space around you, you know you'll be understood and accepted.

However, as part of your personal journey, you are continually changing and evolving – and the way architects and interior designers respond to this is really interesting. Some workspaces are designed to embody the traits that the organisation and its members aspire to. In a space that carries the energy of your ideal future self, you can't help but start to grow into that person, which is a deeply fulfilling experience.

Helping you feel the love

This is perhaps the most important quality of environments that nourish our mind and soul, yet it's so rarely discussed in the context of work experience and performance. We all have a deep desire to love and to be loved. Are you skeptical that love can have a place at work, aside from having close and caring relationships with your colleagues? Just ask any creative professional who is in their element when surrounded by family members – bubbly children or grandchildren, caring parents, or their better half.

And of course, if you have pets, they can brighten your day and make you feel at home wherever you are. You're a different person when your fur or feather babies are around. According to research, employees in dog-friendly workplaces tend to be happier, more relaxed and more social, and interestingly, also more productive and engaged with their work. Sharing your workspace with pets may also bring up some challenges, but you can never underestimate the power of their love.

In corporate offices, putting family photos on desks is often frowned upon or outright forbidden. But when you have the opportunity, why not decorate your workspace with any image that gives you the warm fuzzies? Now, this is not for everyone, but how about photos of cute baby animals? A Japanese study suggests that looking at such pictures can improve focus and the speed and accuracy of work. So if heartwarming photos can bring out your best, display them proudly and let the prickly comments roll off like water from a duck's back.

YOU DON'T WANT TO BE ANYWHERE ELSE

Physical environments influence you in complex and mysterious ways. Your favourite places help you become the best version of yourself and make you feel you belong. There's no formula for creating or finding such spaces, but some of the patterns are clear. Human spaces embody the qualities of natural environments and serve your needs in a balanced way. Every feature of a space contributes to your experience: objects, materials and textures, shapes and forms, proportions, colours, lights and shades, sounds, temperatures, fragrances and movements.

When you find a place where you feel whole, you just know it and you don't want to be anywhere else.

INDIVIDUAL EXERCISES

Write a list of your favourite places in the world. What's special about them? What do they look like? How do they make you feel? ... Next, explore your current options. Can you find places with similar qualities within your workplace or near where you live?

Check out the different spaces in your office, and reflect on which ones you find stimulating, which ones you find peaceful and grounding, and which ones are a bit quirky. How do these spaces influence your mood? And how can they help you get into the right headspace for different activities?

TEAM EXERCISES

Walk through your office together and look at all the different settings. Share your thoughts with each other. Do you see a good variety of styles and vibes? Do you have both relaxing and stimulating spaces? Simple and richly decorated settings? Neat and unpolished rooms? Areas for socialising and for being alone? ... And is there anything missing?

Pick a space in your office that's not very popular and thus rarely used. Have a chat with your team about what the issue might be and how it could be improved. Then roll up your sleeves and do what you can to make that space more attractive. Consider moving things around, bringing in plants and adding new decor. How do you feel about the result?

Brainstorm with your teammates how you could bring humour to your workplace. Then turn the best ideas into a reality. Enjoy!

SHOULD I TIDY UP MY WORKSPACE?

When is it useful to keep my desk perfectly clear?
In what situations can a messy space help me think better?
What is good clutter and what is bad?
'A messy desk is a messy mind' – what's the truth?

Many people prefer to keep their workspaces minimalist and perfectly tidy, while others are in their element in messy environments. Who's getting it right? Well, what works for you largely depends on your personality and on your tasks. There's also good clutter and bad clutter. So rather than choosing a side, you should understand how tidy and messy spaces affect your state of mind.

I see a lot of debates about what makes a supportive and inspiring work environment, but when it comes to the question of clean desks and messy desks, people can butt heads like mountain goats.

Proponents of clean desks tend to stand by the age-old saying, 'A messy desk is a messy mind'. They find it easier to concentrate in perfectly tidy environments, and often argue that any items not required for the task at hand only create distraction. When they see a cluttered workstation, they're likely to draw the conclusion that its owner is either lazy or struggling to stay on top of their work.

Members of the 'Messy Desk Fan Club', on the other hand, can't fathom the idea of keeping their space perfectly organised. Some of them are apologetic about their sloppy habits while others are openly proud of them, feeling validated the famous argument (often attributed to Albert Einstein), 'If a cluttered desk is a sign of a cluttered mind, of what, then, is an empty desk a sign?' Now, I personally feel closer to this second group, and I must say it feels wonderful to know that Thomas Edison, Steve Jobs and Barack Obama all had or have messy desks as well, along with countless other brilliant minds.

When 'messy deskers' see a perfectly organised workspace, they often assume that the person working there is probably rather close-minded, unimaginative and perhaps also a bit unhappy. I've actually heard work-place experts refer to clean desk policies as 'environmental lobotomies'. Now that's a passionate point of view!

Leaders on both sides of the debate naturally want to create the best possi-ble environment for their teams to excel. The problem is when they're abso-lutely convinced that their way of working is the right way, and they expect everyone else around them to follow their example. In many workplaces, employees are not allowed to keep any non-work-related items on their desks or to personalise their work areas. I've also heard about companies where even artworks and pot plants are banned, because the boss finds all this distracting – which is just bizarre ... At the other end of the spectrum are those chaotic offices where clutter has been accumulating for years, if not decades, and no-one is doing anything about it.

Going too far in either direction is rarely a good idea. But what if everyone has a point? Let's see what science says.

TWO SIDES OF THE SAME COIN

Seeing mess all around you may indeed be distracting and even stressful. Research shows that clutter can actually trigger your fight or flight response. When junk is thrown all over your work area or work files take up much of your desk space, it's easy to feel overwhelmed and out of control. You can also waste a lot of time trying to find what you need among the chaos.

A neat and tidy environment can spare you from these issues and even pro-mote certain virtues. For example, it may encourage you to act generously and responsibly – in other words, to be a good citizen. In one study, after completing a task in a tidy room, people were more charitable compared to those who had worked in a cluttered space. Interestingly, they were also more likely to choose a healthy snack over sweets.

Now let's look at the other side of the coin. How can tidiness create problems, and how can mess be beneficial?

Ironically, sterile and non-stimulating environments can make it difficult to focus too, just like untidy workspaces. There's plenty of evidence that on average, people are less productive in sterile, minimalist spaces, compared to rich and stimulating environments. What's more, in a stark and unwelcoming room, you can easily become restless and uncomfortable. All this makes sense when you consider that we humans are wired to feel more at home and safe in spaces that look and feel natural, and nature is anything but tidy and clean. When you see an animal in a barren cage, you feel sorry for it, don't you?

What about creativity and innovation? In an orderly workspace you're more prone to avoid risk and follow conventional thinking, which rarely helps when you're faced with unique challenges. A somewhat chaotic space, on the other hand, may boost your imagination. In fact, the same study which found that orderly environments promoted responsible choices also observed that in an untidy room, participants were able to come up with significantly more creative and original ideas. It seems that the mess around them inspired people to break free from traditions and think unconventionally.

KNOW WHAT WORKS BEST FOR YOU

As you can see, debating who is right or wrong is futile. Whether you perform better in a tidy or in a slightly messy environment largely depends on the **type of work you do**. When your job requires you to think critically, adhere to the norm and stay away from risk – for instance, when you need to manage data, do quality checks or write technical reports – it's a good idea to keep your work area clear. But when you want to think outside the box and explore uncharted territory, a slightly jumbled, laid-back space will probably serve you better. In a rich and homey environment it's also easier to engage in relaxed conversations and build connected relationships. Just think of the types of spaces where you go to catch up with friends.

The way you perceive clutter is also a **matter of perspective**, of course. What one person finds too busy, another may find too sterile. You probably have a sweet spot that's neither too clinical nor too scattered. However, if everything needs to be in perfect order for you to be able to concentrate, you might want to check if this is working for you and your team. And if the contrary is true – you struggle to find a small patch of free surface on your chaotic desk, you keep wasting time searching for what you need, and your colleagues feel disturbed by your mess – you're not just a 'messy desk person'; you have a problem that needs addressing. So make sure you don't go to the extreme, and always be mindful not to impose on others.

And here is one more thing to consider, which is most fascinating in my opinion. When you leave your desk after work without packing things up and then return the following morning, you may find that you get up to speed quicker and pick up where you left off with far less effort. This is because some people rely largely on their visual memory to recall abstract thoughts and concepts. If you happen to be a **visual person**, you can instantly get into a certain headspace just by looking at an image, an object, or your busy desk, for example. However, if you tidy up your space at the end of the day, you may need to spend more time the following morning getting your head around what you need to be doing. In simple terms, your mind will need to reboot.

WHAT IS GOOD CLUTTER?

Not all clutter is created equal. Certain objects in your surroundings can stimulate your productivity and imagination while others restrain your thinking.

Seeing unusual objects that look a bit out of place in a workspace could help you think outside the box. These stimulating objects might be a pile of toys, quirky artworks, or other non-work-related objects you wouldn't expect to see in an office or home office. My favourite piece of 'clutter' I've ever seen in an office was a wooden toy monkey hanging upside down from a desk lamp. Yep, it's difficult to feel constrained by the status quo when a cheeky monkey is smiling right in front of your face.

Playing with tactile objects during a conversation or while contemplating a problem can also stimulate your thinking. While those fidget spinners, squishy toys and fluffy pompoms might look ridiculous in your workspace, it's worth keeping some of them handy.

Happiness is one of the greatest performance boosters, so anything that makes you feel good is worthwhile to have around, such as beautiful or inspiring images or funny drawings that make you smile. Family photos make a difference too. According to a survey, high achievers are more likely to keep photos of their children on their desks, compared to less productive employees.

Items left in plain sight can also influence your personal habits. For example, you'll be inclined to make healthier food choices if you keep nutritious snacks on your desk and hide those packs of chips and chocolate bars in a drawer.

AND WHAT IS BAD CLUTTER?

Just like most people, you're probably overcommitted, and a single look at your to-do list or a mountain of files on your desk could make you feel overwhelmed. So keep any files and documents that are not needed for the task at hand out of sight. Try to put away anything that reminds you of the huge amount of work ahead of you, making you anxious or tempting you to multitask.

The most disturbing item on your desk could actually be your phone. Even when switched to silent and placed face down, it still undermines your focus and productivity (as we uncovered in Choice 5). Our relationships with our phones are extremely complicated, and just looking at them can trigger a cocktail of distracting thoughts and emotions. Therefore, if you don't need to use your phone, it's a good idea to keep it out of sight, and if possible, in another room.

Naturally, you also need to consider information security and confidentiality. If a document shouldn't be seen by visitors, cleaners and perhaps even your colleagues, keep it locked away every time you're away from your desk.

It should go without saying, but don't leave rubbish, food scraps or dirty dishes lying around either. Also make sure your workspace can be easily cleaned. There must be a better place to keep your entire collection of plush kitties or fantasy figurines. (Yep, I've seen it all.) Thinking about hygiene is not very exciting, but a grubby space is a health hazard for anyone around. And let's not even start on how demoralising it is to work among filth.

When you work in a shared setting, there's a whole set of other rules. It's of course common courtesy to always pack up your personal items and leave the space clean and tidy for the next person.

WHAT'S YOUR COMPASS?

When it comes to tidiness, what's guiding your behaviour? Age-old clichés like 'a messy desk is a messy mind'? Wisdom you've learned from your parents or from famous thinkers? Expectations from your colleagues or superiors? Or your lazy habits? ... It's perhaps time to rethink what actually works for you, and how an orderly or a somewhat cluttered space could support what you do.

Your teammates may think and work very differently from you, and that's perfectly okay as long as you can work productively and collaborate seamlessly, without imposing on each other. Think about this for a moment ... Have you ever noticed that a room can seem freezing cold to some people, while being perfectly comfortable for others? Just because someone else's room makes you shiver, if they're happy to work there, why would you tell them to turn up the heat?

When a teammate who is tidier or messier than you is having trouble staying on top of things, have a chat with them first before giving any advice. Their struggle may have something to do with their work habits, but may just as well stem from a completely different source. (Why not give them a copy of this book?)

INDIVIDUAL EXERCISES

Remove every single item from your desk that is not required for the task at hand. See if this makes any difference. How are you feeling? How do you manage with analytical and creative activities? Next, add some good clutter – stimulating and tactile items, and objects that lift your mood. Do you notice any changes in your wellbeing and performance?

Experiment with working on different tasks in tidy and in cluttered spaces. For the first part of this exercise, try to concentrate on a mentally demanding task – for half an hour or so – in a stark, orderly room. Then take a quick break, move to a cluttered space and continue with the same task. Where do you find it easier to focus?
For the second part, try to think outside the box in a neat and tidy room, and then in a somewhat messy space. What do you notice?

TEAM EXERCISES

Discuss in your team who prefers clean desks and who prefers messy desks. What are your arguments and your personal experiences? What can you learn from each other? And what can you agree to disagree on?

For one week, everyone in the team should be allowed to create as much mess as they wish. For another week, everyone should keep their work areas perfectly tidy. Then have a discussion. What have you learned about yourself, about your teammates, and about working together as a team?

CHOICE 30

HOW CAN I DEAL WITH A CHALLENGING WORK ENVIRONMENT?

Great work opportunity – not so great office space. What should I do?

When it comes to working conditions, where should I draw the line?

What should I be flexible about, and what should I not compromise on?

We would all love to work in comfortable, beautiful and inspiring workplaces. But the reality is that many office spaces, old and new, have shortfalls. What should you do when your working conditions are less than ideal? Should you just take a spoonful of cement and get on with your duties, do something about the issue, or stay away from the problem areas completely? This of course depends on the situation. But you must know where to draw the line. Your health and sanity are not worth sacrificing.

I'm fascinated by the intricate ways in which the space around us can shape who we are and what we're able to achieve. My first book, *Create a Thriving Workspace*, is entirely devoted to the subject of positive, high-performance physical work environments. I spent three years researching and writing it, because I wanted to help people make good use of this knowledge. If you'd like to dive a bit deeper into the ins and outs of workspace design, I think you'll get a lot out of reading it.

But let me make this clear: I'm not claiming that the right physical environment is the single key to success. When it comes to your work experience and performance, what matters most is what's inside you. It's possible to produce incredible work almost anywhere, as long as you can breathe and think.

Most workplaces have imperfections. They are designed to meet a range of needs and competing priorities, and are built with limited budgets. If your working conditions are less than ideal, it won't help to approach issues with a sense of entitlement. Ask yourself first how you can improve your environment or work around the problems you're facing. I'm sure you're tough enough to deal with minor inconveniences and discomforts. Some of them might even be good for you.

But in my experience, certain standards are not worth compromising on. I'm sure you agree that sacrificing your health is a bad idea. And you definitely don't want to be hustling in a place that messes with your head, diminishes the quality of your life, or makes you question your integrity. Let me share a few examples.

PUTTING YOU TO SLEEP?

Have you ever been to a place that made you want to sleep? You arrived fully awake and energised, but shortly after you sat down in that room, all your energy just drained out of you. Perhaps you were there to learn something or to come up with new ideas and solve problems, but you just couldn't think. Your brain went on vacation.

Unfortunately, workspaces that do a better job than sleeping pills are all too common. As a workplace specialist, I see a lot of offices – small ones and large ones, brand new interiors as well as old buildings that are overdue for an upgrade – and it seems to me that no building types are exempt from this issue. In some of the offices I've been to, employees actually appeared to move in slow motion, and eventually I also slowed down. This was an eerie experience, but for the people who were used to this environment, it must have felt almost normal.

What is it about a place that puts you to sleep? First and foremost, poor air quality. Without enough fresh, oxygen-rich air, your brain can't function very well. This is a no-brainer (sorry …). Another common issue is unpleasant temperatures. In a warm room you can easily become lethargic, but staying fully awake in a freezing cold space is not any easier. If you're using most of your energy just to keep warm, you won't have much left for high-level thinking.

In new or newly refurbished buildings, the heating, cooling and ventilation systems tend to do a better job. However, there's another issue that's more prevalent in new workspaces than in old ones: gloominess – the sneaky sedative.

In many office buildings, some of the work areas are located away from the windows and rely fully on artificial lighting. And this can spell trouble ... Every area in a modern office is designed to achieve specific lighting levels at floor or desk height, as dictated by building standards. However, despite the floor and the desk being lit up, a room can still feel very dark. When the ceiling and the walls are barely illuminated, and especially if dark colours dominate the room, you feel that something is off. Even the faces of the people you're talking to are in shadow. Your brain falsely registers that it's night, and you start to doze off. In one office where I worked, several of the meeting rooms were so dim that doing anything constructive in them seemed impossible, so I avoided these rooms whenever I could.

Spending long hours in dark or poorly lit spaces can make things even worse, by messing with your circadian cycle and causing sleep problems. And when you don't sleep well at night, you'll naturally find it difficult to stay alert and switched on during the day.

MAKING YOU DEPRESSED?

When we get the chance, most of us prefer to sit near the windows in the office. And this makes perfect sense. Among the many benefits, natural light and decent views help us think sharper and feel more positive. This is why, in some of the best workplaces, every single employee has the option to enjoy daylight and views.

But what if you're not among the lucky ones, and you're confined to an artificially lit room all day? How do you respond? Everyone's different. I've seen teams of geeks blissfully coding away in basements. I'm happy for them, but personally, I'd run screaming. These days I refuse to work and even sleep in windowless rooms. Interestingly, what I need for my sanity is not exactly daylight and views, but simply feeling close to the outdoors and knowing that I can look outside anytime I want to. Ironically, I can sit near a window for hours without opening the blind and still feel fantastic.

Someone I know, a cheerful and energetic person, is hooked on wide open views. He worked for years in a tall commercial tower with sweeping vistas, until his team moved into a dim second-floor office overlooking the stark facade of the building next door. He soon became noticeably sadder, as he missed his connection with the weather. Even the vibrant, friendly culture of the company couldn't compensate for that.

Another person I met, who had to work in an artificially lit room with no connection to the outdoors, developed suicidal thoughts after a few weeks – which is just heartbreaking. Thankfully, he made the decision to change this situation without waiting too long.

Many characteristics can make a space feel depressing. A complete lack of care. A miserable vibe. Monotony and greyness. Sickening colours and lighting. Even a try-hard, alienating design. I've seen it all, and probably you have too.

Early in my career, I worked in an architectural office located in a refurbished industrial building. Through the windows I could see only a large dark shed. I was surrounded by concrete and steel. Perhaps with the intention to make the space more interesting, the designers opted for painting the space ash grey, with pink and orange stripes. I like colours and playful design, but this environment felt claustrophobic and unnatural to me. I was unable to be myself, and I fell into a state of mild anxiety. Only after my contract ended did the world open up for me again.

DRIVING YOU CRAZY?

In the average office, you find no shortage of irritating events and behaviours – silly ringtones, jabbering coworkers, slamming doors, kill-me-now music, you name it. Hopefully you can brush them off. But certain nuisances, in certain places, can really make you feel like you're going insane. Flickering lights and piercing sounds are my personal enemies. I'm just not equipped to block these out, and I believe not many people are.

I once rented a place in a leafy suburb of Melbourne, which was also my home office. When I inspected the property on a Sunday afternoon, everything seemed peaceful and quiet. I noticed that the light rail passed close to the house, but didn't worry about the noise. However, as soon as I moved in, I had the painful realisation that a railroad crossing gate was located just across the corner, and every time the light rail approached, the gate came down with a hammering sound. I heard 'clunk, clunk, clunk' about every five minutes during peak hours. I hoped that I'd soon get used to it, but it only drove me crazier with time. I couldn't think straight or relax. As it turned out, I needed to move out of this place sooner than I expected (for other reasons), which was a blessing in disguise.

Other sources of irritation are less obvious, but can still have a significant impact on your psyche. I'm an introverted person, and as such, quite protective of my personal space. I enjoy working in teams, but when I need to focus on an individual task, I prefer to have no movement around me. In peaceful environments I tend to be much sharper and more and productive.

In one of my old jobs, a manager thought that I needed to be more social, and decided to seat me in the middle of the action, right next to the entrance. In his mind, people walking and chatting around me all day was going to bring out the best in me. Well, it's not hard to guess how that turned out. I became quieter than ever, stressed out and less productive.

What's driving you crazy? It doesn't matter if it seems illogical. Just do what you need to do to preserve your mental and emotional health, so you can create a bright future. Speak up. Stand up for yourself. Look for a place that suits your unique needs.

MAKING YOU QUESTION YOURSELF?

Hopefully, your organisation operates with strong integrity and its values are aligned with yours. But if you ever find yourself in the opposite situation, you'll need to be honest with yourself, and you may have to make some tough decisions.

Unless something changes, you won't find much joy working there or be able to reach your potential. You may even end up shutting down parts of yourself. I've met young people who were seriously worried that in their current jobs they would lose their spark and become someone they didn't want to be.

I believe that at any point in our careers, we have the choice to step off the hamster wheel and reconnect with our true selves. Even the most alien work environment cannot make us forget what's important to us. But you certainly don't want to turn up at your workplace day after day, telling yourself, 'I don't belong'.

The physical environment is only a part of the experience, but it can give you lots of clues and help you make better choices. Several times in my career, I said no to enticing job opportunities because the workplace just didn't live up to the picture described to me. Designers who took pride in creating beautiful environments were putting their own people in bleak offices. Consultants who saw themselves as innovators were working in old-fashioned workplaces in the most traditional ways ... Seeing companies adopting almost nothing from the advice they were giving their clients was a major turn off for me (and still is).

Did I make the right decisions? I have no way of knowing for sure. But here is what I do know: every single time I joined a workplace that ended up crushing my soul, the warning signs were already present from the start. I just foolishly ignored them, blinded by the shower of amazing promises.

Signs that something is out of alignment can sometimes show up in unusual ways. I once worked at a large engineering firm as an environmental consultant. As you'd hope, the office showcased an array of smart engineering solutions. However, from the early days, something didn't feel right ... To get from the entrance to my desk near the window, I needed to walk through a dark and noisy area of the office that accommodated some of the hardest working employees in the company. I crossed that unpleasant space several times a day and rarely saw an empty chair. I can't remember ever seeing people in this team chatting or smiling. Interestingly, they all seemed to be of similar ethnicity, age and gender, which I found rather unsettling – especially because the company was a melting pot of different cultures. I couldn't understand why management didn't make more effort to include this team in the life of the office and create better conditions for them. Just because they didn't complain? It was impossible to shake off the thought that I was contributing to this injustice by being part of this company.

I'm not sure if this story strikes a chord with you. We all have our own values and definitions of integrity. But my point is, when something in your environment seems unacceptable and you can't look in the mirror without shame or guilt, you need to think about the underlying issues and do something. Even when your judgements are biased (which I'm probably also guilty of), they can still taint your experience, and if you ignore what disturbs you, your wellbeing and performance will suffer.

THE WAY FORWARD

There are many ways to deal with a problem when you feel you shouldn't compromise. Whatever situation you're in, it's worth chatting about it with your colleagues and managers. Perhaps you can initiate changes to the space, or you can work flexibly from different locations.

You should also find that you're more resilient and forgiving when you enjoy your job and feel connected to your workmates. Even in an exhausting environment, pursuing a meaningful purpose and feeling part of a great team will help you keep your sanity.

But you should always respect your essential needs and boundaries. You may be strong enough to push through any hardship to meet expectations and avoid rocking the boat, but this is not always the best choice. When you have doubts whether you should settle for a challenging environment, ask yourself:

- 'Can I maintain my physical and mental health in this space?'

- 'Can I work well in these conditions?'

- 'Can I grow personally and professionally?'

- 'Can I keep my self-respect?

- 'And is there anything I can do to get the problem solved?'

INDIVIDUAL EXERCISES

Are there any parts of your workplace where something feels off? Ask yourself: Is this a major issue or only slight discomfort? Do you struggle to think straight? Or do you produce great results in that place, despite the challenging environment?

Notice how you feel at the end of your workdays. Do you ever end up so spent or agitated that you can't even enjoy your free time after work? If yes, could this have anything to do with your work environment?

Pay attention to your internal monologues during work. What thoughts are running through your mind? Do they revolve around the positive challenges of your work? Or do you perhaps tell yourself, over and over again, that something's got to change?

TEAM EXERCISES

Discuss with your team if they find any parts of the office difficult to work in. If yes, look for solutions together. What can you do to fix the problem? How can you work differently so that the issue doesn't affect you?

Run team meetings in different areas of your office. Are there any spaces where people are noticeably more sluggish, distracted and passive? Could the quality of the air or lighting be the issue?

35 SMART CHOICES

CHOICES

PART VI

PART VI

HOW CAN I TURN CHALLENGES INTO OPPORTUNITIES?

AND WHAT ARE MY LIMITS?

How can you give yourself the best chance to do amazing work? Of course, you want to play your natural game, and avoid obstacles and setbacks.

We've already talked about increasing your energy and focus, enhancing your creativity and communication, embracing your playful side, and allowing your personality to shine. We've also looked into minimising distractions and shifting counterproductive habits. Still, there is a missing piece: to thrive at work, you need to be able to identify the real obstacles and the hidden opportunities. In other words, you need to know which situations and choices are your friends, and which are your enemies.

Consider for a moment … What are your relationships with pressure, negative emotions or discomfort, for example? Do they bring out the best in you or do they make you crumble? You probably find that certain challenges tend to stimulate you to raise your game, while others drain your energy and crush your spirit.

But here is the exciting news. When facing unpleasant or trying situations, it's largely your choice what you take from them. With some skill and awareness, you can make friends with pressure, frustrations and uncomfortable experiences, and turn them into a superpower – rather than allowing them to be your kryptonite. And that's real freedom.

A final question – again, a tricky one. Is it always a good idea to give 110%? When you're flooded with work, you may feel it's necessary and noble to push yourself to your limit, work around the clock and cut your sleep short to get things done. But burning the candle at both ends will quickly backfire – affecting not only your physical and mental health but also your performance and your relationships. So be honest about your limits, notice when your 'heroic' efforts are holding you back, and you'll be in the best possible place to bring your magic to life.

CHOICE 31

HOW CAN I PRODUCE GREAT WORK WHEN FEELING LOW?

How can negative emotions affect my performance?

What should I watch out for when I feel frustrated or upset?

How can I turn dark emotions into productive energy?

Work is rarely a walk in the park, and frustrating or disappointing events can occur at any time. In an ideal world you could bounce back in an instant and carry on with high spirits. But unfortunately, low moods sometimes linger – and working in a negative state of mind can spell trouble. To remain productive, you need to understand how negative emotions can affect your performance, and then work around those challenges. What's more, you could even learn to use them to your advantage!

Think back to a moment when you were super productive. You were on a mission to move mountains. Your mind was sharp and your focus was clear. Everything was flowing and you were ticking off one task after the other with ease.

What was your mood like? … Pretty good, I imagine.

To be on top of your game, positive emotions can help enormously. It's now a well-known fact that happiness boosts performance – we know this from experience and it's also confirmed by a large body of research. One landmark study revealed that 'happiness raises nearly every business and educational outcome: raising sales by 37%, productivity by 31%, and accuracy on tasks by 19%'.

With this knowledge, organisations worldwide are now making increased efforts to create positive experiences for their teams, placing happiness and wellbeing at the centre of their culture. And you're probably doing your best to stay positive yourself, not only to be able to work better, but because happiness is a worthwhile goal in itself.

UPS AND DOWNS ARE INEVITABLE

But what happens when something dampens your spirit?

You don't need to look too far to find alarming news. But even when you don't need to deal with major crises or threats and business is running as usual, you still have your ups and downs. Life is often a roller-coaster, and it can be difficult to shelter yourself from unpleasant situations and experiences.

On some days you're lured into frustrating arguments. On others, you need to deal with demanding clients or digest the disappointing news that you've missed out on an important opportunity. With a heavy heart and troubled mind, it's not easy to maintain focus and momentum. The work that normally energises you may mean very little to you at this time. You might find that your mind often goes blank and your sense of control vanishes as soon as something ruins your mood.

Of course, you're still doing your best to get on with your duties. But if you ignore the impact of negative emotions, you could make a real mess of your work and perhaps create more problems than you had before.

LOW MOODS CAN LINGER

There's no shortage of good advice on how to manage negative thoughts and bounce back. You can practise mindfulness, focus on something positive, talk to a friend, go for a walk, do some exercise, listen to music, seek professional help … the list goes on.

But let's face it, sometimes those low moods linger. Perhaps you feel so deflated that you can't even be bothered doing anything about the issue. Or your problems are so enormous that you can't rise above.

However, you certainly don't want your negative emotions to create further drama. It's therefore useful to understand how low moods can influence different aspects of your work – especially because, while you're consumed by emotions, you may not even notice the damage you might be causing.

EMOTIONS CAN CHANGE EVERYTHING

If happiness boosts performance, there's an inevitable flipside – unhappiness can present serious disadvantages at work, if you're not careful. Here is just a handful of the many ways negative emotions can affect your performance:

- It's nearly impossible to think creatively when feeling down.

- You tend to make more mistakes and poorer decisions.

- It's unlikely that you can handle complicated situations and challenges.

- You see negativity even where there isn't any, and make biased judgements.

- You perceive risks to be greater than they actually are.

- You communicate less clearly and effectively.

- Your words can become more cynical and critical than you intend them to be.

- You're less likely to succeed in sales.

- You find it harder to empathise with others.

- You may become irritable, and accidentally hurt or lash out at people.

- It's very difficult to learn new skills or retain information in a negative state.

- You struggle with self-discipline, and thus you're more likely to give in to unproductive habits such as self-distraction and procrastination.

- Your ethics and morals may differ compared to when you feel fine, and consequently you might say or do something you'll regret later. (Simply put, sad and frustrated people more often act like jerks.)

As you can see, unpleasant emotions – just like positive ones – can filter into every tiny segment of your performance. There's a good reason for all this: your physiology and brain chemistry undergo significant changes when you fall into in a negative state, and parts of your brain actually shut down.

LEAVE NO CHANCE FOR MISTAKES

So, what can you do when you feel down and you've got work to do?

First and foremost, acknowledge how you're feeling. You might also want to let people around you know that you are not quite yourself at the moment. But please don't criticise yourself for the state you're in – I can't see how that could possibly be useful.

Choose simple, straightforward activities you can easily manage – tasks that require little creativity and emotional investment. Avoid making big decisions, initiating difficult conversations and perhaps even giving feedback. Once you've completed your work, ask someone to review it carefully. In situations like this, a thorough check is needed more than ever.

If you handle your emotions intelligently and organise your tasks well, your work will keep rolling without a major hiccup. You'll probably bounce back more quickly and have fewer reasons to be worried later on.

HARNESS YOUR EMOTIONS

While preventing mistakes is a great starting point, there are also bigger questions to ask:

- Should you always try to shake off any negative feelings before launching into work?

- Could you benefit somehow from feeling sad, frustrated or angry?

- Is there an opportunity for you to harness these emotions to create something valuable?

When it comes to optimal conditions for high performance, as I've learned during my life and career, nothing is black and white – absolutely nothing, apart from the need for oxygen. There are exceptions to every rule. So, even though in general it's a good idea to tame raw emotions at work, rolling with them also has some upsides.

Psychologists and personal development teachers tend to agree that fully feeling and expressing a spectrum of emotions is critical to working through personal issues, developing emotional intelligence and maintaining a healthy psyche. However, what I'd like to explore now is when and how a hot head or a heavy heart can sometimes help produce amazing results.

THIS COULD BE A TURNING POINT

Have you seen the movie *Jerry Maguire*? In one of the early scenes, Maguire, a sports agent, finds himself in a confronting situation, which forces him to face the reality that he has been absorbed into the unethical culture of his industry. He experiences an emotional breakdown, which he turns into a breakthrough. He works through the night with unprecedented clarity, energy and passion, and creates a heartfelt and inspiring mission statement that sets the course for his future career.

This is a dramatised story of course, but it tells a lot of truth. Facing frustrations and being pushed to the edge can sometimes force us to make critical decisions that we've previously avoided, and propel us into a state of remarkable productivity and clarity.

In my own career, I've achieved numerous breakthroughs while feeling frustrated. For example, I once received a critique for a research paper I'd written that I felt was unreasonable. In a dedicated attempt to prove my point, I came up with a design framework which later became the most often used tool in my consulting practice, as well as the central framework of my first book, *Create a Thriving Workspace*.

TURN ALL THAT NEGATIVITY INTO SOMETHING VALUABLE

We all find ourselves in situations at times that make us feel agitated, regardless of our industries and roles. I'm particularly triggered by narrow-mindedness, incongruence, and the lack of respect some folk show for others' time. Whenever I see a promising opportunity evaporate or large amounts of work go to waste because of a communication breakdown, or I find out about one of my teammates or clients shooting themselves in the foot due to negligence ... well, I'm not thrilled.

When possible, I first try to deal with the issue directly. But when the problem is beyond my power or I feel I'm banging my head against a brick wall, I often can't help but put my thoughts on paper and share them with my tribe. I know that the problems I'm dealing with are not uncommon, and that some people out there might benefit from my experiences and insights. Interestingly, I've written some of my most well-received articles in this not-so-pleasant headspace.

When I find myself in a situation that worries me or pushes my buttons, there's also probably something I need to learn.

And here is the beauty in this process: to get things off my chest in a constructive fashion, rather than having a self-indulgent rant, I need to think through the issue rationally, from different angles. This always helps me sort out my thoughts and draw useful conclusions. And the icing on the cake? Once I feel I've got something valuable out of a bad situation, all that fog in my head evaporates and I can finally carry on, fully focused and level-headed.

MOVING FORWARD ...

Negative emotions can work for or against you. The question is whether you're able to use them to move forward, or you allow them to hold you back and perhaps even do some damage.

Anger or frustration, at times, could give you the drive and focus to produce transformative work. Just ask Jerry Maguire. Doubt or self-doubt can motivate you to expand your knowledge, ask better questions and explore new avenues with an open mind. Feeling intimidated by seemingly impossible goals or challenges can provoke you to seek innovative ideas and take worthwhile risks. And essentially any painful experience could be that last straw that makes you say, 'That's enough, it's time for change'.

Learning to master emotions is a lifelong journey. But once you recognise that it's possible to use them to your advantage, you're a huge step ahead. If you pressure yourself and your teammates to put on a happy face every day, those emotions will not disappear – they will likely get suppressed and continue sabotaging your work. But if you use them well, they can help you achieve real breakthroughs.

If you look at high-performing teams in action, you often see the expression of a variety of feelings and emotions: excitement, anticipation, passion, curiosity, determination ... and even some frustration and nerves. What you don't often see are peaceful faces with smiles of contentment.

At work, there should be times for channelling unpleasant feelings into creating positive change, and times for staying level-headed and rational – including the time when you double-check the piece of work that you've produced with a foggy head, and when you decide whether to hit the 'send' button. When you get this right, your work will reflect creativity, professionalism and passion.

INDIVIDUAL EXERCISES

Make a list of the tasks you can safely work on even when you're not in a great headspace – activities you can complete on autopilot, and which don't involve creative challenges or critical decisions. Whenever you feel low, use this list to get on with your day ... What do you notice? Are you able to stay productive? Do you find that ticking off a few simple tasks helps you feel better?

When you're feeling really upset for some reason, stop for a moment and pay attention to the emotions you're experiencing. Notice where you're feeling them in your body. Acknowledge them for now, rather than trying to fight them ... What exactly do they signal? What do you need to let go of? What do you need to do differently? And what do you need to change about yourself?

TEAM EXERCISES

Ask your teammates to think of a time in the past when they were able to channel negative emotions into productive work, and thus managed turn painful situations into advantages. Share your stories with each other ... What great things have some of you accomplished that you wouldn't have achieved without those triggers?

Pick an unresolved problem that tends to stir up a lot of emotions in your team. Act out the situation through role-play, with each team member representing a different emotion (such as anger, regret, shame, worry, frustration, confusion, optimism and so on) ... What do the different emotions have to say? What purpose do they serve? How can they help your team move forward?

CHOICE 32

HOW CAN I MAKE PRESSURE MY FRIEND?

When can pressure be useful, and when can it create problems?

What does it take to work well in demanding situations?

How can I leverage pressure to improve my performance?

Tight deadlines, high expectations, high stakes ... Such testing situations are all too common in the workplace. The question is, does pressure bring out the best in you or does it crush you? It's largely your choice. By understanding the nature of pressure, you can turn it into an advantage and use it as a powerful force to elevate your performance.

'Do you work well under pressure?' When I ask people this question they usually answer with a confident yes or no. You probably also have a clear idea of how well you perform in demanding situations.

Can you perhaps relate to one of the following characters?

The first person, let's call her Nina, receives a difficult engineering assignment which is due in 12 weeks. Failing to complete it on time or to the required standard could put her career in jeopardy. Nina is facing 12 intense weeks with little time for family and friends, or even sleep. She's not sure how to go about the task or where to find all the information she needs in order to do a great job. Nonetheless, she knows that succeeding will bring her a step closer to her lifelong goal. So she launches into the challenge with enthusiasm and a creative spirit, and systematically tackles one obstacle after the other. When the big day comes, she presents an impressive solution that exceeds even her own expectations.

Peter, our second character, is asked by a colleague to help with an urgent project. He needs to analyse data from a company survey and to present the results in a report by the end of the week. The task is not particularly complicated, but Peter has never done this type of analysis before, and since the whole team is busy, he needs to figure out by himself exactly what to do. In addition, the amount of data to go through is vast. Peter is not confident that he's able to meet the deadline, even if he works around the clock. When he raises his concerns with his team, he receives little support or acknowledgement. Instead, his work ethic is doubted. Peter powers through the week, though he feels resentful and thus fails to keep his colleagues in the loop. He miraculously manages to complete the report in time, but the project leader only finds out about it by accident.

The third person, junior designer Adrian, recently joined a small firm, following the promise of creative opportunities and increased responsibilities. However, he doesn't feel trusted – or even treated as an adult. His boss often stands behind him, watching his every move and pointing out every single perceived mistake he makes, even in front of visiting clients. Adrian is also unclear about his role and responsibilities. He's frequently asked to abandon what he's doing and to jump in to finish a colleague's tasks, which they should have completed days earlier. He's trying hard to learn and grow, and to fit in. But as the weeks pass, his optimism fades and he becomes increasingly tense and agitated. Eventually he decides to leave, and his boss also thinks that it's time for him to go.

FRIEND OR FOE?

It's useful to understand whether you tend to thrive, produce mixed results, or crumble in high-pressure situations. With this knowledge, you can better prepare for difficult times – which are sometimes unavoidable – and seek ideal conditions for you to excel.

However, whether you work well under pressure is not a yes/no question. How you perform depends on a variety of factors.

Amount of pressure

We all need at least a little pressure to get things done. You want to do work that matters – where something meaningful is at stake. If you didn't care about the results of your efforts, you'd be bored and unmotivated, and you would struggle to concentrate.

In contrast, too much pressure can be crippling. It triggers stress and anxiety, and inhibits certain functions of the brain, including creative and analytical thinking.

The sweet spot is usually somewhere in the middle. A moderate amount of pressure can motivate you to learn, grow and push your own limits. It helps you stay focused, engaged and productive.

In the first story, Nina wouldn't have been able to expand her own limits without feeling the weight of the situation. But since her career was on the line, she was all in.

Type of work

In certain circumstances, significant pressure could propel you to excel. For example, high expectations from your team or clients, or a sense of urgency, can force you to take positive risks and to approach problems in new ways.

In the face of great demands, it's also easier to be disciplined and to focus on boring, routine tasks like turning survey data into hundreds of Excel charts. In the second story, where Peter needed to complete a monotonous task, the extremely tight deadline was actually helpful, because it prompted him to concentrate and work without wasting a single moment.

You too have probably had the experience of performing small miracles in a state of near panic, as you were racing towards the finish line.

There are of course many types of work where significant pressure doesn't help. For example, you don't want too much tension while learning a new skill or focusing on an unfamiliar task. In the third story, Adrian, our junior designer, crumbled under the pressure partly because he didn't even have the chance to settle into his new role.

It's also better to evaluate large amounts of information and develop solutions to complicated problems in a relatively relaxed environment. In high-demand situations, you're more likely to assess options in a haphazard manner and reach conclusions too early.

Calm and friendly surroundings are more conducive to creative ideas as well. Innovative solutions are often born from daydreaming, playing spontaneously and exploring seemingly crazy scenarios. None of these can happen when you feel rushed or on edge.

What the situation means to you

High-pressure events often promise great opportunities and rewards along with potential obstacles and threats. If you live up to the challenge, you'll grow your confidence, earn greater appreciation from your teams and clients, and put a dent in the universe. If you fail, you might need to face some loss, embarrassment and career setback. Either way, you'll surely gain valuable knowledge and experience.

It's largely up to you what you focus on. And interestingly, this can determine how you think and act – whether pressure brings out the best or the worst in you.

If you see an event as a positive challenge or an opportunity, your performance will increase, as shown by science. You'll feel more motivated, engaged and energised. Your brain will function at a higher level, so you'll also be sharper, more focused and more resourceful. While savouring the challenge, you'll be kinder and more helpful towards your colleagues, and more ready to listen to feedback and advice.

In light of this, you can probably guess what's likely to happen when you see a high-pressure situation as an obstacle or a threat. With less oxygen reaching your brain, you'll make poorer judgements and decisions, and find it difficult to manage your emotions and behaviour. In this state, chances are you'll act somewhat irrationally and fall into unproductive patterns. And it's highly unlikely that you'll be nominated for the coveted 'Coworker of the Week' award.

Your relationship with stress and the people around you

So why do some people choose to look at the upsides, while others become fixated with the downsides, when faced with high demands? According to studies, it largely comes down to your resilience – your ability to rebound from difficult, stressful events.

If you're a resilient person, you're more likely to focus on what could go right, and as a result, raise your performance. But if you're sensitive to adversity, your thoughts are drawn to what could go wrong, which could send you into a spin.

Your take on the situation is also strongly influenced by the culture of your organisation and your relationship with your team. In a trusting and supportive environment, it's easier to focus on the upsides. But when you're exposed to a toxic culture, you'll see negativity everywhere.

Nina had well-meaning mentors who may not have had all the answers but were committed to listening to her and giving her honest advice. This gave her the strength and confidence to aim high.

Peter felt positively challenged, but also imposed upon and mistreated. Overcome by resentment, he decided to hide in his bubble and communicate very little, which of course didn't make life easy for the rest of his team.

And as Adrian became overwhelmed by frequent criticism, embarrassment and unreasonable demands, he lost sight of the opportunities of his job and ended up in a state of fight or flight. Literally. He kept defending himself until he decided he had to leave.

WHAT CAN YOU DO TO IMPROVE YOUR PERFORMANCE?

Almost everyone works well under the right amount of pressure in the right environment. However, even the toughest person will struggle when the wrong buttons are pressed.

It may not come as a surprise to you that in all three stories I shared my own experiences (I just changed the names and gender). There have been times when pressure inspired me to reach for the stars, and other times when it reduced me to an antisocial mess.

If you find yourself in difficult situations like these, the question you should ask is: 'Do I use pressure well to improve my performance?'

There are a number of actions you can take to make friends with pressure and use it to your advantage.

Are you feeling a bit bored or unmotivated? Ramp up the pressure a little. Set deadlines for yourself. Find someone who is willing to hold you accountable. Take new initiatives. Start working on a problem that's been nagging you for a long time but you've never addressed. Reignite your passion and remind yourself of the big-picture purpose of your work.

Are the demands you're facing all too much and therefore clouding your mind? You need to reduce some of the pressure you're experiencing. Perhaps you can push back a deadline or lighten your workload, but even when that's not possible, you should still be able to nurture your body and mind. Find a pleasant and comfortable place to work and block out all distractions. Allow at least a little time for breaks, social activities and self-care. The load on you will feel lighter. (By acting on the ideas in this book and developing powerful new habits, you'll find that a lot of the harmful stress you might be experiencing right now will fade away.)

Are you anxious or stressed about what might happen if you fail? Remind yourself of the opportunities inherent in the challenge, all the possible benefits and rewards, and what you could learn even if you do happen to fail.

Is there no love or trust in the team? Work on your relationships. Spend time with your workmates, talk things through openly and honestly, and invest in your social connections. Have fun and laugh together. Ensure your goals and values are aligned. Agree on which behaviours are encouraged and which are unacceptable.

Is pressure getting the best of you? Build up your resilience. Resilience consists of a range of skills that can be learned and strengthened. If you're ready, you can easily find credible, practical advice to develop yourself.

LESS STRESS, MORE EXCITEMENT

Pressure can be your friend or your enemy, depending on the situation, your personality and your workplace culture. With an empowered mindset and great work relationships, you'll naturally handle challenging situations better. And by understanding the nature of pressure, you'll know when to avoid it, reduce it, or take advantage of it.

None of these will make work super easy. Adrenaline will still be high, but you'll experience less stress and more excitement. You'll have a good chance to achieve things you never thought possible. And when you look back from the finish line, you may come to the conclusion that you wouldn't have done it any other way.

INDIVIDUAL EXERCISES

Experiment with completing different creative and non-creative tasks, with and without tight deadlines. Assess your efficiency and the quality of the results. When were the deadlines helpful, and when did they hinder your performance?

When you're faced with a demanding situation, assess the pros and cons in order to put things in perspective. Be realistic. What's the worst possible thing that can happen? What's the best possible thing that can happen? What is *likely* to happen? And what can you learn from this challenge?

TEAM EXERCISES

Share your stories with one another about the times when pressure brought out the best in you. Also talk about the occasions when pressure crushed you. Can you relate to each other's experiences? What are your teammates' relationships like with pressure? And in light of this, how can you better support each other and improve your teamwork?

Split your team into two groups. Give both groups the same problem to solve, but one should meet a very tight timeframe while the other should have a more relaxed one. Then evaluate each team's performance. Do you see a difference in the quality of the two solutions?

SHOULD I ALWAYS TRY TO GIVE 110%?

What can happen when I try to be a superhero?

What can go wrong when I spread myself too thin?

What does it take to be both empathetic and strategic?

Why is it a good idea to put my own needs first?

Do you see yourself as a superhero at times, smashing through obstacles and pushing yourself to the limit? If you do, not only your health and wellbeing are at stake, but also your productivity and the quality of your work. Making things worse, when you get caught up in your 'mission', you could inadvertently distance yourself from the very people you wish to engage. You'll probably achieve more and develop stronger relationships if you slow down a little and look after your needs first.

The days before the internet and personal computers are a fading memory for most of us, if we're old enough to remember at all. Imagine manually adding up numbers on a paper spreadsheet, or typing documents with a typewriter and then retyping them because you've made a mistake. At university, I used to spend long hours correcting architectural drawings using tracing paper, technical ink pens and razor blades. Opting for such archaic methods today would be a joke.

Over the past few decades, work has been transformed in ways previously unimaginable, and we too must adapt. Without clairvoyant powers, it's difficult to envision what our jobs and daily routines will look like in, say, five or ten years, but the trends are clear. We're doing fewer and fewer repetitive and routine tasks that can be completed by machines, and more and more activities that require artistry, creative thinking and people skills.

To remain efficient and competitive, we need to hone those aspects of our intelligence that machines can't possess, including intuition and empathy. We can only solve burning problems and create value when we deeply understand the people we serve and collaborate with. Humans are emotion-driven beings with many idiosyncrasies and flaws – and we'd better embrace this fact if we want to be able to work effectively in teams and help our clients succeed.

DO WE EXPECT TOO MUCH OF OURSELVES?

Our societal norms are also shifting, and it seems that we are getting better and better at accepting others for who they are, with all their human flaws and differences. On the other hand, our expectations of ourselves haven't changed that much since the era when we actually had to work – in some ways – like machines.

Most of us still struggle to accept ourselves fully, with all our physical and emotional needs, imperfections and (perceived) weaknesses. We find it more convenient to look outside of ourselves – and be smart, understanding and supportive about other people's issues – rather than learning to be kind to ourselves.

Acknowledging your own limitations is admittedly difficult. In this highly competitive world, you may feel you need to be on top of your game all the time. Even on your most productive days you might be pretty hard on yourself. When you notice a lapse in your energy and focus, make some mistakes or fail to progress with your tasks as planned, you're probably inclined to push yourself to up your game. Chances are, you often treat yourself in ways you would never treat others, and you actually see this as a heroic act.

WHY IS THIS A PROBLEM?

When you stretch yourself too thin, you tend to ignore your own personal needs. Despite working insane hours, you don't take nearly enough – or maybe any – breaks during the day. You're likely to eat poorly, skip exercise and cut back on sleep. Ultimately, you put your physical and mental health on the line and risk burnout.

The quality of your work also suffers. It's hard to think clearly and intelligently with a run-down body and mind, and therefore you're prone to make mistakes and poor decisions.

In this state, it's hard to think strategically about work and to set the right priorities. You can easily get caught up in the details and lose sight of the bigger picture. While you may feel that you're getting a lot done, in reality you're probably not very effective. You operate in a constant state of urgency, and as a result, you don't allow yourself enough time to explore ideas or to contemplate. Consequently, you try to come up with solutions to problems in a state of mind that's not very conducive to creative thinking.

To add fuel to the fire, you communicate poorly and infrequently. You rush through conversations, choose the wrong platforms to discuss issues, and often leave problems unresolved. As you are fixated on getting things done, investing in your work relationships becomes a low priority, which can eventually erode personal connections and trust.

These are well-researched and frequently discussed problems. However, one issue that I find especially intriguing is getting very little airtime: by working through thick and thin like a wannabe superhero, you might be distancing yourself from the very people you're trying to engage and serve.

EMPATHY AND LOGIC DON'T MIX

You are an empathetic being by nature – even if you feel you don't have an empathetic personality or particularly strong skills to put yourself in other people's shoes. Your brain in fact has an in-built 'empathy function' which is automatically activated when needed – as long as you're mentally healthy and fresh. When you engage with someone whose thoughts and feelings you wish to understand and relate to, a specific neural network fires up that allows you to identify with what the other person is going through.

In contrast, when life presents you with a logical challenge, a different network switches on in your brain. This part of your mind is highly active while you're analysing data, developing plans and strategies, or writing technical reports, for example.

Alternating between these two modes of thinking allows you to look at issues holistically and to understand their practical as well as their human

and ethical implications. But here's the catch: you can't think both ana-
lytically and empathetically at the same time. You might know this from
experience, and it's also proven by science. As one of these networks is
activated, the other is inevitably repressed due to a biological constraint.

When you need to work around the clock, you're probably being kept busy
with mostly cerebral tasks as opposed to empathy-inducing activities. And
the issue is, if you're overworked and exhausted, you can actually get stuck in
this analytical mode. Even when the time comes for you to make a personal
connection with someone, the empathy function simply won't switch on.

So what can happen when you try to get to know a person – or a team – in
this state of mind? You could spend hours or days collecting information
about them, but they will remain strangers to some extent. You might
methodically decipher their problems and needs, and come up with some
sort of an answer through a series of logical conclusions. But without being
able to truly relate to their issues, you'll have a slim chance of offering them
the best possible solution. And it's equally unlikely that they will have an
amazing experience working with you.

Let me share some of my observations and experiences.

SUPERHEROES ONLY DO HALF THE JOB

My job as a workplace consultant and work style coach involves deep conversations with business leaders and employees, creative problem-solving
sessions, as well as long hours doing research, analysing data and writing
reports. And like most of us, at times I need to perform small miracles to
meet expectations and deadlines.

How do I try to achieve the seemingly unachievable? Well, sometimes I work
around the clock, ticking off tasks like there's no tomorrow, determined
to redefine what's humanly possible. I forget about breaks and weekends,
telling myself, 'I will eat properly, exercise and rest later'.

I'm proud of the fact that I have an excellent track record of meeting deadlines. However, at some point in recent years I started to question if I'm
actually serving my team and my clients the best I can when I take on the
persona of a superhero.

When I'm on a mission, I find it rather difficult to empathise with other people's personal needs and vulnerabilities. In turn, they might also find it more difficult to open up to me about their deepest thoughts – their visions and passions, wild ideas, hopes and fears. Who could blame them? You probably wouldn't feel comfortable either exposing your vulnerable side to someone who powers through like a superhero, would you?

I certainly can't see myself having a heart-to-heart with Superman. But if I were to meet Clark Kent, I'd probably feel more relaxed to show my real self … Perhaps there's a reason why in superhero stories, it's always the real, flawed, down-to-earth version of the person who eventually finds love. And in real life, people who respect their own needs and limitations have the greatest relationships.

'No profound thoughts today'

A few years ago, at the end of an especially long and exhausting day, I bumped into a dear mate from my professional network. 'Hi John,' I said. 'It's so lovely to see you. I always enjoy talking to you, because we have such profound conversations, but sadly that's not going to happen today. I'm just not in the right frame of mind, because I've been processing data all day without a break.' (I must have expressed myself less eloquently, because at that point even constructing complete sentences was a challenge.) He was surprised, but once he noticed my blank gaze he understood what was going on.

To be honest, this is all I remember from that encounter. In that state, I was simply unable to connect with a person I would normally click with in an instant. And I certainly didn't have the mental capacity to engage in deep discussions or be excited by inspirational ideas.

Insane schedules

I've also been on the other side of somewhat similar scenarios. I recall, for instance, numerous catch-ups with colleagues after they had been running back-to-back meetings and workshops all day every day for a week, and doing additional work at night and on the weekend. On other occasions, my teammates had returned to the office straight from the airport, after landing from an overnight flight following a gruelling overseas trip.

During these catch-ups, although my colleagues were obviously spent, we had constructive discussions about facts and figures, systems and patterns. However, there was absolutely no place in our conversations for out-of-the-box ideas, playful approaches or intuition. On a few occasions, I would have also loved to explore with them how we could take our collaboration to the next level, or to talk through some sensitive issues, but those discussions died before they began.

Considering my teammates' busy schedules, all this made sense. They were all switched on, creative and caring professionals – just very much overworked – so I saw these uneasy moments as tiny hiccups in our communication. Still, I was left with a few nagging thoughts … What if the dozens of interviews and workshops my colleagues had facilitated the previous week had an equally detached and rational tone? How would that affect the quality of our company's service, and our relationships with our clients and their teams? If I had been in my teammates' shoes, I probably would have struggled to bring my best game.

TAKE OFF YOUR CAPE

Working efficiently and meeting deadlines are of course important, but you must also keep your eyes on the big picture. You won't be able to work well in a team and produce real value unless your empathy function operates seamlessly.

How can you achieve this? Take off your cape …

Prioritise your health and wellbeing. Take breaks during the day, step away from the pressures of work, and spend time with activities that nourish your body and soul.

Look after your social ties. Even during the most hectic times, you should be able to spend a few relaxed moments with your teammates. Communicate patiently, listen deeply and express yourself freely.

Allow time for expansive, creative thinking and contemplation. Revisit your purpose frequently and see whether you're heading in the right direction.

These are all common-sense practices that many of us tend to neglect. Acting on them will take a bit of time, but the benefits are substantial.

By slowing down a little, you'll be able to stay on course and reach your goals more quickly, without sacrificing your health and sanity. You'll work smarter, tackle tasks more effectively and find it easier to stay on top of difficult situations. You'll become more agile and influential – and aren't these the true qualities of modern-day heroes?

Who do you need to be?

When studying life coaching, I learned that mental states are contagious. If I'd like to help a person to relax, it's best if I make myself relaxed first. And if I'd like to help them feel enthusiastic about something, I should first tap into my own enthusiasm.

The way I see it, the same law applies (to some extent) to essentially any knowledge- and service-based role. If you want your teammates, clients and prospects to be honest about their limitations and to acknowledge their need for help, you should be prepared to do the same. When you want them to pursue what's best for them and think freely about possibilities, you should also be in that headspace. And if the people you work with would love to become superheroes themselves for a little while, that's a perfect time for you to see yourself as invincible too.

So before you put yourself second in order to perform that small miracle, why not ask yourself: 'What do my teams and clients really need? How do I want them to show up? And who do I need to be so that I can understand them, relate to them, and help them thrive?'

INDIVIDUAL EXERCISES

When you're going through a super intense period at work, spare five minutes before you knock off to jot down a list of the activities you focused on during the day. When things slow down a little, have a look at your lists. Did you make the right choices and priorities? Did you work effectively?

Pick a piece of work you produced during an extremely busy period in your life and have a good look at it. Is it your best work? Is it as useful, engaging and insightful as it could be? Or could you perhaps have done a better job with a relaxed mind?

Reflect on what you need to know about your clients and your teammates to give them the best possible support. What are their limitations and challenges? What do they need help with? Also look inwards for a moment. Are you honest with yourself and your team about your own limitations and challenges? And are you willing to ask for help when you're overwhelmed?

TEAM EXERCISES

Share with each other what 'work ethic' and 'professionalism' mean to you. How can you best support one another and serve your clients? And how much personal sacrifice should you be willing to make when the stakes are high?

Discuss with your teammates what should happen if any of you feel you have too much on your plate. How far should you push yourselves? What should you do when you feel you can't meet a deadline without jeopardising your health? When is it appropriate to slow down, to ask for help or to change plans?

Have a frank conversation with your teammates. Ask them what it's like for them to work with you during those periods when you push yourself to the limit and work around the clock. Also share your own experiences of engaging with your teammates when they are overworked.

HOW COMFORTABLE DO I REALLY NEED TO BE?

How do comfortable and uncomfortable environments influence my thinking?

How can certain types of discomfort help me reach my goals?

What are the risks of chasing comfort?

What kinds of discomfort should I avoid?

You need a reasonable amount of comfort to be able to focus and work productively. However, certain types of discomfort are actually beneficial to your performance and even the quality of your life. When you develop a healthy relationship with discomfort, your whole mindset shifts. You become more resilient and better prepared for change. You also give yourself a much better chance of reaching your most ambitious goals.

ISN'T IT NICE TO BE TREATED LIKE ROYALTY

The Edge, located in Amsterdam, is a remarkable office building. In fact, it's seen as one of the most (if not the most) intelligent buildings in the world. Among its many impressive features, The Edge can read your mind … Well, almost. The building recognises your car as soon as you reach the car park and points you to a vacant parking space. It also knows your schedule, including who you're meeting today, and directs you to your optimal working or meeting space. What's more, the lighting and temperature are adjusted to your preference wherever you go. Even the coffee machines can recognise you as you approach and remember exactly how you like your cuppa.

In a building like this, you can feel comfortable all year round, whatever you do. You don't need to worry about distractions or waste your precious mental energy on mundane activities and decisions. You can put all your focus into the things that matter most.

Sometimes I wish I worked in an office like this. I'd surely be able to get things done more quickly and easily … But is that *really* the case?

COMFORT IS RELATIVE

In recent years, I've been spending a lot of time in my home office – my own cosy bubble. At home, nothing stops me from making myself comfortable. I don't need to worry about commuting, let alone parking. I can wear comfy clothes and set up the space to my liking. The usual distractions of the office are non-existent.

However, on some days I still can't get settled. I feel restless and irritable. Although I don't have to listen to creative ringtones or the chatter of coworkers, I just can't ignore the noises coming from the street – traffic, construction works, lawn mowers, leaf blowers, crying babies, you name it. Even the slightest sound can disrupt my thinking. Sometimes I wish those darned birds and crickets would just stop chirping for a moment so I can focus … What's wrong with me? The truth is that working from home a lot has made me hypersensitive to noise. The environment that used to feel peaceful and quiet to me often seems very busy now, and I'm more easily distracted than ever.

ARE WE LOSING OUR RESILIENCE?

It doesn't take long to get used to comfort. In many offices, for example, people are constantly fighting over the thermostat. Unless the temperature is perfect, they just can't concentrate. In other workplaces you don't see such arguments, but for an obvious reason: employees simply have no control over the air-conditioning system. Why aren't they given this option? Because designers and mechanical engineers know too well that in any open office – apart from highly intelligent buildings like The Edge – there will always be people who feel either too hot or cold. Therefore, allowing employees to collectively decide about the temperature in a room is a recipe for trouble.

True, we all find different environments comfortable; however, it's also clear that as a developed society, we're losing our resilience. Many of us live in air-conditioned homes, drive air-conditioned cars and work in air-conditioned offices. And when we spend little time exposed to the elements, it's no surprise that we become highly sensitive to variations in temperature – just like I've become more sensitive to noise in my usually quiet home.

It appears that as we grow more accustomed to an easy life, our comfort zones are shrinking, and we need near-perfect physical conditions to feel well. But more importantly, our relationship with discomfort, in general, is shifting. As we're getting softer, we're increasingly tempted to run away from any sort of hardship, including mental and emotional challenges.

WHAT KIND OF LIFE ARE WE CREATING?

We naturally want to feel well and to get things done with minimal pain and effort. The promise of an easier and more pleasant life has been inspiring innovation throughout history. Without this desire, no-one would have invented the wheel, the telephone or the light bulb, for example.

I feel lucky to live at a time and place where our basic needs are easily met. An ever-growing range of innovative products and services are available to us, designed to reduce friction in our lives. Many of the mundane tasks our parents and grandparents had to do themselves can now be outsourced to machines or automated using clever software.

But – and there is a but – we're in a self-perpetuating cycle. The more comfortable we become, the more comfort we desire, and so we keep innovating and making life even *easier*. 'Why would this be a problem?' you may ask. 'We are smart enough to shape the world to our needs, so what's wrong with being a bit spoiled?'

Well, I can think of a number of problems with this attitude. Our growing need for comfort and convenience drives many lifestyle choices and consumption habits that are destroying the planet. Just think about the volume of resources we turn into waste in the name of convenience. While we rely heavily on digital technologies to stay connected with the world, our friends and family, and even our own bodies, we're losing our emotional and body intelligence. And despite living an increasingly comfortable life, we fail to recognise this, and many of us struggle to find true happiness and fulfilment.

By avoiding hardship we're in fact making ourselves smaller. While this may sound like a cliché, challenges are part of a rich and purposeful life. They help us learn and grow. Few things are more satisfying than achieving a difficult goal. And after doing something physically or mentally testing, having the chance to relax can feel like heaven.

I find it particularly interesting that certain types of discomfort, such as exercising, feeling hot or cold, or experiencing hunger for short periods, can trigger biological processes in the body that contribute to health and longevity.

THE ROCKY PATH TO SUCCESS

The path to creating positive change is never short on uncomfortable situations and decisions. To improve on the status quo, you may need to call out the elephant in the room and set a bold vision for the future. You can only innovate successfully if you're willing to take risks and accept failure.

To develop your knowledge and skills, you need to ask lots of questions, learn and unlearn. You've got to engage with people who think differently from you, and let go of old ideas that no longer serve you. Sometimes you need to say 'sorry' or 'I was wrong'. Working through disagreements and conflicts is another important aspect of teamwork, along with showing vulnerability at times.

To evolve professionally and personally, you also have to be honest with yourself, recognise your weaknesses and take on feedback. And of course, what better way to grow than facing new experiences, experimenting with different ideas and routines, and constantly improving the way you work? I'm sure you agree, these aspects of work are rarely easy or comfortable, but they certainly make work more exciting and rewarding.

MODERATE DISCOMFORT COULD BE YOUR ALLY

Put simply, discomfort at work is necessary – but it's not a 'necessary evil'. It can actually help you work more effectively. Just think about it …

While in your perfect environment you're more inclined to slow down, slight discomfort can motivate you to focus and get things done more quickly. You probably also need some level of emotional pressure to perform at your best, as we established earlier.

When you feel at ease, you're more likely to become complacent. On the other hand, irritations and frustrations can provoke you to address nagging problems you've been ignoring.

Of course, you want to avoid extreme emotional and physical hardship, but moderate discomfort could boost your productivity in unusual ways. Let me share a few examples of both types of experiences.

I've spent many years of my life in freezing cold offices where my fingers were shivering as I typed. I also had the misfortune of having to do mental work in temperatures of over 30 degrees. I know I'm not alone. Working in such conditions is zero fun, and the brain just doesn't want to cooperate. Heat can drain your energy and make it very difficult to handle complex decisions, while cold can cause you to feel disconnected from others. And in both conditions, you're likely to work slower than usual, become easily distracted and produce errors.

On the other hand, feeling a little warm or cool can help you excel in specific tasks. In warmer environments you tend to be more empathetic, friendly and trusting towards others. You're also prone to feel less guarded or risk-averse, and thus to think more expansively. So when you're a bit toasty, you might do really well in artistic tasks, people-centric activities and creative collaboration. In contrast, feeling a bit chilly can make you more alert, and help you tackle challenges that require abstract thinking (such as developing conceptual models or brainstorming names for new products).

Too much noise – when you can't even hear your own thoughts – is rarely useful for focused mental work. However, as I mentioned earlier, some people find it easier to get into their groove and come up with creative ideas in buzzing environments with moderate background noise.

Dealing with frequent distractions and having to switch your attention all the time can take a lot out of you. It's difficult to think rationally with a scattered, exhausted mind. Having said that, even when you're feeling spent, it's still in your power to create magic. This could be a good time to tune out, forget about rules and logic, and allow your imagination to take off.

WHAT YOU SHOULD AVOID

Keep in mind that certain types of discomfort provide next to no benefit. For example, you definitely want to avoid eye strain and glare. Equally, do whatever you can to prevent intense physical pain and muscle fatigue. An invasion of your personal space and privacy is not nice either – let alone having to deal with unpleasant odours, like a coworker's exotic lunch – and I can't think of any potential upside to these irritations.

Specific sounds designed to trigger automatic stress responses in the body can be detrimental to mental performance. I'm talking about my personal kryptonite: those high-pitched beeping sounds emitted by construction equipment and service vehicles, as well as many everyday appliances like digital lockers and dishwashers. These noises may serve a purpose, but not when you're trying to think straight. So I always try to block them out as if my life depends on it.

GIVE YOURSELF THE BEST CHANCE

You've probably noticed that many of the work practices discussed in this book are somewhat uncomfortable. Standing up, moving around or working with tactile tools all require some effort, just like experimenting with new ways of working, changing your environment or adopting new habits.

Just make sure you don't allow comfort to weigh you down. I bet you don't want to end up working the same way as, sadly, millions of people do world-wide – glued to their desks, sitting in the same spot, in front of the same screen, and falling into the same productivity traps every single day, all day. By developing a healthy relationship with discomfort, you're giving yourself the best chance to succeed – whatever success means to you – while enjoying the journey.

WHAT IT TAKES TO RISE ABOVE COMFORT

It's possible to engineer discomfort into your work environment. In *Create a Thriving Workspace* I talk about a piece of furniture designed at the Stanford d.school (Hasso Plattner Institute of Design). The so-called 'Periodic Table' is a unique invention; it's intended to be unpleasant to work on, whether you're sitting or standing, and thus it prompts you to move around and engage in active collaboration.

You may choose to go down a similar path and make your environment purposefully challenging. However, you probably already have enough hurdles to jump. My advice is, just stay self-aware. Before you decide about where and how you should work, check in with yourself – and answer honestly: 'Am I giving myself the best chance to succeed? Or am I submitting to convenience and inertia?'

If you're concerned about having to deal with too much discomfort, let me assure you that you'll be fine. You're highly adaptable, and it's just as easy to build up your resilience as it is to lose it. Let me illustrate this with a personal story.

Years ago I spent a few weeks exploring Madagascar with my then partner, during the heat of the summer. It's a stunning country, but the trip was far from luxurious. Early in our travels we stayed one night in a guest house in a largish town. The room was very basic and battered. Cold shower. Stuffy air. Lousy bed. A single light bulb hanging on a wire. Swarms of mosquitoes … The following morning we headed to the country for about a fortnight to visit a few small villages. Most of these settlements had limited electricity and water. Others had zero infrastructure. On some nights we slept in a tent or under the stars. We bathed in the muddy river. We drank lukewarm water. We rode on a zebu cart over giant potholes. We had an incredible time, but it was hardly relaxing … Towards the end of our trip we went back to the guest house where we had stayed earlier. And guess what? It felt like a luxury resort. We actually had a proper bed. And a bathroom, with some water pressure. We even had chilled drinks! I had the best sleep that night. I had everything I needed.

Developing yourself and your work style is a journey – it has its challenges and rewards. And if you throw yourself into it, you'll arrive at a place where many things can bring you comfort and satisfaction, and very few things can drag you down.

INDIVIDUAL EXERCISES

Write a list of your long-time professional and personal goals. How many of these are you on track with? And how many of them do you keep delaying because the road to achieving them is uncomfortable? What needs to happen for you to get started?

Pick a simple activity you know is good for you but you don't do very often because it's a bit uncomfortable. (For example, standing while working, stepping away from your desk when you take a break, or moving between different settings during the day.) Do this activity every day for three weeks. Then check with yourself: How uncomfortable is it now, compared to when you started? What has changed?

TEAM EXERCISES

Start a team session in a comfortable setting, perhaps in a lounge space with sofas. Then halfway through, make yourself a bit uncomfortable. Perhaps stand up or move to a meeting space with very basic seating, and continue the meeting. How is the conversation changing? Are your team's pace, mood and focus any different compared to when you started? What can you learn from this experience?

Chat with your teammates about some of the achievements you're most proud of. What did it take for you to succeed? Did you need to leave your comfort zone? And if you were faced with a similar challenge again, how would you feel about it?

Discuss with your team which parts of your workplace you find a bit uncomfortable. Brainstorm how you could use this to your advantage.

CHOICE 35

IS IT A GOOD IDEA TO TRADE SLEEP TIME FOR PRODUCTIVE TIME?

How does sleep affect my skills, emotions and behaviour?

What can happen when I sacrifice sleep for work?

How can I get enough sleep and still get a lot done?

Sleep is not just a necessity but a wonderful gift to your body and mind, supporting your health, wellbeing and brain power. Still, sometimes you might feel inclined to cut your sleep short to get ahead with your duties. When this becomes a habit, your performance and life quality will inevitably suffer. There are smarter ways to stay productive. Start prioritising sleep, and you'll have more valuable hours in a day than ever.

What if I told you that I usually sleep around eight hours a night and rarely use an alarm clock to wake up? And that despite the advice from many 'success gurus', I refuse to cut my sleep short just to squeeze a couple of extra 'productive' hours into my day? Do you get the impression that I'm lazy and uncommitted, or that I'm giving myself the best chance to reach my potential?

We hear about people like Elon Musk or Barack Obama who sleep about six hours a night. Oprah Winfrey can function well on five and a half hours. Marissa Mayer, Yahoo's former CEO, is known to sleep just four hours when she's super busy. Their stories suggest that sleeping is a waste of time if you want to be successful. (Interestingly, almost no-one talks about the fact that Roger Federer sleeps about twelve hours a day.)

Sleeping long hours can seem like luxury these days, wherever you work and whatever you do. Some people perceive it as a sign of weakness, whereas staying up late, waking up early, and thus missing out on sleep due to work commitments is often regarded as a sign of a great work ethic.

I know people who take pride in routinely cutting down on sleep so that they can fit more into their days. Sometimes they work 16 to 18 hours straight, travelling to meetings, running interviews and workshops, and consolidating information. No doubt, they are committed to giving 100%. But is this really the best use of their time and energy?

SLEEP IS TRANSFORMATIVE

During sleep, a great deal of physical and neurological changes occur in our bodies. Some of them serve our physical health, including cell regeneration and hormonal regulation. Others support our psychological wellbeing. For instance, REM sleep is believed to help process emotions. Sleep also prepares us for optimum mental performance; for example, our memories from the day before get consolidated, and the brain is prepared for new learnings. Without sufficient sleep, we can't absorb new information and we struggle to recall memories.

Sleeping affects our most valuable skills, including our ability to concentrate, think clearly and communicate effectively. It influences our capacity to be creative, solve problems and make intelligent decisions. Not surprisingly, we tend to work more slowly and less accurately when underslept – even on basic tasks – and the slightest complexity can defeat us.

Interestingly, lack of sleep impacts our cognitive abilities in similar ways to consuming alcohol. Our reaction time slows down, we struggle to focus, and we make more mistakes. A study found that after being awake for 17 to 19 hours, our performance declines to the same extent as having a blood alcohol level of 0.05%. And if we stay up a few more hours, the impact is equivalent to a blood alcohol content of 0.1%.

Our mood and emotional intelligence are also affected; for example, we tend to be more level-headed, optimistic and empathic when feeling well rested, and more anxious, inflexible and irritable when sleep deprived. In a less than optimal state, we're not great at handling conflict either.

In fact, lack of sleep can take a toll on our relationships. A study that looked at supervisors' sleeping patterns found that on days they hadn't had sufficient sleep, employees saw them as more abusive, less charismatic and less self-controlled than otherwise. As a result, employees were less engaged, even when they themselves were fully rested.

CAN WE PUSH THROUGH?

We all have a lot on our plates, and sometimes it seems necessary to work late nights or get up super early to keep up. We feel we should be tough enough to overcome such a 'mundane inconvenience' as missing out on a few hours of sleep.

At the same time, we know too well that we're doing ourselves and every-one around us a disservice when this becomes a routine. I know people who regularly pull all-nighters to meet deadlines, and after presenting their solutions to the client, they crash spectacularly every single time. In fact, they know in advance that they shouldn't schedule any important activities for the two days following a client meeting.

I learned during my university years that I can act like a warrior for a few days – or even a few weeks – but there will always be a cost. Sleepless periods are inevitably followed by bleak and unproductive days. During this time, I usually feel pessimistic and antisocial. I spend long hours pro-crastinating, shuffling things around, or staring at the screen blankly while bingeing on chocolate.

Sacrificing sleep to get things done is like taking one step forward and two steps back. You might achieve a great deal while pushing yourself to the limit, but later on you'll slow down so much, or make so many mistakes, that your overall productivity will significantly suffer. This can become a self-perpetuating cycle. When you fall behind, there's even more pressure on you to catch up, so you're more likely to miss out on sleep again.

Sadly, some organisations expect people to be fully productive even when sleep deprived, which makes my blood boil. We're biological beings, not machines! There've been times when I felt some of my colleagues were actu-ally testing me. On one occasion, after landing from a 6 am flight to see an interstate client, I was asked to quickly pull together a presentation before the meeting. Another time, after working a couple of late nights to meet an important deadline, a teammate asked me to prepare a complex proposal on the same day. All this frenzy could have been easily avoided with a bit of forward thinking – but in this team, considering our own wellbeing and limitations were just not cool. And although I managed to hit the mark most of the time, there was always a comedown, sooner or later.

THERE ARE NO SHORTCUTS

Many people claim they can get by on just six hours of sleep or less each night. In truth, only around 1% of the population are naturally 'short sleepers'. Scientists believe this is due to genetic disposition, and if you're not among the lucky ones, you can't train yourself to need less sleep. If you drink coffee to get through the day or tend to sleep in on weekends, these might be signs that you're chronically sleep deprived.

Studies show that the vast majority of healthy adults need seven to nine hours of sleep every night. While good habits and lifestyle choices – such as nutritious diet, exercise, meditation and other restorative breaks – can certainly help maintain your physical and mental energy, none of these can substitute for quality sleep time.

Sleeping is not something you can catch up on either. It's not a debt you can pay off. It can be tempting to sleep late on weekends, but this habit could do more harm than good. As shown by research, inconsistent sleeping patterns disrupt your circadian rhythm, essentially making you feel jet-lagged.

In a nutshell, there are no shortcuts. Sleep is not a luxury but a biological necessity. No other creatures in nature willfully deprive themselves of sleeping, which is worth contemplating.

SLEEP IS A TRUE GIFT

Rather than trying to hack the system, I find myself looking at the body's innate intelligence with increasing appreciation. Although there are many things we don't understand about sleep, it's clear that it is an incredible gift to our bodies and minds.

In fact, good sleep is a recipe for a long and healthy life. It boosts your immune system, maintains your DNA, slows down ageing, preserves your memory and mental sharpness, and reduces the risk of numerous diseases, including dementia, heart disease, type 2 diabetes and cancer. When you sleep well and enough, you also experience less physical pain, and lower your chances of suffering from obesity and depression.

Put simply, sleep buys you a lot of quality time – years, if not decades. Why would you want to trade this for getting a few hours ahead here and there with your duties?

SLEEP MORE **AND** ACHIEVE MORE

'Easier said than done,' I hear you say. You're stretched thin, both at work and at home. And when urgent tasks are piling up, you can't just drop everything and depart to dreamland. (Even if you went to bed, your troubling thoughts would keep you awake.)

Thankfully, there are a few things you can do to break the cycle.

Get more organised

To start with, check whether you and your team could become better organised. I know this seems like trivial advice, but in my experience, most late-night and predawn working sessions could be avoided with better communication and planning. In my view, working intelligently is also way cooler than acting like a superhuman and ending up completely deflated.

Travel wisely

When you need to travel a couple of hours for a meeting or event, leaving early in the morning may look like the easier and cheaper option. You can fit the whole trip into a single day and you don't need to organise accommodation. But if you think about it, the productivity you'll lose after a very short night and an exceptionally long day also has a cost. Keep this in mind before organising your trips. Sometimes getting there a day early is a smarter choice.

Work on your culture

I encourage you to look at your values and priorities, and discuss them with your teams and clients, ensuring that everyone is on the same page. Is it worth sacrificing your health and your long-term productivity to meet certain deadlines? Does it reflect badly on you if you close your laptop at a reasonable hour, even when the pressure is on? Will it create any problems if you ask for more time? And is it really a sign of weakness or incompetence when you say you need help? You may find out that some of the things you used to stress about are not actually problems.

Get better quality sleep

Finally, while you can't negotiate the amount of quality sleep you need, you can certainly work towards spending fewer hours in bed. There are many ways to improve your sleep and reduce the amount of time you waste counting sheep, tossing and turning. Here are just a few tips from experts:

- Try to go to bed and wake up at the same time each day, even on week-ends and holidays. Once your body gets used to the routine, you'll fall asleep more easily and sleep better.

- Make sure your bedtime aligns with your circadian rhythm. (We touched on this in Choice 2, 'What should I do at different times of the day?')

- Avoid using screens, and unwind before bedtime. If there's a lot on your mind, empty your thoughts on a piece of paper; you can revisit them tomorrow.

- Exercise during the day, but not too close to bedtime.

- Maintain a healthy diet, and avoid caffeine, alcohol, sugar and heavy meals late in the day.

- Make sure your bedroom has a calming, peaceful ambience.

- Keep your bedroom cool, so that your body temperature can drop a little.

If you find yourself lying awake for too long, get up and do something relaxing. Only return to bed when you feel sleepy. This way your brain can learn to associate your bed with sleeping, rather than with sleeplessness.

PRIORITISING SLEEP IS A SMART CHOICE

For the sake of your health, wellbeing and performance, you need to make sleep a priority, challenge the stigma around sleeping long hours, and have a hard look at how you define work ethic and performance.

Once you start to prioritise sleep, you'll no doubt reap the rewards. Instead of working extra hours for diminishing returns, you'll find it easier to get on a roll, and likely achieve more in a day than you have done in the past.

And guess what! After spending less time sitting in front of your screen and more time doing other things you love – thus feeling happier, healthier and more relaxed – you will sleep even better.

INDIVIDUAL EXERCISE

Keep a 'sleep diary' for a few weeks. Each day, note down when you went to sleep, when you woke up, and how well you were sleeping. If your mind was active at some point at night, write down what was going on. Also rate each day (perhaps on a scale from 0 to 10) how effective you were at work, and how you were feeling overall. Look at your notes at the end of each week. Do you notice any interesting patterns?

TEAM EXERCISES

Have a discussion about sleep and work performance. What does sleeping eight hours a day say about a person? Is it possible to meet work demands without sacrificing sleep? How can you organise yourselves more effectively? What should you do when there's not enough time in the day to get everything done? When are you expected to work late nights or early mornings? And when is it okay to ask for help or to push back a deadline?

Experiment with implementing a 'sleep policy' for a month. During this time, everyone in the team should prioritise sleep over deadlines. After the month is over, get together for a discussion. How did you find the experience? Did you manage to stick to the rule? Did you encounter any problems? Did you notice any change in your health, mood or performance? And what about your relationships, teamwork and culture?

THIS IS NOT THE END

Few things compare to the joy of solving a big problem, creating something extraordinary or changing lives for the better, using your experience and talent ... Or when you find a deep connection with others, tap into your flow and put something of yourself into what you're doing. In these moments you're not 'working' – you're living your purpose.

This experience is almost addictive. We're hardwired to learn and grow, explore new aspects of ourselves and express our uniqueness. We're meant to create beautiful and exciting things, and to improve the lives of those we care about. If you feel your current job is less than fulfilling, just think about what makes you feel truly alive when you're not working.

Some people call me naive (and I call these folk cynics, so we're all square), but I believe that work can be an amazing source of happiness and satisfaction. And almost any role has the potential to enrich your life and give you a sense of contribution, if you approach it with skill and wit.

Don't get me wrong; I know all too well that work can be very trying at times, no matter which way you attack it. I've had my fair share of battles and sleepless nights, even while writing this book (just ask my partner). But I rarely back down from meaningful challenges, because I know that with the right work habits and strategies, I'll overcome them sooner rather than later – and with less effort.

What the future holds

By looking at the trends, it's clear that we're not heading towards the 'utopian dream' where all the difficult jobs are done by machines. As far as we can foresee, the real challenges will be left for us humans to solve. I'm talking about complex tasks and problems that require unique insights, ingenuity and emotional intelligence to overcome.

Sources of stress, distractions and demands are not going to dry up either. We can expect the continued flood of information, along with a lot of noise. And people will always be people – often unpredictable, biased, emotion-driven and irrational. Put simply, our days will be riddled with booby traps as much as they are today. And if we're not prepared, we'll quickly get caught up in the hamster wheel, see our plans hijacked, and find ourselves reacting to issues like puppets as our attention is pulled in myriad directions.

Unskillful strategies to keep our heads above water will only create more problems while pushing us towards burnout. Working longer hours or tackling larger to-do lists, for example, are anything but a smart approach in the knowledge economy. These primitive performance measures really should have been left in the Industrial Age.

Different experiences and different results

I'm sure you agree, it's time to work smarter. In today's society, you can only achieve meaningful change if you play to your strengths while putting your heart and soul into what you do. You need to recognise and *own* the choices available to you about when, where and how you work. You need to appreciate the value of your unique qualities, honour your individual work style, and add your own rules to the collective 'rule book'.

Early in this book, I invited you to ask yourself, 'What does high performance mean to me?' We talked about the fact that you can often recognise your most powerful moments by experiencing certain thoughts and emotions. So I encourage you to pay attention to the subtle signs of your body and mind – if they give you a 'green light', you're probably on the right track.

Following your authentic path is not necessarily comfortable, but is always rewarding. Let me illustrate this with a quick example. There have been a number of times in my career when I was on the verge of completing a major project and I was 90% happy with the results (which I guess is not bad for a borderline perfectionist). But instead of smoothing out the edges, something compelled me to pull the whole thing apart and recreate it from scratch. Now, this might sound like pointless fussiness, but whenever I acted on my gut feeling, the final result turned out to be a game changer, yielding significant and lasting value for my teams and clients. Over and over again, my instinct has been proven to be right.

This 'green light' of course looks and feels different for everyone. But once you know how to tap into your genius, your experience and your results transform. Ideas start to come to you, and you bring powerful solutions to life without the hard labour.

You've come a long way

At the start of this book I outlined six critical skills and attributes that should help you THRIVE in your career: being a *Team player*, *Honest* and *humane*, *Responsive*, *Intelligent*, *Venturous*, and an *Eternal learner*. By reading *35 Smart Choices* and acting on some of the ideas we've explored, you've made massive headway in each of these skills. Well done!

In plain terms, you've learned to be a more proficient and empathetic communicator, ready to build trusting relationships and to collaborate with people from all walks of life. You've become more agile and flexible, and thus better prepared to tackle the ever-changing challenges of modern work. You now know better than ever how to bring out the best in yourself and others, and how to approach different tasks and problems effectively. You set better priorities and make wiser decisions, even in complex and difficult situations. You're hopefully more confident to pursue big goals and bold visions, and left with a strong desire to constantly learn and evolve.

With these skills and attributes, you should be able to progress towards your goals faster – and perhaps even reach beyond your dreams – while savouring every step. And just as importantly, you should find it much easier to demonstrate the value you bring to your teammates, leaders and clients – and subsequently, to advance your career. Because THRIVE-ing professionals are the very people who can solve our society's biggest problems, make the greatest contribution towards positive change, and help progressive organisations fulfil their purpose.

This is not the end of the road

After reading this far, you know well that you'll never 'arrive'. When it comes to exploring your work style and improving the way you work, there's no such thing as a final destination. The world is constantly shifting. Work and business is constantly changing … And so are you, as you embrace life's experiences and venture into new territories.

I hope you see this as good news. Whether you're a keen traveller, sports fan, art enthusiast, people person, nature lover or game player – for example – you know how much more fun it is to dive into new experiences as opposed to doing what you've always done.

So I invite you to continue experimenting with new ways of working – and to do this with the same level of energy that you to devote to your (other) passions in life. Keep this book handy, and revisit these 35 Choices frequently. Don't hesitate to try new things, and also look out for other powerful choices within your reach that are not discussed in this book. If you look around with eyes wide open, you'll notice them everywhere.

See you around … and keep sharing your magic!

SOURCES

Here is a list of articles, research papers and summaries, reports, blog posts, books, videos and podcasts to complement the insights and advice shared in the main text. Whether you're an enthusiast of the subjects we've explored or you're studying them through the eyes of an academic, I trust that some of these sources will meet your interest. (Note that all web links were live at the time of publication.)

While you're digging deeper into a topic, you may come across conflicting findings and advice. Well, that's life … But I'm confident that you're able to think critically about the information you take in – and especially after reading this book, you're able to decide what works for you and what doesn't.

Please feel free to contact me to discuss any of the material referenced here, or if you seek additional information.

Let's get started

Mattingly, Stephen M., Julie M. Gregg, Pino Audia, Ayse Elvan Bayraktaroglu, Andrew T. Campbell, Nitesh V. Chawla, Vedant Das Swain, et al. 'The Tesserae Project: Large-Scale, Longitudinal, In Situ, Multimodal Sensing of Information Workers'. *Extended Abstracts of the 2019 CHI Conference on Human Factors in Computing Systems*, 2019. https://doi.org/10.1145/3290607.3299041.

'Mobile-Sensing System Makes Assessing Worker Performance Easier'. *Big News Network*, 2019. https://www.bignewsnetwork.com/news/261651778/mobile-sensing-system-makes-assessing-worker-performance-easier.

'Pink Drinks Can Help You Run Faster and Further, Study Finds'. *University of Westminster*, 2021. https://www.westminster.ac.uk/news/pink-drinks-can-help-you-run-faster-and-further-study-finds.

PART I: HOW CAN I BUILD MOMENTUM AND MAKE THE MOST OF MY DAY?

Choice 1: How should I plan my day to make the most of it?

Amabile, Teresa, and Steven J. Kramer. 'The Power of Small Wins'. *Harvard Business Review*, 2011. https://hbr.org/2011/05/the-power-of-small-wins.

DeMelo, Juno. 'Precrastination: When the Early Bird Gets the Shaft'. *The New York Times*, 2019. https://www.nytimes.com/2019/03/25/smarter-living/precrastination-when-the-early-bird-gets-the-shaft.html.

Eltringham, Mark. 'Riffing on the Issue of Workplace Design and Creativity'. *Workplace Insight*, 2019. https://workplaceinsight.net/riffing-on-the-issue-of-workplace-design-and-creativity/.

Grant, Adam. 'Productivity Isn't About Time Management. It's About Attention Management.' *The New York Times*, 2019. https://www.nytimes.com/2019/03/28/smarter-living/productivity-isnt-about-time-management-its-about-attention-management.html.

Newport, Cal. *Deep Work: Rules for Focused Success in a Distracted World.* Grand Central Publishing, 2016.

Choice 2: What should I do at different times of the day?

Carey, Benedict. 'Twitter Study Tracks When We Are :)'. *The New York Times*, 2011. https://www.nytimes.com/2011/09/30/science/30twitter.html.

Carr, Coeli. 'Doctors More Likely to Prescribe Antibiotics Later in the Day'. *The Pharmaceutical Journal* 293, no. 7832, 2014. https://pharmaceutical-journal.com/article/news/doctors-more-likely-to-prescribe-antibiotics-later-in-the-day.

Chen, Jing, Baruch Lev, and Elizabeth Demers. 'The Dangers of Late-Afternoon Earnings Calls'. *Harvard Business Review*, 2013. https://hbr.org/2013/10/the-dangers-of-late-afternoon-earnings-calls.

Dai, Hengchen, Katherine L. Milkman, David A. Hofmann, and Bradley R. Staats. 'The Impact of Time at Work and Time Off From Work on Rule Compliance'. *American Psychological Association* 100, no. 3, 2014. https://www.apa.org/pubs/journals/releases/apl-a0038067.pdf.

Hines, Carolyn B. 'Time-of-Day Effects on Human Performance'. *Journal of Catholic Education* 7, no. 3, 2004. https://doi.org/10.15365/joce.0703072013.

Imber, Amantha. 'Here's Why You Should Never Hold Management Meetings in the Afternoon'. *Business Insider*, 2018. https://www.businessinsider.com.au/ideal-meeting-times-2018-2.

Linder, Jeffrey A., Jason N. Doctor, Mark W. Friedberg, Harry Reyes Nieva, Caroline Birks, Daniella Meeker, and Craig R. Fox. 'Time of Day and the Decision to Prescribe Antibiotics'. *JAMA Internal Medicine* 174, no. 12, 2014. https://doi.org/10.1001/jamainternmed.2014.5225.

'Morningness Eveningness Questionnaire - Are You an Owl or a Lark?'. *Sleepsurge.* https://sleepsurge.com/morningness-eveningness-questionnaire/.

Pink, Daniel H. *When: The Scientific Secrets of Perfect Timing.* Riverhead Books, 2018.

Pink, Daniel H., and Tony Robbins. 'Timing Is Everything: Daniel Pink on the Best Time for Meetings, Taking Breaks and Creative Breakthroughs'. *Tony Robbins Podcast*, 2019. https://www.tonyrobbins.com/podcasts/timing-is-everything/.

Suni, Eric, and Anis Rehman. 'Sleep Drive and Your Body Clock'. *Sleep Foundation*, 2021. https://www.sleepfoundation.org/circadian-rhythm/sleep-drive-and-your-body-clock.

Vetter, Céline, Dorothee Fischer, Joana L. Matera, and Till Roenneberg. 'Aligning Work and Circadian Time in Shift Workers Improves Sleep and Reduces Circadian Disruption'. *Current Biology* 25, no. 7, 2015. https://doi.org/10.1016/j.cub.2015.01.064.

Choice 3: How can I maximise my mental energy?

Gilsinan, Kathy. 'The Buddhist and the Neuroscientist: What Compassion Does to the Brain'. *The Atlantic*, 2015. https://www.theatlantic.com/health/archive/2015/07/dalai-lama-neuroscience-compassion/397706/.

Lee, Jooa Julia, Francesca Gino, and Bradley R. Staats. 'Rainmakers: Why Bad Weather Means Good Productivity'. *Journal of Applied Psychology* 99, no. 3, 2014. https://www.apa.org/pubs/journals/features/apl-a0035559.pdf.

Lieberman, Charlotte. 'Why You Procrastinate (It Has Nothing to Do with Self-Control)'. *The New York Times*, 2019. https://www.nytimes.com/2019/03/25/smarter-living/why-you-procrastinate-it-has-nothing-to-do-with-self-control.html.

Mark, Gloria, Daniela Gudith, and Ulrich Klocke. 'The Cost of Interrupted Work: More Speed and Stress'. *CHI '08: Proceedings of the SIGCHI Conference on Human Factors in Computing Systems*, 2008. https://doi.org/10.1145/1357054.1357072.

Newport, Cal. 'Why You Should Quit Social Media'. *TEDxTysons*, 2016. https://www.ted.com/talks/cal_newport_why_you_should_quit_social_media.

Schipper, Ori. 'Workplace Interruptions Lead to Physical Stress'. *ETH Zurich*, 2020. https://ethz.ch/en/news-and-events/eth-news/news/2020/10/workplace-interruptions-lead-to-physical-stress.html.

'Think Better – Neuroscience: The Next Competitive Advantage'. *Steelcase*, 2015. https://www.steelcase.com/research/articles/topics/open-plan-workplace/think-better/.

Tubbs, Sara. 'Multitasking in the Workplace Can Lead to Negative Emotions'. *University of Houston*, 2020. https://www.uh.edu/news-events/stories/2020/may-2020/05112020-multitasking-in-workplace-and-negative-emotions.

Urban, Tim. 'Inside the Mind of a Master Procrastinator'. *TED*, 2016. https://www.ted.com/talks/tim_urban_inside_the_mind_of_a_master_procrastinator.

Choice 4: How can I stay focused?

Arantes, Beatriz. 'Neuroscience: The Next Great Competitive Advantage'. *Work&Place*, 2015. https://workplaceinsight.net/wp-content/uploads/2015/12/Work-Place6.pdf.

Brown, Derren. 'Trains ... Of Thought', 2006. https://www.youtube.com/watch?v=6bkleuxpvxY.

Goldfarb, Anna. 'Stop Letting Modern Distractions Steal Your Attention'. *The New York Times*, 2019. https://www.nytimes.com/2019/03/26/smarter-living/stop-letting-modern-distractions-steal-your-attention.html.

Herrera, Tim. 'How to Actually, Truly Focus on What You're Doing'. *The New York Times*, 2019. https://www.nytimes.com/2019/01/13/smarter-living/how-to-actually-truly-focus-on-what-youre-doing.html.

Imber, Amantha. 'What Super Productive People Do Differently'. *Harvard Business Review*, 2020. https://hbr.org/2020/12/what-super-productive-people-do-differently.

Medina, John. *Brain Rules: 12 Principles for Surviving and Thriving at Work*. Pear Press, 2008.

Tonietto, Gabriela N., Selin A. Malkoc, and Stephen M. Nowlis. 'When an Hour Feels Shorter: Future Boundary Tasks Alter Consumption by Contracting Time'. *Journal of Consumer Research* 45, no. 5, 2019. https://doi.org/10.1093/jcr/ucy043.

Weinschenk, Susan. 'The True Cost of Multi-Tasking: You Could Be Losing up to 40% of Your Productivity.' *Psychology Today Australia*, 2012. https://www.psychologytoday.com/au/blog/brain-wise/201209/the-true-cost-multi-tasking.

Choice 5: When and why is it a good idea to work unplugged?

'Anatomy of Work Index 2021: Overcoming Disruption in a Distributed World'. *Asana*, 2021. https://asana.com/resources/anatomy-of-work.

'Communications Market Report'. *Ofcom*, 2018. https://www.ofcom.org.uk/research-and-data/multi-sector-research/cmr/cmr-2018.

Goldhill, Olivia. 'Scientists Made People Turn off Their Notifications for a Day, and Saw an Effect Years Later'. *Quartz*, 2017. https://qz.com/1046312/scientists-made-people-turned-off-their-notifications-for-a-day-and-saw-an-effect-years-later/.

'How Many Productive Hours in a Work Day? Just 2 Hours, 23 Minutes ...'. *Vouchercloud*. https://www.vouchercloud.com/resources/office-worker-productivity.

Knight, Will. '"Info-Mania" Dents IQ More than Marijuana'. *New Scientist*, 2005. https://www.newscientist.com/article/dn7298-info-mania-dents-iq-more-than-marijuana/.

'Lecturer Takes Laptops and Smart Phones Away and Musters Student Presence'. *University of Copenhagen*, 2020. https://science.ku.dk/english/press/news/2020/lecturer-takes-laptops-and-smart-phones-away-and-musters-student-presence/.

Pattison, Kermit. 'Worker, Interrupted: The Cost of Task Switching'. *Fast Company*, 2008. https://www.fastcompany.com/944128/worker-interrupted-cost-task-switching.

Schaffhauser, Dian. 'Report: Even the Mere Presence of a Smartphone Makes You Dumber'. *THE Journal*, 2018. https://thejournal.com/articles/2018/04/09/even-the-mere-presence-of-a-smartphone-makes-you-dumber.aspx.

Ward, Adrian F., Kristen Duke, Ayelet Gneezy, and Maarten W. Bos. 'Brain Drain: The Mere Presence of One's Own Smartphone Reduces Available Cognitive Capacity'. *Journal of the Association for Consumer Research* 2, no. 2, 2017. https://doi.org/10.1086/691462.

Zerkel, Joshua. 'The Simple 3-Step Process for Combating Workplace Stress'. *Fast Company*, 2019. https://www.fastcompany.com/90383370/3-ways-to-combat-workplace-stress.

Choice 6: When should I take a break?

Ariga, Atsunori, and Alejandro Lleras. 'Brief Diversions Vastly Improve Focus, Researchers Find'. *ScienceDaily*, 2011. https://www.sciencedaily.com/releases/2011/02/110208131529.htm.

Carnegie, Dale. *How to Stop Worrying and Start Living*. Simon and Schuster, 1948.

Danziger, Shai, Jonathan Levav, and Liora Avnaim-Pesso. 'Extraneous Factors in Judicial Decisions'. *Proceedings of the National Academy of Sciences* 108, no. 17, 2011. https://doi.org/10.1073/pnas.1018033108.

Friedman, Ron. 'Schedule a 15-Minute Break Before You Burn Out'. *Harvard Business Review*, 2014. https://hbr.org/2014/08/schedule-a-15-minute-break-before-you-burn-out.

Gifford, Julia. 'The Secret of the 10% Most Productive People? Breaking!' *DeskTime*, 2018. https://desktime.com/blog/17-52-ratio-most-productive-people/.

Hirsh, Arthur. 'You Can Take a Break from Practice – but Not for Too Long, Study Shows'. *Johns Hopkins University*, 2017. https://hub.jhu.edu/2017/12/18/how-long-to-break-practice-to-improve-learning/.

Seiter, Courtney. 'The Science of Breaks at Work: How to Be More Productive By Changing the Way You Think About Downtime'. *Buffer* , 2014. https://buffer.com/resources/science-taking-breaks-at-work/.

Vozza, Stephanie. 'This Is How Many Minutes of Breaks You Need Each Day'. *Fast Company*, 2017. https://www.fastcompany.com/40487419/this-is-how-many-minutes-of-breaks-you-need-each-day.

Choice 7: What should I do during my break time?

Ducharme, Jamie. 'Being Bored Can Be Good for You – If You Do It Right. Here's How'. *Time*, 2019. https://time.com/5480002/benefits-of-boredom/.

Kimura, Tsukasa, Tatsuya Yamada, Yohko Hirokawa, and Kazumitsu Shinohara. 'Brief and Indirect Exposure to Natural Environment Restores the Directed Attention for the Task'. *Frontiers in Psychology* 12, 2021. https://doi.org/10.3389/fpsyg.2021.619347.

'Napping May Not Be Such a No-No'. *Harvard Health*, 2009. https://www.health.harvard.edu/newsletter_article/napping-may-not-be-such-a-no-no.

Newport, Cal. 'Why You Should Quit Social Media'. *TEDxTysons*, 2016. https://www.ted.com/talks/cal_newport_why_you_should_quit_social_media.

Popescu, Adam. 'Keep Your Head Up: How Smartphone Addiction Kills Manners and Moods'. *The New York Times*, 2018. https://www.nytimes.com/2018/01/25/smarter-living/bad-text-posture-neckpain-mood.html.

Rosenfeld, Jordan. '8 Scientific Benefits of Napping'. *Mental Floss*, 2019. https://www.mentalfloss.com/article/502902/8-scientific-benefits-napping.

Sianoja, Marjaana, Christine J. Syrek, Jessica de Bloom, Kalevi Korpela, and Ulla Kinnunen. 'Enhancing Daily Well-Being at Work through Lunchtime Park Walks and Relaxation Exercises: Recovery Experiences as Mediators'. *Journal of Occupational Health Psychology* 23, no. 3, 2018. https://doi.org/10.1037/ocp0000083.

Whillans, Ashley. 'Time Confetti and the Broken Promise of Leisure'. *Behavioral Scientist*, 2020. https://behavioralscientist.org/time-confetti-and-the-broken-promise-of-leisure/.

PART II: HOW CAN I COLLABORATE BETTER WITH OTHERS?

Choice 8: When should I work alone, and when should I collaborate with my team?

Bernstein, Ethan, Jesse Shore, and David Lazer. 'How Intermittent Breaks in Interaction Improve Collective Intelligence'. *Proceedings of the National Academy of Sciences* 115, no. 35, 2018. https://doi.org/10.1073/pnas.1802407115.

Obama, Barack. *A Promised Land*. Crown, 2020.

'Problem-Solving Techniques Take on New Twist'. *The Harvard Gazette*, 2018. https://news.harvard.edu/gazette/story/2018/08/collaborate-on-complex-problems-but-only-intermittently/.

Repenning, Nelson P., Don Kieffer, and James Repenning. 'A New Approach to Designing Work'. *MIT Sloan Management Review*, 2017. https://sloanreview.mit.edu/article/a-new-approach-to-designing-work/.

Riedl, Christoph, and Anita Williams Woolley. 'Successful Remote Teams Communicate in Bursts', *Harvard Business Review*, 2020. https://hbr.org/2020/10/successful-remote-teams-communicate-in-bursts.

Choice 9: How should we run meetings to ensure problems are actually solved?

Desai, Teja Lele. 'Informal Meetings Are Key to Innovative Ideas'. *Mint*, 2019. https://www.livemint.com/mint-lounge/business-of-life/informal-meetings-are-key-to-innovative-ideas-1553022288691.html.

Fradera, Alex. 'Minimalist, Anonymous Rooms Are Probably Not a Good Place to Do Teamwork'. *The British Psychological Society – Research Digest*, 2016. https://digest.bps.org.uk/2016/05/25/minimalist-anonymous-rooms-are-probably-not-a-good-place-to-do-teamwork/.

Gelsomini, Mirko, Giulia Leonardi, and Franca Garzotto. 'Embodied Learning in Immersive Smart Spaces'. *Association for Computing Machinery*, 2020. https://doi.org/10.1145/3313831.3376667.

Greenaway, Katharine H., Hannibal A. Thai, S. Alexander Haslam, and Sean C. Murphy. 'Spaces That Signal Identity Improve Workplace Productivity'. *Journal of Personnel Psychology* 15, no. 1, 2016. https://doi.org/10.1027/1866-5888/a000148.

Knapp, Jake. 'Google Ventures: Your Design Team Needs a War Room. Here's How to Set One Up'. *Fast Company*, 2014. https://www.fastcompany.com/3028471/google-ventures-your-design-team-needs-a-war-room-heres-how-to-set-one-up.

Knight, Andrew P., and Markus Baer. 'Get Up, Stand Up: The Effects of a Non-Sedentary Workspace on Information Elaboration and Group Performance'. *Social Psychological and Personality Science* 5, no. 8, 2014. https://doi.org/10.1177/1948550614538463.

Paul, Annie Murphy. 'How to Think Outside Your Brain'. *The New York Times*, 2021. https://www.nytimes.com/2021/06/11/opinion/brain-mind-cognition.html.

'The Science of Collaboration: How the Body Activates the Brain and Makes Ideas Better'. *Steelcase 360 Magazine*, 2019. https://www.steelcase.com/research/360-magazine/new-work-new-rules/.

Witthoft, Scott, and Scott Doorley. *Make Space: How to Set the Stage for Creative Collaboration*. John Wiley & Sons, 2012.

Choice 10: Where should we meet?

Farnan, Keith, Carl Hutchinson, Kerry Godliman, Romesh Ranganathan, Richard Herring, Phil Wang, Chris Turner, et al. '"The Staff Are like Gin-Pouring Ninjas": Standups Pick the Best Comedy Clubs'. *The Guardian*, 2015. https://www.theguardian.com/stage/2015/jun/15/standups-on-comedy-clubs-andrew-maxwell-richard-herring-rachel-parris-romesh-ranganathan.

Gluckselig, Katie, Rebecca Milne, and Scott Fallick. 'Not Just Child's Play: How Playful Environments Contribute to Innovation'. *Perkins Eastman*, 2018. https://www.perkinseastman.com/white-papers/.

Usher, Neil. 'A Unity of Opposites at Sky Central'. *Workplace Insight*, 2017. https://workplaceinsight.net/unity-opposites-sky-central/.

Ware, Jim. 'The Main Challenge of Modern Working Life: Finding the Place Just Right to Meet'. *Workplace Insight*, 2018. https://workplaceinsight.net/main-challenge-modern-working-life-finding-place-just-right-meet/.

Choice 11: Who should I sit with in the office?

Behr, Adam. 'Two of Us: Inside John Lennon's Incredible Songwriting Partnership with Paul McCartney'. *The Conversation*, 2020. http://theconversation.com/two-of-us-inside-john-lennons-incredible-songwriting-partnership-with-paul-mccartney-147857.

Corsello, Jason, and Dylan Minor. 'Want to Be More Productive? Sit Next to Someone Who Is'. *Harvard Business Review*, 2014. https://hbr.org/2017/02/want-to-be-more-productive-sit-next-to-someone-who-is.

Gino, Francesca, Shahar Ayal, and Dan Ariely. 'Contagion and Differentiation in Unethical Behavior: The Effect of One Bad Apple on the Barrel'. *Psychological Science* 20, no. 3, 2009. https://doi.org/10.1111/j.1467-9280.2009.02306.x.

Housman, Michael, and Dylan Minor. 'Organizational Design and Space: The Good, the Bad, and the Productive'. *Social Science Research Network*, 2016. http://dx.doi.org/10.2139/ssrn.2805578.

Lestrange, Geoffroy de. 'Watch Where You Sit: New Workplace Setups Could Hit Productivity'. *Workplace Insight*, 2020. https://workplaceinsight.net/watch-where-you-sit-new-workplace-setups-could-hit-productivity/.

Stone, Emily. 'Sitting Near a High-Performer Can Make You Better at Your Job'. *Kellogg Insight*, 2017. https://insight.kellogg.northwestern.edu/article/sitting-near-a-high-performer-can-make-you-better-at-your-job.

'Toxic Employees in the Workplace - Hidden Costs and How to Spot Them'. *Cornerstone*, 2015. https://www.cornerstoneondemand.com/resources/whitepapers/toxic-employees-workplace-hidden-costs-and-how-spot-them.

Choice 12: What kinds of relationships should I cultivate at work?

'Guide: Understand Team Effectiveness'. *Google*. https://rework.withgoogle.com/print/guides/5721312655835136/.

Heffernan, Margaret. 'Forget the Pecking Order at Work'. *TEDWomen*, 2015. https://www.ted.com/talks/margaret_heffernan_forget_the_pecking_order_at_work.

Hülsheger, Ute R., Neil Anderson, and Jesus F. Salgado. 'Team-Level Predictors of Innovation at Work: A Comprehensive Meta-Analysis Spanning Three Decades of Research'. *Journal of Applied Psychology* 94, no. 5, 2009. https://doi.org/10.1037/a0015978.

Pizag, Anetta. 'Why You Need to Discuss Company Values with Your People'. *Pizag*, 2019. https://pizag.com.au/2019/05/27/why-you-need-to-discuss-company-and-team-values-with-your-people/.

Rock, David, Heidi Grant, and Jacqui Grey. 'Diverse Teams Feel Less Comfortable – and That's Why They Perform Better'. *Harvard Business Review*, 2016. https://hbr.org/2016/09/diverse-teams-feel-less-comfortable-and-thats-why-they-perform-better.

Smith, Mickey B., Aaron D. Hill, J. Craig Wallace, Tessa Recendes, and Timothy A. Judge. 'Upsides to Dark and Downsides to Bright Personality: A Multidomain Review and Future Research Agenda'. *Journal of Management* 44, no. 1, 2018. https://doi.org/10.1177/0149206317733511.

Van Kleef, Gerben A., Christina Anastasopoulou, and Bernard A. Nijstad. 'Can Expressions of Anger Enhance Creativity? A Test of the Emotions as Social Information (EASI) Model'. *Journal of Experimental Social Psychology* 46, no. 6, 2010. https://doi.org/10.1016/j.jesp.2010.05.015.

Wallace, Craig. 'The Scientific Case for Hiring a Narcissist'. *Quartz*, 2019. https://qz.com/work/1767917/the-scientific-case-for-hiring-a-narcissist/.

Choice 13: How much of my personality should I bring to my professional life?

'Bo Burnham Had a Hard Time Just Holding Coffee Cups While Filming "Promising Young Woman"'. *TheWrap*, 2020. https://www.youtube.com/watch?v=7ifY2Ri_6RE.

Choice 14: How can I build better relationships at work?

Bannister, Emma. 'Reinventing Water Cooler Chats: Fostering Social Interaction Is Key to Increasing Workplace Productivity'. *SmartCompany*, 2019. https://www.smartcompany.com.au/people-human-resources/productivity/water-cooler-chats/.

Brown, Brené. *Braving the Wilderness*. Random House, 2017.

Brown, Brené. 'Why Experiencing Joy and Pain in a Group Is So Powerful'. *Greater Good*, 2019. https://greatergood.berkeley.edu/article/item/why_experiencing_joy_and_pain_in_a_group_is_so_powerful.

Cao, Jiyin, Dejun Tony Kong, and Adam D. Galinsky. 'Breaking Bread Produces Bigger Pies: An Empirical Extension of Shared Eating to Negotiations and a Commentary on Woolley and Fishbach (2019)'. *Psychological Science* 31, no. 10, 2020. https://doi.org/10.1177/0956797620939532.

Crudo, Ben. 'I Wanted to Be Friends with All My Employees. Now I Have 100'. *Fast Company*, 2019. https://www.fastcompany.com/90424402/i-wanted-to-be-friends-with-all-my-employees-now-i-have-100.

Deusen, Meg Van. 'The Power of Eye Contact – A Stress Reducer'. *Sight On Stress*, 2019. http://www.sightonstress.com/the-power-of-eye-contact-a-free-and-easy-stress-reducer/.

Edmondson, Amy C., and Thomas Chamorro-Premuzic. 'Today's Leaders Need Vulnerability, Not Bravado'. *Harvard Business Review*, 2020. https://hbr.org/2020/10/todays-leaders-need-vulnerability-not-bravado.

Headlee, Celeste. 'Ten Ways to Have Better Conversations'. *VitalSmarts Video*, 2018. https://www.youtube.com/watch?v=-iOr-Z_qNAo&t=1187s.

Headlee, Celeste. *We Need to Talk: How to Have Conversations That Matter.* Harper Wave, 2017.

Heffernan, Margaret. 'The Human Skills We Need in an Unpredictable World'. *TEDSummit*, 2019. https://www.ted.com/talks/margaret_heffernan_the_human_skills_we_need_in_an_unpredictable_world.

Irwin, Amy, and Ceri T. Trevethan. 'Five Ways Rudeness Can Actually Be a Positive Experience'. *The Conversation*, 2019. http://theconversation.com/five-ways-rudeness-can-actually-be-a-positive-experience-125447.

Jarick, Michelle, Kaitlin E. W. Laidlaw, Eleni Nasiopoulos, and Alan Kingstone. 'Eye Contact Affects Attention More than Arousal as Revealed by Prospective Time Estimation'. *Attention, Perception, & Psychophysics* 78, 2016. https://doi.org/10.3758/s13414-016-1085-8.

Low, Luisia. 'It Could Pay to Get Personal at Work – Here's Why'. *The University of Sydney*, 2019. https://www.sydney.edu.au/news-opinion/news/2019/07/17/It-could-pay-to-get-personal-at-work-heres-why.html.

Wingard, Jason. 'Loneliness Is Crippling Workplace Productivity: Here's the Leadership Prescription'. *Forbes*, 2020. https://www.forbes.com/sites/jasonwingard/2020/02/14/loneliness-is-crippling-workplace-productivity-heres-the-leadership-prescription/.

Woolley, Kaitlin, and Ayelet Fishbach. 'Shared Plates, Shared Minds: Consuming From a Shared Plate Promotes Cooperation'. Psychological Science 30, no. 4, 2019. https://doi.org/10.1177/0956797619830633.

Choice 15: How can we do great work and have a great time?

Aleida, Teresa, and Cecily Josten. 'Not a Joke: Leveraging Humour at Work Increases Performance, Individual Happiness, and Psychological Safety'. *LSE Business Review*, 2021. https://blogs.lse.ac.uk/businessreview/2021/04/28/not-a-joke-leveraging-humour-at-work-increases-performance-individual-happiness-and-psychological-safety/.

Andrew, Tarvin. 'The Skill of Humor'. *TEDxTAMU*, 2017. https://www.youtube.com/watch?v=MdZAMSyn_As&t=3s.

Brown, Tim. 'Tales of Creativity and Play'. *TED Serious Play*, 2008. https://www.ted.com/talks/tim_brown_tales_of_creativity_and_play.

Desai, Teja Lele. 'Informal Meetings Are Key to Innovative Ideas'. *Mint*, 2019. https://www.livemint.com/mint-lounge/business-of-life/informal-meetings-are-key-to-innovative-ideas-1553022288691.html.

Gluckselig, Katie, Rebecca Milne, and Scott Fallick. 'Not Just Child's Play: How Playful Environments Contribute to Innovation'. *Perkins Eastman*, 2018. https://www.perkinseastman.com/white-papers/.

Huang, Li, Francesca Gino, and Adam D. Galinsky. 'The Highest Form of Intelligence: Sarcasm Increases Creativity for Both Expressers and Recipients'. *Organizational Behavior and Human Decision Processes* 131, 2015. https://doi.org/10.1016/j.obhdp.2015.07.001.

Ma, Moses. 'The Power of Humor in Ideation and Creativity'. *Psychology Today Australia*, 2014. https://www.psychologytoday.com/au/blog/the-tao-innovation/201406/the-power-humor-in-ideation-and-creativity.

Mayo Clinic Staff. 'Stress Relief from Laughter? It's No Joke'. *Mayo Clinic*, 2021. https://www.mayoclinic.org/healthy-lifestyle/stress-management/in-depth/stress-relief/art-20044456.

McDowell, Tiffany. 'Are You Having Fun Yet?' *Deloitte Insights*, 2019. https://www2.deloitte.com/us/en/insights/topics/talent/making-work-fun-competitive-advantage.html.

Pizag, Anetta. 'Is There a Place for Humour in Your Workspace?' *Pizag*, 2016. https://pizag.com.au/2016/02/16/workplace-design-with-a-pinch-of-humour/.

Rober, Mark. 'The Super Mario Effect: Tricking Your Brain into Learning More'. *TEDxPenn*, 2018. https://www.ted.com/talks/mark_rober_the_super_mario_effect_tricking_your_brain_into_learning_more.

Stamato, Philip. 'The Credibility of Late Night Comedy'. *Vulture*, 2017. https://www.vulture.com/2017/06/the-credibility-of-late-night-comedy.html.

PART III: HOW CAN I MASTER REMOTE WORKING?

Choice 16: When should I meet others face to face?

Epley, Nicholas, and Justin Kruger. 'When What You Type Isn't What They Read: The Perseverance of Stereotypes and Expectancies over e-Mail'. *Journal of Experimental Social Psychology* 41, no. 4, 2005. https://doi.org/10.1016/j.jesp.2004.08.005.

Fayard, Anne-Laure, John Weeks, and Mahwesh Khan. 'Designing the Hybrid Office'. *Harvard Business Review*, 2021. https://hbr.org/2021/03/designing-the-hybrid-office.

Graber, Sean. 'Why Remote Work Thrives in Some Companies and Fails in Others'. *Harvard Business Review*, 2015. https://hbr.org/2015/03/why-remote-work-thrives-in-some-companies-and-fails-in-others.

Gupta, Alisha Haridasani. 'It's Not Just You: In Online Meetings, Many Women Can't Get a Word In'. *The New York Times*, 2020. https://www.nytimes.com/2020/04/14/us/zoom-meetings-gender.html.

Hietanen, Jonne, Mikko Peltola, and Jari K. Hietanen. 'Psychophysiological Responses to Eye Contact in a Live Interaction and in Video Call'. *Psychophysiology* 57, no. 6, 2020. https://doi.org/10.1111/psyp.13587.

Kerr, Fiona. 'Look Into My Eyes'. *TEDxNorthernSydneyInstitute*, 2016. https://www.youtube.com/watch?v=019Z0dAzNsQ.

Kerr, Fiona, and Leikki Maze. 'The Art & Science of Looking Up: Transforming Our Brains, Bodies, Relationships and Experience of the World by the Simple Act of Looking Up.' *Look Up*, 2019. https://www.lookup.org.au/report.

Lufkin, Bryan. 'What If You Never Saw Your Colleagues in Person Again?' *BBC Worklife*, 2018. https://www.bbc.com/worklife/article/20180130-what-if-you-never-saw-your-colleagues-in-person-again.

Middlemiss, Nicola. 'Binary Bores Could Be Destroying Your Workplace Culture'. *Human Resources Director*, 2017. https://www.hcamag.com/nz/specialisation/hr-technology/binary-bores-could-be-destroying-your-workplace-culture/150687.

Nutt, Amy Ellis. 'Science Shows Why It's Important to Speak – Not Write – to People Who Disagree with You'. *The Washington Post*, 2017. https://www.washingtonpost.com/news/speaking-of-science/wp/2017/11/27/people-may-seem-more-reasonable-when-you-hear-them-rather-than-read-their-words/.

Repenning, Nelson P., Don Kieffer, and James Repenning. 'A New Approach to Designing Work'. *MIT Sloan Management Review*, 2017. https://sloanreview.mit.edu/article/a-new-approach-to-designing-work/.

Van Deusen, Meg. 'The Power of Eye Contact: A Free and Easy Stress-Reducer'. *Sight On Stress*, 2019. http://www.sightonstress.com/the-power-of-eye-contact-a-free-and-easy-stress-reducer/.

Choice 17: Should I work from home or go to the office today?

Burns, Caroline. 'The Productivity Illusion – Office or Home, Which Place Is More Productive?' *LinkedIn*, 2021. https://www.linkedin.com/pulse/productivity-illusion-office-home-which-place-more-productive/.

'Competing in the Post-COVID Era: The Case for Place and the Need to Get It Right'. *Steelcase*, 2020. https://www.steelcase.com/research/articles/topics/post-covid-workplace/competing-post-covid-era/.

Ma, Liang, and Runing Ye. 'Walking and Cycling to Work Makes Commuters Happier and More Productive'. *The Conversation*, 2019. http://theconversation.com/walking-and-cycling-to-work-makes-commuters-happier-and-more-productive-117819.

Oldman, Tim. 'Why Workplace – A Leader's Guide to Rebuilding the Post-Pandemic Workplace'. *Leesman*, 2021. https://www.leesmanindex.com/whats-your-workplace-why/.

Ramachandran, Vignesh. 'Four Causes for "Zoom Fatigue" and Their Solutions'. *Stanford News*, 2021. https://news.stanford.edu/2021/02/23/four-causes-zoom-fatigue-solutions/.

Spataro, Jared. 'The Future of Work – the Good, the Challenging & the Unknown'. *Microsoft 365 Blog*, 2020. https://www.microsoft.com/en-us/microsoft-365/blog/2020/07/08/future-work-good-challenging-unknown/.

'Your Workplace of the Future: All You Need to Know to Plan Your Future Workplace Strategy'. *Leesman*, 2020. https://www.leesmanindex.com/your-workplace-of-the-future/.

Choice 18: How can we communicate better in virtual meetings?

Graber, Sean. 'Why Remote Work Thrives in Some Companies and Fails in Others'. *Harvard Business Review*, 2015. https://hbr.org/2015/03/why-remote-work-thrives-in-some-companies-and-fails-in-others.

Gupta, Alisha Haridasani. 'It's Not Just You: In Online Meetings, Many Women Can't Get a Word In'. *The New York Times*, 2020. https://www.nytimes.com/2020/04/14/us/zoom-meetings-gender.html.

Headlee, Celeste. 'Ten Ways to Have Better Conversations'. *VitalSmarts Video*, 2018. https://www.youtube.com/watch?v=-iOr-Z_qNAo&t=1187s.

Kraus, Michael W. 'Voice-Only Communication Enhances Empathic Accuracy'. *American Psychologist* 72, no. 7, 2017. https://doi.org/10.1037/amp0000147.

Nowakowska, Agata. 'Body Language Still Matters When You Are Working Online'. *Workplace Insight*, 2021. https://workplaceinsight.net/body-language-still-matters-when-you-are-working-online/.

Choice 19: How can we collaborate more effectively in a hybrid team?

Adegbuyi, Fadeke. 'How to Be Remote-First When You Still Have an Office'. *Ambition & Balance by Doist*, 2020. https://blog.doist.com/remote-first/.

Bartel, Caroline A., Amy Wrzesniewski, and Batia M. Wiesenfeld. 'Knowing Where You Stand: Physical Isolation, Perceived Respect, and Organizational Identification Among Virtual Employees'. *Organization Science* 23, no. 3, 2012. https://doi.org/10.1287/orsc.1110.0661.

Dvorak, Nate. 'Create Your Hybrid Workplace Strategy with 7 Questions'. *Gallup*, 2021. https://www.gallup.com/workplace/351797/create-hybrid-workplace-strategy-questions.aspx.

Nickless, Rachel. 'Ever Heard of "Distance Bias" at Work? You Might Want to Change Desks'. *Commercial Real Estate*, 2019. https://www.commercialrealestate.com.au/news/ever-heard-of-distance-bias-at-work-you-might-want-to-change-desks-15598/.

'The Future of Work Is Hybrid: Here's How to Thrive in the New Normal'. *IDEO U*, 2021. https://www.ideou.com/blogs/inspiration/the-future-of-work-is-hybrid.

'Breaking Down the Distance Barrier: How to Do Teamwork When You Can't Be with Your Team'. *Steelcase*, 2020. https://www.steelcase.com/research/articles/topics/working-from-home/breaking-distance-barrier/.

Woolf, David. 'Designing Space for Virtual Collaboration in an Untethered World'. *Workplace Insight*, 2017. https://workplaceinsight.net/designing-space-for-virtual-collaboration-in-an-increasingly-untethered-world/.

Choice 20: How can we collaborate better remotely?

Akitunde, Tomi. 'How Remote Workers Are Creatively Battling Social Isolation'. *Dropbox Blog*, 2020. https://blog.dropbox.com/topics/work-culture/how-remote-workers-are-creatively-battling-social-isolation.

Choudhury, Prithwiraj (Raj). 'Our Work-from-Anywhere Future'. *Harvard Business Review*, 2020. https://hbr.org/2020/11/our-work-from-anywhere-future.

Feldman, Elana, and Melissa Mazmanian. 'Why Time Signals Still Matter When Working Remotely'. *MIT Sloan Management Review*, 2020. https://sloanreview.mit.edu/article/why-time-signals-still-matter-when-working-remotely/.

Peach, Venessa. 'Remote, but Not Forgotten: Eight Ways to Build a Brilliant Online Workspace'. *SmartCompany*, 2020. https://www.smartcompany.com.au/people-human-resources/remote-work/build-online-workspace/.

Riedl, Christoph, and Anita Williams Woolley. 'Successful Remote Teams Communicate in Bursts'. *Harvard Business Review*, 2020. https://hbr.org/2020/10/successful-remote-teams-communicate-in-bursts.

Sjolie, Ela. 'The Hidden Threat of the Home Office'. Norwegian *SciTech News*, 2020. https://norwegianscitechnews.com/2020/10/the-hidden-threat-of-the-home-office/.

Sowierszenko, Magda. 'How to Build Inclusive Communication and Collaboration in Digital Workplace'. *Remote-How*, 2020. https://remote-how.com/blog/how-to-build-inclusive-communication-and-collaboration-in-digital-workplace.

Sowierszenko, Magda. 'Practicing Empathy with Your Virtual Team'. *Remote-How*, 2020. https://remote-how.com/blog/practicing-empathy-with-your-virtual-team.

Tank, Aytekin. 'Delivering Constructive Criticism Remotely – without Sinking Employee Morale'. *Fast Company*, 2020. https://www.fastcompany.com/90497622/delivering-constructive-criticism-remotely-without-sinking-employee-morale.

Yang, Longqi, David Holtz, Sonia Jaffe, Siddharth Suri, Shilpi Sinha, Jeffrey Weston, Connor Joyce, et al. 'The Effects of Remote Work on Collaboration among Information Workers'. *Nature Human Behaviour*, 2021. https://doi.org/10.1038/s41562-021-01196-4.

Zenger, Jack, and Joseph Folkman. 'Your Employees Want the Negative Feedback You Hate to Give'. *Harvard Business Review*, 2014. https://hbr.org/2014/01/your-employees-want-the-negative-feedback-you-hate-to-give.

Choice 21: How can I look after myself better while working from home?

Bloom, Nicholas. 'The Productivity Pitfalls of Working from Home in the Age of COVID-19'. *Stanford News*, 2020. https://news.stanford.edu/2020/03/30/productivity-pitfalls-working-home-age-covid-19/.

Friedman, Arik. 'Proof the Workday Is Longer since COVID'. *Work Life by Atlassian*, 2020. https://www.atlassian.com/blog/teamwork/data-analysis-length-of-workday-covid.

Herrera, Tim. 'Don't Work on Your Party Laptop or Party on Your Work Laptop'. *The New York Times*, 2020. https://www.nytimes.com/2020/10/23/smarter-living/what-not-to-do-work-computer.html.

Howe, Lauren C., Ashley Whillans, and Jochen I. Menges. 'How to (Actually) Save Time When You're Working Remotely'. *Harvard Business Review*, 2020. https://hbr.org/2020/08/how-to-actually-save-time-when-youre-working-remotely.

Levenson, Alec, and Patrick McLaughlin. 'New Leadership Challenges for the Virtual World of Work'. *MIT Sloan Management Review*, 2020. https://sloanreview.mit.edu/article/new-leadership-challenges-for-the-virtual-world-of-work/.

Rothbard, Nancy P. 'Building Work-Life Boundaries in the WFH Era'. *Harvard Business Review*, 2020. https://hbr.org/2020/07/building-work-life-boundaries-in-the-wfh-era.

Rothe, Peggie. 'The Home Stretch'. *Leesman*, 2021. https://www.leesmanindex.com/the-home-stretch/.

Singer-Velush, Natalie, Kevin Sherman, and Erik Anderson. 'Microsoft Analyzed Data on Its Newly Remote Workforce'. *Microsoft Workplace Insights*, 2020. https://workplaceinsights.microsoft.com/workplace-analytics/microsoft-analyzed-data-on-its-newly-remote-workforce/.

Smith, Jayne. 'Majority of Employees Struggling with "Always on" Work Culture'. *Workplace Insight*, 2020. https://workplaceinsight.net/majority-of-employees-struggling-with-always-on-work-culture/.

'The Hidden Bias of Working From Home'. *Steelcase*, 2021. https://www.steelcase.com/research/articles/topics/work-better/hidden-bias-working-home/.

Warzel, Charlie. 'You Are Not Working From Home'. *The New York Times*, 2020. https://www.nytimes.com/2020/05/26/opinion/work-from-home.html.

Wilser, Jeff. 'The Pandemic of Work-From-Home Injuries'. *The New York Times*, 2020. https://www.nytimes.com/2020/09/04/well/live/ergonomics-work-from-home-injuries.html.

'Working From Home: Real Life Lessons'. *Steelcase*, 2020. https://www.steelcase.com/research/articles/topics/working-from-home/working-home-real-life-lessons/.

Xiao, Yijing, Burcin Becerik-Gerber, Gale Lucas, and Shawn C. Roll. 'Impacts of Working From Home During COVID-19 Pandemic on Physical and Mental Well-Being of Office Workstation Users'. *Journal of Occupational and Environmental Medicine* 63, no. 3, 2021. https://doi.org/10.1097/JOM.0000000000002097.

PART IV: HOW CAN I GET INTO THE RIGHT FRAME OF MIND?

Choice 22: How can I get motivated?

Alexander, Verda. 'I've Been Designing Offices for Decades. Here's What I Got Wrong'. *Fast Company*, 2019. https://www.fastcompany.com/90373440/ive-been-designing-offices-for-decades-heres-what-i-got-wrong.

Amabile, Teresa, and Steven J. Kramer. 'The Power of Small Wins'. *Harvard Business Review*, 2011. https://hbr.org/2011/05/the-power-of-small-wins.

Bailey, Catherine, and Adrian Madden. 'What Makes Work Meaningful – Or Meaningless'. *MIT Sloan Management Review*, 2016. https://sloanreview.mit.edu/article/what-makes-work-meaningful-or-meaningless/.

Fraser-Thill, Rebecca. 'How to Spot Valuable Moments at Work'. *Forbes*, 2019. https://www.forbes.com/sites/rebeccafraserthill/2019/08/20/how-to-spot-valuable-moments-at-work/.

'Self-Determination Theory'. *Wikipedia*. https://en.wikipedia.org/w/index.php? title=Self-determination_theory.

Shanafelt, Tait D., Colin P. West, Jeff A. Sloan, Paul J. Novotny, Greg A. Poland, Ron Menaker, Teresa A. Rummans, and Lotte N. Dyrbye. 'Career Fit and Burnout Among Academic Faculty'. *Archives of Internal Medicine* 169, no. 10, 2009. https://doi.org/10.1001/archinternmed.2009.70.

Steinmetz, Janina, and Ayelet Fishbach. 'We Work Harder When We Know Someone's Watching'. *Harvard Business Review*, 2020. https://hbr.org/2020/05/we-work-harder-when-we-know-someones-watching.

Choice 23: How can I use my body to hack my brain?

Clayton, Russell, Christopher Thomas, and Jack Smothers. 'How to Do Walking Meetings Right'. *Harvard Business Review*, 2015. https://hbr.org/2015/08/how-to-do-walking-meetings-right.

Knight, Andrew P., and Markus Baer. 'Get Up, Stand Up: The Effects of a Non-Sedentary Workspace on Information Elaboration and Group Performance'. *Social Psychological and Personality Science* 5, no. 8, 2014. https://doi.org/10.1177/1948550614538463.

Link, Jeff. 'Can Steelcase's Office of the Future Make Corporate America Rethink the Drab Modern Workplace?' *Fast Company*, 2017. https://www.fastcompany.com/40448771/can-steelcases-office-of-the-future-make-corporate-america-rethink-the-drab-modern-workplace.

Merchant, Nilofer. 'Sitting Is the Smoking of Our Generation'. *Harvard Business Review*, 2013. https://hbr.org/2013/01/sitting-is-the-smoking-of-our-generation.

Reynolds, Gretchen. 'Work. Walk 5 Minutes. Work.' *The New York Times*, 2016. https://www.nytimes.com/2016/12/28/well/move/work-walk-5-minutes-work.html.

'The Science of Collaboration: How the Body Activates the Brain and Makes Ideas Better'. *Steelcase 360 Magazine*, 2019. https://www.steelcase.com/research/360-magazine/new-work-new-rules/.

Ward, Thomas. 'Can a Simple Walk Improve Your Creative Thinking?' *Psychology Today Australia*, 2017. https://www.psychologytoday.com/au/blog/creativity-you/201703/can-simple-walk-improve-your-creative-thinking.

Wasmer Andrews, Linda. 'Walking Can Lift Your Mood, Even When You Don't Expect It To'. *Psychology Today Australia*, 2016. https://www.psychologytoday.com/au/blog/minding-the-body/201608/walking-can-lift-your-mood-even-when-you-dont-expect-it.

Wong, May. 'Stanford Study Finds Walking Improves Creativity'. *Stanford News*, 2014. https://news.stanford.edu/2014/04/24/walking-vs-sitting-042414/.

Choice 24: What kinds of tools and technologies should I use?

Bell, Genevieve. 'Fast, Smart and Connected: How to Build Our Digital Future'. *Australian Broadcasting Corporation*, 2017. https://www.abc.net.au/radionational/programs/boyerlectures/genevieve-bell-fast-smart-connected-how-build-digital-future/9062060.

Brahm, Ajahn. 'Energy in Our Body and Mind from Inspiration'. *Buddhist Society of Western Australia*, 2018. https://www.youtube.com/watch?v=VWz3LAAj-J0.

Curtis, Keith. 'How Visual Storytelling Can Spark Innovation without Tech'. *Atlanta Inno*, 2019. https://www.bizjournals.com/atlanta/inno/stories/from-the-community/2019/06/05/how-visual-storytelling-can-spark-innovation.html.

Heffernan, Margaret. 'The Human Skills We Need in an Unpredictable World'. *TEDSummit*, 2019. https://www.ted.com/talks/margaret_heffernan_the_human_skills_we_need_in_an_unpredictable_world.

Knapp, Jake. 'Google Ventures: Your Design Team Needs A War Room. Here's How To Set One Up'. *Fast Company*, 2014. https://www.fastcompany.com/3028471/google-ventures-your-design-team-needs-a-war-room-heres-how-to-set-one-up.

'Lecturer Takes Laptops and Smart Phones Away and Musters Student Presence'. *University of Copenhagen*, 2020. https://science.ku.dk/english/press/news/2020/lecturer-takes-laptops-and-smart-phones-away-and-musters-student-presence/.

Lyon, Martha. 'Take Notes by Hand for Better Long-Term Comprehension'. *Association for Psychological Science*, 2014. https://www.psychologicalscience.org/news/releases/take-notes-by-hand-for-better-long-term-comprehension.html.

'Productivity Paradox'. *Wikipedia*. https://en.wikipedia.org/w/index.php?title=Productivity_paradox.

Robinson, Bryan. 'Is Your Computer Screen Stealing Your Breath? 6 Tips to Avoid Risks of Screen Apnea'. *Forbes*, 2020. https://www.forbes.com/sites/bryanrobinson/2020/11/14/is-your-computer-screen-stealing-your-breath-6-tips-to-avoid-screen-apnea/.

'The Neurological and Creative Toll of Digital Overload'. *MIT Sloan Management Review*, 2020. https://sloanreview.mit.edu/article/the-neurological-and-creative-toll-of-digital-overload/.

VanHemert, Kyle. 'The Engineer of the Original Apple Mouse Talks About His Remarkable Career'. *Wired*, 2014. https://www.wired.com/2014/08/the-engineer-of-the-original-apple-mouse-talks-about-his-remarkable-career/.

Weir, Kirsten. 'Turning Classrooms into Learning Laboratories'. *American Psychological Association* 49, no. 1, 2018. https://www.apa.org/monitor/2018/01/classrooms-laboratories.

Choice 25: Should I listen to music at work?

Chu, Melissa. '5 Types of Music That Increase Your Productivity, According to Science'. *Jumpstart Your Dream Life*, 2018. https://medium.com/jumpstart-your-dream-life/5-types-of-music-that-increase-your-productivity-according-to-science-6214d5a5fe3f.

Gillett, Rachel. 'The Best Music to Listen to for Optimal Productivity, According to Science'. *Business Insider Australia*, 2015. https://www.businessinsider.com.au/the-best-music-for-productivity-2015-7.

Grills, Chad. 'The Science Backed Ways Music Affects Your Brain and Productivity'. *Mission.Org*, 2017. https://medium.com/the-mission/the-science-backed-ways-music-affects-your-brain-and-productivity-e11145079305.

Kniffin, Kevin M., Jubo Yan, Brian Wansink, and William D. Schulze. 'The Sound of Cooperation: Musical Influences on Cooperative Behavior'. *Journal of Organizational Behavior* 38, no. 3, 2017. https://doi.org/10.1002/job.2128.

Lashbrooke, Barnaby. 'Can Music and Sound Change the Tune of Remote Worker Productivity?' *Forbes*, 2020. https://www.forbes.com/sites/barnabylashbrooke/2020/07/29/can-music-and-sound-change-the-tune-of-remote-worker-productivity/.

Murphy, Cheryl. 'Music Can Change (the Way We See) the World'. *Scientific American*, 2012. https://blogs.scientificamerican.com/guest-blog/music-can-change-the-way-we-see-the-world/.

Reinoso-Carvalho, Felipe, Laura Gunn, German Molina, Takuji Narumi, Charles Spence, Yuji Suzuki, Enrique ter Horst, and Johan Wagemans. 'A Sprinkle of Emotions vs a Pinch of Crossmodality: Towards Globally Meaningful Sonic Seasoning Strategies for Enhanced Multisensory Tasting Experiences'. *Journal of Business Research* 117, 2020. https://doi.org/10.1016/j.jbusres.2020.04.055.

Ritter, Simone M., and Sam Ferguson. 'Happy Creativity: Listening to Happy Music Facilitates Divergent Thinking'. *PLOS ONE* 12, no. 9, 2017. https://doi.org/10.1371/journal.pone.0182210.

Schellenberg, E. Glenn, Takayuki Nakata, Patrick G. Hunter, and Sachiko Tamoto. 'Exposure to Music and Cognitive Performance: Tests of Children and Adults'. *Psychology of Music* 35, no. 1, 2007. https://doi.org/10.1177/0305735607068885.

Team Tony. 'Music and Your Brain: Music Makes You Smarter, Happier and More Productive – but Why?'. *Tony Robbins*. https://www.tonyrobbins.com/mind-meaning/music-and-your-brain/.

Viney, Liam. 'Good Vibrations: The Role of Music in Einstein's Thinking'. *The Conversation*, 2016. http://theconversation.com/good-vibrations-the-role-of-music-in-einsteins-thinking-54725.

Choice 26: How can I invite creative inspiration?

Eltringham, Mark. 'Riffing on the Issue of Workplace Design and Creativity'. *Workplace Insight*, 2019. https://workplaceinsight.net/riffing-on-the-issue-of-workplace-design-and-creativity/.

Epstein, Dan. 'Pearl Jam's "Ten": 10 Things You Didn't Know'. *Rolling Stone*, 2016. https://www.rollingstone.com/feature/pearl-jams-ten-10-things-you-didnt-know-250550/.

Epting, Claire. '10 Amazing Movies with Incredibly Short Production Schedules'. *ScreenCrush*, 2020. https://screencrush.com/movies-with-the-shortest-production-schedules/.

Farhadi, Afsheen. '10 Novels Written in About a Month'. *Bookstr*, 2015. https://bookstr.com/list/10-novels-written-in-about-a-month/.

Gilbert, Elizabeth. *Big Magic: How to Live a Creative Life, and Let Go of Your Fear.* Bloomsbury Publishing, 2015.

Gilbert, Elizabeth. 'Your Elusive Creative Genius'. *TED*, 2009. https://www.ted.com/talks/elizabeth_gilbert_your_elusive_creative_genius.

Goodchild, Paul. 'Adversity and Chaos Can Help to Foster Creativity'. *Workplace Insight*, 2019. https://workplaceinsight.net/adversity-chaos-can-often-help-foster-personal-creativity/.

McCready, Mike, and Steve Gleason. 'Behind the Glass: Soul to Soul with Steve Gleason and Guest Mike McCready'. *Team Gleason*, 2020. https://www.youtube.com/watch?v=nQHmNl0aMMw.

Pearl Jam, and Mark Richards. 'Pearl Jam & Surfer Mark Richards Full Length Interview – Lightning Bolt'. *Pearl Jam*, 2014. https://www.youtube.com/watch?v=BTj9jGkG_Ow&t=1641s.

Springsteen, Bruce, and Zane Lowe. 'Bruce Springsteen – Apple Music "Letter To You" Interview'. *Bruce Springsteen*, 2020. https://www.youtube.com/watch?v=PhkL4K7Esc0.

PART V: WHAT KINDS OF SPACES HELP ME THRIVE?

Choice 27: Where should I go when I need a creative boost?

'360 Focus: Creativity, Work and the Physical Environment'. *Steelcase*, 2017. https://www.steelcase.com/360-focus-creativity/.

Boyd, William, A. L. Kennedy, Nicola Barker, Joan Bakewell, and Daljit Nagra. '"Where Do I Think Best? In Bed" – Authors Reveal Their Dream Retreats'. *The Guardian*, 2017. http://www.theguardian.com/books/2017/dec/29/where-do-i-think-best-bed-authors-reveal-their-ideal-retreats.

De Paoli, Donatella, Erika Sauer, and Arja Ropo. 'The Spatial Context of Organizations: A Critique of "Creative Workspaces"'. *Journal of Management & Organization* 25, no. 2, 2019. https://doi.org/10.1017/jmo.2017.46.

Judkis, Maura. 'Stairs to Nowhere Are Everywhere These Days. Where Are They Taking Us?' *The Washington Post*, 2019. https://www.washingtonpost.com/lifestyle/style/stairs-to-nowhere-are-everywhere-these-days-where-are-they-taking-us/2019/10/04/482d41c8-d8c6-11e9-bfb1-849887369476_story.html.

Link, Jeff. 'Can Steelcase's Office of the Future Make Corporate America Rethink the Drab Modern Workplace?' *Fast Company*, 2017. https://www.fastcompany.com/40448771/can-steelcases-office-of-the-future-make-corporate-america-rethink-the-drab-modern-workplace.

Mehta, Ravi, Rui (Juliet) Zhu, and Amar Cheema. 'Is Noise Always Bad? Exploring the Effects of Ambient Noise on Creative Cognition'. *Journal of Consumer Research* 39, no. 4, 2012. https://doi.org/10.1086/665048.

Choice 28: What kind of places help me feel well and happy?

'Benefits of Taking Fido to Work May Not Be Far "Fetched"'. *VCU News*, 2012. https://www.news.vcu.edu/article/benefits_of_taking_fido_to_work_may_not_be_far_fetched.

Browning, Bill, Chris Garvin, Catie Ryan, Namita Kallianpurkar, Leslie Labruto, Siobhan Watson, and Travis Knop. 'The Economics of Biophilia'. *Terrapin Bright Green*, 2012. https://www.terrapinbrightgreen.com/report/economics-of-biophilia/.

Browning, William, Catherine Ryan, and Joseph Clancy. '14 Patterns of Biophilic Design'. *Terrapin Bright Green*, 2014. https://www.terrapinbrightgreen.com/reports/14-patterns/.

Candido, Christhina, Samin Marzban, Shamila Haddad, Martin Mackey, and Angela Loder. 'Designing Healthy Workspaces: Results from Australian Certified Open-Plan Offices'. *Facilities* 39, no. 5/6, 2020. https://doi.org/10.1108/F-02-2020-0018.

Foreman, Anne M., Margaret K. Glenn, B. Jean Meade, and Oliver Wirth. 'Dogs in the Workplace: A Review of the Benefits and Potential Challenges'. *International Journal of Environmental Research and Public Health* 14, no. 5, 2017. https://doi.org/10.3390/ijerph14050498.

Klotz, Anthony C. 'Creating Jobs and Workspaces That Energize People'. *MIT Sloan Management Review*, 2020. https://sloanreview.mit.edu/article/creating-jobs-and-workspaces-that-energize-people/.

Knight, Craig, and S. Alexander Haslam. 'The Relative Merits of Lean, Enriched, and Empowered Offices: An Experimental Examination of the Impact of Workspace Management Strategies on Well-Being and Productivity'. *Journal of Experimental Psychology: Applied* 16, no. 2, 2010. https://doi.org/10.1037/a0019292.

Nieuwenhuis, Marlon, Craig Knight, Tom Postmes, and S. Alexander Haslam. 'The Relative Benefits of Green versus Lean Office Space: Three Field Experiments'. *Journal of Experimental Psychology: Applied* 20, no. 3, 2014. https://doi.org/10.1037/xap0000024.

Nittono, Hiroshi, Michiko Fukushima, Akihiro Yano, and Hiroki Moriya. 'The Power of Kawaii: Viewing Cute Images Promotes a Careful Behavior and Narrows Attentional Focus'. *PLoS ONE* 7, no. 9, 2012. https://doi.org/10.1371/journal.pone.0046362.

Pizag, Anetta. 'Is There a Place for Humour in Your Workspace?' *Pizag*, 2016. https://pizag.com.au/2016/02/16/workplace-design-with-a-pinch-of-humour/.

Schwab, Katharine. 'What Is Biophilic Design, and Can It Really Make You Happier and Healthier?' *Fast Company*, 2019. https://www.fastcompany.com/90333072/what-is-biophilic-design-and-can-it-really-make-you-happier-and-healthier.

'Study Indicates Pet Friendly Companies Are More Likely to Attract, Engage and Retain Employees'. *Nationwide*, 2018. https://news.nationwide.com/study-indicates-pet-friendly-companies-are-more-likely-to-attract-engage-and-retain-employees/.

'The Power of Puppies: Looking at Cute Images Can Improve Focus'. *Association for Psychological Science*, 2015. https://www.psychologicalscience.org/news/minds-business/the-power-of-puppies-looking-at-cute-images-can-improve-focus.html.

'Window Views and Smaller Offices Improve Productivity'. *UCL News*, 2021. https://www.ucl.ac.uk/news/2021/apr/window-views-and-smaller-offices-improve-productivity.

Choice 29: Should I tidy up my workspace?

Ferrari, Joseph R., and Catherine A. Roster. 'Delaying Disposing: Examining the Relationship between Procrastination and Clutter across Generations'. *Current Psychology* 37, 2018. https://doi.org/10.1007/s12144-017-9679-4.

Feuer, Jack. 'The Clutter Culture'. *UCLA Magazine*, 2012. http://magazine.ucla.edu/features/the-clutter-culture/.

Lucid Content Team. 'Productivity Survey: Want to Be a Go-Getter? WFH, Take More Vacation, and Get a Dog'. *Lucidchart*, 2019. https://www.lucidchart.com/blog/productivity-survey.

Rogers, Caroline J., and Rona Hart. 'Home and the Extended-Self: Exploring Associations between Clutter and Wellbeing'. *Journal of Environmental Psychology* 73, 2021. https://doi.org/10.1016/j.jenvp.2021.101553.

University of Exeter. 'Designing Your Own Workspace Improves Health, Happiness and Productivity'. *ScienceDaily*, 2010. https://www.sciencedaily.com/releases/2010/09/100907104035.htm.

Vohs, Kathleen D., Joseph P. Redden, and Ryan Rahinel. 'Physical Order Produces Healthy Choices, Generosity, and Conventionality, Whereas Disorder Produces Creativity'. *Psychological Science* 24, no. 9, 2013. https://doi.org/10.1177/0956797613480186.

Ward, Adrian F., Kristen Duke, Ayelet Gneezy, and Maarten W. Bos. 'Brain Drain: The Mere Presence of One's Own Smartphone Reduces Available Cognitive Capacity'. *Journal of the Association for Consumer Research* 2, no. 2, 2017. https://doi.org/10.1086/691462.

Winerman, Lea. 'A Messy Desk Encourages a Creative Mind, Study Finds'. *American Psychological Association*, 2013. https://www.apa.org/monitor/2013/10/messy-desk.

Choice 30: How can I deal with a challenging work environment?

Allen, Joseph G. 'Research: Stale Office Air Is Making You Less Productive'. *Harvard Business Review*, 2017. https://hbr.org/2017/03/research-stale-office-air-is-making-you-less-productive.

'Future Workplace Wellness Study'. *Future Workplace*, 2019. https://view.com/sites/default/files/documents/workplace-wellness-study.pdf.

'Health & Happiness Petal: Creating Environments That Optimize Physical and Psychological Health and Well Being'. *Living Building at Georgia Tech*. https://livingbuilding.gatech.edu/health-happiness-petal.

Heerwagen, Judith. 'Psychosocial Value of Space'. *Whole Building Design Guide*, 2017. https://www.wbdg.org/resources/psychosocial-value-space.

'Living Building Challenge 4.0: A Visionary Path to a Regenerative Future'. *International Living Future Institute*, 2019. https://living-future.org/wp-content/uploads/2019/04/Living-Building-Challenge-4.0.pdf.

Sander, Libby (Elizabeth). 'Research Shows If You Improve the Air Quality at Work, You Improve Productivity'. *The Conversation*, 2017. http://theconversation.com/research-shows-if-you-improve-the-air-quality-at-work-you-improve-productivity-76695.

WBDG Sustainable Committee. 'Enhance Indoor Environmental Quality (IEQ)'. *Whole Building Design Guide*, 2021. https://www.wbdg.org/design-objectives/sustainable/enhance-indoor-environmental-quality.

'WELL Building Standard – WELL v2 – Air'. *International WELL Building Institute*, 2021. https://v2.wellcertified.com/wellv2/en/air.

'WELL Building Standard – WELL v2 – Light'. *International WELL Building Institute*, 2021. https://v2.wellcertified.com/wellv2/en/light.

PART VI: HOW CAN I TURN CHALLENGES INTO OPPORTUNITIES? AND WHAT ARE MY LIMITS?

Choice 31: How can I produce great work when feeling low?

Achor, Shawn. *Happiness Advantage: The Seven Principles of Positive Psychology That Fuel Success and Performance at Work.* Crown Publishing Group, 2010.

Achor, Shawn. 'The Happiness Dividend'. *Harvard Business Review*, 2011. https://hbr.org/2011/06/the-happiness-dividend.

Brown, Brené. *Rising Strong: The Reckoning. The Rumble. The Revolution.* Spiegel & Grau, 2015.

Fox, Jason. 'It's Not All Black and White: The Three Hidden Benefits of Doubt'. *Professional Planner*, 2016. https://www.professionalplanner.com.au/2016/04/its-not-all-black-and-white-the-three-hidden-benefits-of-doubt/.

Goodchild, Paul. 'Adversity and Chaos Can Help to Foster Creativity'. *Workplace Insight*, 2019. https://workplaceinsight.net/adversity-chaos-can-often-help-foster-personal-creativity/.

Minchin, Tim, and Judd Apatow. 'Upright Q&A with Tim Minchin & Judd Apatow'. *ATX TV...from the Couch!'*, 2020. https://www.youtube.com/watch?v=OZMFM2t-7vA.

Proto, Eugenio. 'Are Happy Workers More Productive?' *IZA World of Labor*, 2016. https://doi.org/10.15185/izawol.315.

Team Tony. 'What is Emotional Mastery? Learning Emotional Mastery Puts You in Control of Your Life'. *Tony Robbins*. https://www.tonyrobbins.com/mind-meaning/be-the-master-of-your-emotions/.

Choice 32: How can I make pressure my friend?

Brown, Brené. 'Brené on Anxiety, Calm + Over/Under-Functioning'. *Brené Brown Podcast*, 2020. https://brenebrown.com/podcast/brene-on-anxiety-calm-over-under-functioning/.

Brown, Brené. *The Gifts of Imperfection: Let Go of Who You Think You're Supposed to Be and Embrace Who You Are.* Hazelden Publishing, 2010.

Chajut, Eran, and Daniel Algom. 'Selective Attention Improves under Stress: Implications for Theories of Social Cognition'. *Journal of Personality and Social Psychology* 85, no. 2, 2003. https://doi.org/10.1037/0022-3514.85.2.231.

Crum, Alia, and Thomas Crum. 'Stress Can Be a Good Thing If You Know How to Use It'. *Harvard Business Review*, 2015. https://hbr.org/2015/09/stress-can-be-a-good-thing-if-you-know-how-to-use-it.

Fried, Jason, and David Heinemeier Hansson. *It Doesn't Have to Be Crazy at Work*. Harper Business, 2018.

Gino, Francesca. 'Are You Too Stressed to Be Productive? Or Not Stressed Enough?' *Harvard Business Review*, 2016. https://hbr.org/2016/04/are-you-too-stressed-to-be-productive-or-not-stressed-enough.

Keinan, Giora. 'Decision Making under Stress: Scanning of Alternatives under Controllable and Uncontrollable Threats'. *Journal of Personality and Social Psychology* 52, no. 3, 1987. https://doi.org/10.1037/0022-3514.52.3.639.

Mitchell, Marie S., Mary Marwitz, Rebecca L. Greenbaum, and Ryan M. Vogel. 'How to Encourage Better Performance without Straining Employees'. *LSE Business Review*, 2019. https://blogs.lse.ac.uk/businessreview/2019/07/18/how-to-encourage-better-performance-without-straining-employees/.

Urban, Tim. 'Inside the Mind of a Master Procrastinator'. *TED*, 2016. https://www.ted.com/talks/tim_urban_inside_the_mind_of_a_master_procrastinator.

Young, Emma. 'The Effect of Emotions on Your Behaviour Depends Partly on Your Expectations'. *Research Digest*, 2017. https://digest.bps.org.uk/2017/10/20/the-effect-of-emotions-on-your-behaviour-depends-partly-on-your-expectations/.

Choice 33: Should I always try to give 110%?

Agarwal, Ritu, and Peter Weill. 'The Benefits of Combining Data with Empathy'. *MIT Sloan Management Review*, 2012. https://sloanreview.mit.edu/article/the-benefits-of-combining-data-with-empathy/.

Case Western Reserve University. 'Empathy Represses Analytic Thought, and Vice Versa: Brain Physiology Limits Simultaneous Use of Both Networks'. *ScienceDaily*, 2012. https://www.sciencedaily.com/releases/2012/10/121030161416.htm.

Choice 34: How comfortable do I really need to be?

Alexander, Verda. 'I've Been Designing Offices for Decades. Here's What I Got Wrong'. *Fast Company*, 2019. https://www.fastcompany.com/90373440/ive-been-designing-offices-for-decades-heres-what-i-got-wrong.

Bargh, John A., and Idit Shalev. 'The Substitutability of Physical and Social Warmth in Daily Life'. *American Psychological Association* 12, no. 1, 2012. https://doi.org/10.1037/a0023527.

Belkin, Liuba Y., and Maryam Kouchaki. 'Too Hot to Help! Exploring the Impact of Ambient Temperature on Helping'. *European Journal of Social Psychology* 47, no. 5, 2017. https://doi.org/10.1002/ejsp.2242.

Chang, Tom Y., and Agne Kajackaite. 'Battle for the Thermostat: Gender and the Effect of Temperature on Cognitive Performance'. *PLoS ONE* 14, no. 5, 2019. https://doi.org/10.1371/journal.pone.0216362.

IJzerman, Hans, Angela K. Y. Leung, and Lay See Ong. 'Perceptual Symbols of Creativity: Coldness Elicits Referential, Warmth Elicits Relational Creativity'. *Acta Psychologica* 148, 2014. https://doi.org/10.1016/j.actpsy.2014.01.013.

Quin, Michael. 'Can't Concentrate at Work? This AI System Knows Why', *RMIT*, 2020. https://www.rmit.edu.au/news/all-news/2020/jun/office-comfort-and-concentration.

Randall, Tom. 'The Smartest Building in the World: Inside the Connected Future of Architecture'. *Bloomberg*, 2015. http://www.bloomberg.com/features/2015-the-edge-the-worlds-greenest-building/.

Rock, David, Heidi Grant, and Jacqui Grey. 'Diverse Teams Feel Less Comfortable – and That's Why They Perform Better'. *Harvard Business Review*, 2016. https://hbr.org/2016/09/diverse-teams-feel-less-comfortable-and-thats-why-they-perform-better.

Sinclair, David. *Lifespan: Why We Age – and Why We Don't Have To*. Atria Books, 2019.

Syndicus, Marc, Bettina S. Wiese, and Christoph van Treeck. 'In the Heat and Noise of the Moment: Effects on Risky Decision Making'. *Environment and Behavior* 50, no. 1, 2018. https://doi.org/10.1177/0013916516680700.

Witthoft, Scott, and Scott Doorley. *Make Space: How to Set the Stage for Creative Collaboration*. John Wiley & Sons, 2012.

Young, Emma. 'Cold Days Can Make Us Long For Social Contact – But Warming Up Our Bodies Eliminates This Desire'. *Research Digest*, 2020. https://digest.bps.org.uk/2020/01/27/cold-days-can-make-us-long-for-social-contact-but-warming-up-our-bodies-eliminates-this-desire/.

Choice 35: Is it a good idea to trade sleep time for productive time?

Aubrey, Sophie. 'Getting by on Six Hours? Welcome to the "Sleepless Elite"'. *The Sydney Morning Herald*, 2019. https://www.smh.com.au/lifestyle/health-and-wellness/getting-by-on-six-hours-welcome-to-the-sleepless-elite-20191030-p535sr.html.

Chamorro-Premuzic, Tomas. 'Why You Should Choose Sleep Over Work'. *Harvard Business Review*, 2020. https://hbr.org/2020/09/why-you-should-choose-sleep-over-work.

Guadagni, Veronica, Ford Burles, Silvana Valera, Emeleigh Hardwicke-Brown, Michele Ferrara, Tavis Campbell, and Giuseppe Iaria. 'The Relationship between Quality of Sleep and Emotional Empathy'. *Journal of Psychophysiology* 31, no. 4, 2017. https://doi.org/10.1027/0269-8803/a000177.

Laber-Warren, Emily. 'New Office Hours Aim for Well Rested, More Productive Workers'. *The New York Times*, 2018. https://www.nytimes.com/2018/12/24/well/mind/work-schedule-hours-sleep-productivity-chronotype-night-owls.html.

Lee, Soomi, Orfeu M. Buxton, Ross Andel, and David M. Almeida. 'Bidirectional Associations of Sleep with Cognitive Interference in Employees' Work Days'. *Sleep Health* 5, no. 3, 2019. https://doi.org/10.1016/j.sleh.2019.01.007.

Suni, Eric, and Abhinav Singh. 'How Much Sleep Do We Really Need?' *Sleep Foundation*, 2021. https://www.sleepfoundation.org/how-sleep-works/how-much-sleep-do-we-really-need.

Tigar, Lindsay. 'The 6 Most Dangerous Sleeping Habits for Professionals'. *Ladders*, 2019. https://www.theladders.com:443/career-advice/the-6-most-dangerous-sleeping-habits-for-professionals-2.

Walker, Matt. 'Sleep Is Your Superpower'. *TED*, 2019. https://www.ted.com/talks/matt_walker_sleep_is_your_superpower.

Walker, Matthew. 'How to Boost Your Business? Let Workers Sleep'. *The Guardian*, 2018. http://www.theguardian.com/commentisfree/2018/mar/26/succeed-business-sleep-profits-employees-bosses.

Walker, Matthew. *Why We Sleep: The New Science of Sleep and Dreams*. Penguin, 2017.

Williamson, A. M., and Anne-Marie Feyer. 'Moderate Sleep Deprivation Produces Impairments in Cognitive and Motor Performance Equivalent to Legally Prescribed Levels of Alcohol Intoxication'. *Occupational and Environmental Medicine* 57, no. 10, 2000. https://doi.org/10.1136/oem.57.10.649.

SPECIAL THANKS

This book would have turned out very differently – or may not have even seen the light of the day – without the generosity and wisdom of many people.

I'm grateful to all organisations and individuals who openly share their knowledge via mainstream and social media, with the intention to make this world a smarter and better place.

I appreciate the contribution of every person I've ever worked with who has enriched my life with (sometimes glorious and sometimes confronting) stories and learnings.

I'd like to thank each member of the Workplace Revolution Community, led by Caroline Burns, for their incredible knowledge and insights about everything workplace, as well as their fun vibes and camaraderie.

Andrew Griffiths, my amazing coach and mentor, has been an invaluable source of wisdom, inspiration and support from the moment the idea of this book was conceived till the completion of the finishing touches. Andrew, thank you for your guidance, and for setting an example worth striving for – by making this world a better place through caring, respect, authenticity and integrity.

Don Beckley, my wonderful partner, has put up with more of my quirks than I'm willing to share on paper. He's been there for me through thick and thin – always with a huge smile and heart – and was immensely helpful and generous with his time and ideas at every phase of the production of this book. Don, I can't thank you enough.

My parents, András and Zsuzsa Pizág, would have loved to have seen this book come to life. They taught me to approach challenges with curiosity, intelligence and a pinch of humour. They encouraged me to set ambitious goals and pursue high standards. Bandi, Zsuzsa, I hope you'd be proud.

LET'S KEEP IN TOUCH

I hope this is not a final goodbye. If any of the insights or stories in this book resonate with you – or perhaps you think differently about certain issues – I'd love to hear about your experiences. I always enjoy good conversations about people, places and performance.

If you choose to run with some of the suggestions and strategies, I'd be very happy to learn about your journey and your results. What has changed in your work life? How have your choices influenced the performance and culture of your team, and the way you work together? Please share your stories with me.

And if you – or the people you collaborate with – could use a bit of help in improving your work practices or adopting new strategies, I'm here to assist. Let's have a chat and explore how I could support you. It would be my pleasure to guide you or your teams towards enhanced performance and a more fulfilling work experience.

Please email me at **anetta@pizag.com.au**.

ABOUT ANETTA PIZAG

Driven by curiosity

Anetta is a workplace design consultant and strategist, work style coach and author. She is fascinated by human nature, and how our environments and actions can shape our experiences and results. Her calling is to help people create a better quality life for themselves and others through curiosity, self-awareness and intelligence.

When it comes to finding innovative solutions to problems, Anetta sees no boundaries. She believes that essentially any places and experiences can teach us something about smarter ways of living and working. In fact, she often has light-bulb moments while enjoying music and movies, exploring the outdoors, or just people watching from a cafe with a mug of hot chocolate.

A unique combination of experiences

Anetta understands people, places and performance; she has training and experience in architecture, building engineering, evidence-based design research, coaching and business leadership. With these skills and expertise, Anetta knows how to implement effective workplace strategies and practices that promote individual and business success.

Early in her career, Anetta worked in Europe, New Zealand and Australia for over a decade as an architect and environmental consultant. Exploring the world of psychology became a turning point. She started to view space design and user experience from the inside out, and it became clear to her that high-performance environments and work practices are as unique as each of us.

Seeing issues from all perspectives

Anetta has seen a large variety of workplaces – through the eyes of a designer, researcher, workplace consultant, corporate employee, small business team member and business owner – and had plenty of opportunities to learn from the challenges and triumphs of her clients and teams, as well as her own experiences.

In recent years, Anetta has also witnessed first hand how the world of work has transformed. Forward-thinking organisations are now seeking switched on, flexible employees and partners who are able to think freely, organise themselves effectively and solve problems with little supervision. She has also noticed, however, that many organisations still approach professional development and change management in traditional ways. And unless people are supported and trusted to embrace their individual work styles, work performance and culture inevitably suffer.

Helping teams and individuals

Anetta's mission is to help people be their best selves every day, by giving them the right physical space, training and coaching support to do quality work and thrive.

As a workplace design consultant and strategist, Anetta helps create human-centric, future-ready workplaces that enable people to effectively tackle the ever-changing challenges of work while maintaining a healthy body and mind. Through close collaboration with leaders, managers and team members, she also develops tailored work practices that optimise individual and team performance, enable agility and promote engagement.

As a work style coach, Anetta guides and educates people to explore their unique work styles, and to make conscious, informed choices about when, where and how they work.

Anetta is a firm believer in lifelong learning, and she's constantly evolving her own work style. When she embarked on this journey, she couldn't find the guidance she needed in books or training programmes, so she learned much through trial and error. With this book, as well as her consulting and coaching services, Anetta offers a smoother, faster path to self-discovery, which could save readers years of hit and miss.

Clients and collaboration partners

Anetta works with a variety of organisations, large and small, including legal and financial firms, engineering and tech companies, design and media businesses, as well as education and government bodies. She collaborates closely with leaders, managers, HR professionals and employees involved in workplace change projects such as office relocations and upgrades, technology and cultural transformations, and the adoption of new work practices. She also supports teams and individuals who simply want to be better at what they do.

Her clients are unified by their commitment to excellence, their passion for creating positive change, and their genuine appreciation and care for their colleagues and teams. They strive to create a great workplace where people show their real selves, work to their strengths, and achieve ambitious goals through powerful teamwork.

Create a Thriving Workspace

Anetta's first book, *Create a Thriving Workspace: 7 essential design principles for positive high-performance physical work environments*, presents a simple framework and a comprehensive range of practical solutions for creating people-centric, results-oriented work environments.

www.35smartchoices.com

anetta@35smartchoices.com

www.pizag.com.au

anetta@pizag.com.au

www.linkedin.com/in/anettapizag/